James Geddes Craighead

**Scotch and Irish Seeds in American Soil**

The early History of the Scotch and Irish Churches, and their Relations to the

Presbyterian Church of America

James Geddes Craighead

**Scotch and Irish Seeds in American Soil**
The early History of the Scotch and Irish Churches, and their Relations to the Presbyterian Church of America

ISBN/EAN: 9783337115845

Printed in Europe, USA, Canada, Australia, Japan

Cover: Foto ©ninafisch / pixelio.de

More available books at **www.hansebooks.com**

# Scotch and Irish Seeds

# In American Soil:

THE EARLY HISTORY OF THE SCOTCH AND IRISH CHURCHES, AND THEIR RELATIONS TO THE PRESBYTERIAN CHURCH OF AMERICA.

BY THE
Rev. J. G. CRAIGHEAD, D.D.

---

PHILADELPHIA:
PRESBYTERIAN BOARD OF PUBLICATION,
No. 1334 Chestnut Street.

Entered according to Act of Congress, in the year 1878, by
THE TRUSTEES OF THE
PRESBYTERIAN BOARD OF PUBLICATION,
In the Office of the Librarian of Congress, at Washington.

WESTCOTT & THOMSON,
*Stereotypers and Electrotypers, Philada.*

# PREFACE.

Two objects have been before my mind while preparing this volume:

First, to show the indebtedness of the American Presbyterian Church to the churches of Scotland and Ireland for the elements which entered into its original constitution, as also for its subsequent rapid growth and influence. In attempting this it was thought to be more important to bring clearly to view the principles and character of the ministers and members of those churches who came to this country, and identified themselves with the Presbyterian Church, than simply to point out their number or the periods of their arrival. Numbers alone might have been of comparatively little value, as they might have proved the means of discord, and consequently a source of weakness rather than of strength. But if the character of a people is strong, reliable, courageous, based on correct principles and built up into symmetry by conscientious adherence to convictions of right and duty, their numbers may be small and yet their influence be powerful and permanent.

If, then, we would understand how valuable was the contribution that Scotland and Ireland made to the Presbyterianism of this country, we must consider the previous religious condition of each, and the influences, favorable or otherwise, under which the religious life of the people was developed. In this way we can see how these future colonists were educated and disciplined in the Old World for the great work God in his providence had for them to do in the New.

The second object was to bring into proper prominence and perspicuity the principles of religious and civil freedom for which the Presbyterians of Scotland and Ireland so long battled, and to maintain which all of them were called to endure protracted persecution, and many thousands of them to lay down their lives. As the union of Church and State in those countries was so close and dependent, so the relation between civil and religious liberty was so intimately conjoined that those who contended for the one necessarily promoted the other; and, as a matter of fact, the two have ever existed together and neither can long survive without the other. The Presbyterians, therefore, while contending even unto blood for the headship of Christ over his Church, and for its freedom from the yoke of kingly or priestly authority, were naturally and necessarily the friends and supporters of the rights of the people as against the usurpations and exactions of despotic rulers.

In the perusal of this history the reader will notice: First, that the views of these Presbyterians were more accurate respecting religious liberty than were those of the Puritans who settled New England. Under the latter a law was enacted in Massachusetts in 1631 uniting the Church and State, with the provision that no one should vote unless he had been baptized in his youth and was a church member. Their desire was to found a theocracy, and therefore they adopted measures to unite the religious and civil power practically. Our Presbyterian fathers, on the other hand, distinctly discerned the separate province or sphere of each; and while unwilling to allow the Church to be controlled by the secular power, they neither asked its help nor depended upon it for authority or support. From their entrance into this country, as may be seen by their conduct in Virginia and New York, they opposed everything that looked like a union of Church and State or any dependence of the Church on the arm of civil power.

The second noticeable thing is, that in the long contests between these monarchical governments and their subjects, the natural and constant allies of despotism were the Romish and Episcopal hierarchies. These were ever the most dangerous as well as the most inveterate enemies of the nonconformists when they were resisting tyrants. Presbyterians, at least, had most to dread from Episcopal prelates, and from them they suffered most. The Episcopal Church was more frequently in the ascendant, and had much the greater influence with the civil rulers. This influence it almost invariably used to oppress all outside of its own communion. If, then, in our endeavor to present a truthful picture of these times we have occasionally spoken with severity of the prelates of the Established Church of England and Ireland, it is because the facts of history have compelled the statements.

In describing the development of these fundamental principles in these countries I have had no wish to undervalue the part taken by the Puritans from England, the Dutch from Holland, or the Huguenots from France, in their steadfast maintenance of those principles both in Europe and in this country. While the writer believes that the Scotch and the Scotch-Irish had clearer conceptions of the relations which ought to exist between the Church and the State, and were consequently foremost and most resolute in their defence of the same, he freely acknowledges that civil and religious liberty in America had no abler champions than were the emigrants from those countries. Of this fact he would have made more frequent mention had it come within the scope of the present volume, and had not this congenial subject been treated already by many and more competent writers.

It is greatly to be desired that the youth of the Presbyterian Church of this country should familiarize themselves with the history of the perscutions and sufferings endured by their Scotch and Scotch-Irish ancestors, and with the character and services of those heroes of the Church who maintained with such fortitude their conscientious views of civil and religious liberty, and who, in coming to America, brought their principles with them and did so much to have them engrafted into our republican institutions. Such an acquaintance with the origin and defence of the great cardinal principles of the polity and government of the Presbyterian Church would inevitably lead them to reverence the memories of the departed worthies of the Church, and to love and perpetuate their simple and scriptural faith and forms of worship.

It is impossible to state with any accuracy all the sources of information from which I have derived the materials for this volume. For those which pertain to the history of the Scotch and Irish churches I am indebted of necessity to the standard histories of those countries. The facts connected with the emigration from those lands, and the influence of the colonists upon Church and State in America, have been gleaned from a large number of volumes and pamphlets. Not unfrequently much care and research have been requisite to discover or verify a single incident or event; but the labor has been one of love, and rendered from a desire to be useful.

# CONTENTS.

## HISTORY OF THE SCOTCH CHURCH.

### CHAPTER I.

FROM THE INTRODUCTION OF CHRISTIANITY TO THE ACT OF PARLIAMENT, 1592, RATIFYING THE GENERAL ASSEMBLY OF SCOTLAND.

Characteristics of Scotch Presbyterianism—Its three cardinal principles—Introduction of Christianity—The pope asserting his supremacy—Obstacles to the Reformation—Defenders of the gospel—Patrick Hamilton—The first martyr—Effects of his death—Many embrace the doctrines preached—Persecutions by Cardinal Beaton—George Wishart—His preaching and martyrdom—Beaton's retributive death—Warning unheeded by his successor—Death of Walter Mill—The first Covenant adopted at Edinburgh—Its provisions—Conflict between the queen and Reformers—John Knox—His great influence—Protestant nobility meet at Perth—Duplicity of the queen—Reformers increase—Knox at St. Andrews—Meeting of a free Parliament—Petition of Protestants—*First Confession of Faith*—Necessity of a national ecclesiastical organization—The first General Assembly—Book of Discipline—Its provisions—Two objects secured—Superintendents—Tulchan bishops—Queen Mary's return to Scotland—Efforts to restore popery—Her measures resisted—Knox's successful opposition—The Church prosperous—Opposition of the queen and regent Morton—Andrew Melville returns to Scotland—Chief opponent of Morton—A commission reports a system of ecclesiastical polity—*Second Book of Discipline*—Its provisions—Conflict of the

Assembly with King James and his Parliament—Remonstrance presented to the king by Melville—Black Acts of Parliament—Clergy obliged to fly—Patriotism and good conduct of Presbyterians—Secures more favor from the king—His eulogy on the Church of Scotland—Parliament ratifies the Constitution of the Church............ ............... 19

## CHAPTER II.
### From the Charter of the Church to the Renewal of the National Covenant.

Bad faith of James—Conspiracy of popish earls—The danger averted—Two of the conspirators excommunicated—Roman Catholic earls; their proposed recall—Melville confronts the king—Deceitful conduct of the king—Assaults the Church—King claims absolute power—Resistance by Presbyterians—Ministers of Edinburgh expelled—The corrupt Assembly at Perth—Advisory council for the king—The Church represented in Parliament—Prelacy triumphant—Three ministers made bishops—Aberdeen Assembly the last free one—Clergy banished—Melville summoned to London and banished—Bishops appointed permanent moderators of Assembly—Their civil jurisdiction restored—Court of High Commission—The king visits Scotland—New Confession of Faith—Five Articles of Perth ratified—Constitution of the Church subverted—Persecutions by Court of High Commission—Ministers banished—Congregations left without ordinances—Death of King James—Charles I. adopts his father's policy—Great revival of religion—Book of Canons and Liturgy prepared—Riot at Edinburgh at its introduction—The kingdom aroused—People flock to Edinburgh—The National Covenant enthusiastically renewed—THE SECOND REFORMATION IN SCOTLAND................................................ 63

## CHAPTER III.
### From Subscribing the Covenant to the Restoration of Charles II.

Despair of prelates, and the defeat of their schemes—Deputations sent to the king—He tries to negotiate with the

Covenanters—Failure of Hamilton, the king's commissioner—Concessions made—General Assembly at Glasgow—Efforts of Hamilton—The Assembly triumphs—The whole fabric of prelacy swept away—Vital principles vindicated—King enraged, and prepares for war—Preparations of Presbyterians—They march to Dunse Law—The king hesitates, and accedes to articles of peace—The peace a brief one—War again determined upon—Covenanters march to the Tweed—Treaty of Ripon—Petitions to Parliament for uniformity of worship in the two kingdoms—Action of the Assembly—The **Covenanters** join their English brethren—The Solemn **League** and Covenant—The Westminster Assembly of Divines—Importance of **their** work—Difficulties—Uniformity not secured—The General Assembly ratifies the Confession of Faith of the Westminster divines—Presbyterian system long unmolested............................................................................. 86.

## CHAPTER IV.

### From the Restoration of Charles II. to his Death, in 1685.

Restoration of Charles II.—No guarantees exacted—A **council** of state favors prelacy—The illegal Parliament of 1661—**Their** despotic acts—Purpose **to destroy the** Church—Marquis **of Argyle and** Guthrie **executed—The king, by** proclamation, restores prelacy—Four **bishops** consecrated—Only Episcopalians allowed to preach and teach—Act of Glasgow—Four hundred ministers banished—Field-meetings—Bishop's **drag-net—Court of High Commission again erected**—Curate **spies—Persecution—James Turner and his** "lambs"—Cruelty of the **soldiers—The rising of** Pentland—**Covenanters dispersed—Death of Hugh McKail—Soldiers instigated to cruelty by the curates and Archbishop Sharp—His death—The** persecuted on the defensive—Battle of Drumclog—Dissensions—Battle **of Bothwell Bridge—Terrible cruelties—Deaths of Cameron, Cargill and** Hackson—**The Test Act**—Proceedings against **the earl of Argyle—Further persecutions—Resistance of the persecuted—Their** declaration—The Bloody Act—Death **of Charles II**............ 103

## CHAPTER V.

### From the Accession of James VII. to the Emigration of Presbyterians to America.

PAGE

Accession of James VII.—Proceedings of the new Parliament—The king's schemes to restore popery—Attempt of Argyle—Capture and death—Presbyterians persecuted and banished—Parliament will not yield to the king—Passes three acts of indulgence—Clergy return to Scotland—Strict Covenanters reject the king's acts—Death of Renwick—Landing of Prince of Orange—The Revolution—Ineffectual attempts to introduce Episcopacy in Scotland—The system a nondescript Church—Slavish and persecuting—Covenanters refuse to fellowship prelacy—Meeting of Parliament—Abolishes the prelatic Church—Ratifies the Confession of Faith and establishes the Presbyterian Church—Patronage done away—Meeting of the General Assembly—Desire of the king that all Protestants unite in same church government—Origin of moderate party—The Revolution settlement a calamity—Connection between religious and civil liberty—The principles contended for in Scotland—Dear to them—Brought to America—Element of power in the Presbyterian Church in America.................................................... 126

---

# HISTORY OF THE IRISH CHURCH.

## CHAPTER VI.

### From the Introduction of the Reformed Religion in Ireland to the Great Revival of 1625.

American Presbyterian Church indebted to the Irish—Gospel introduced in Ireland in second century—Irish Church independent until twelfth century—Then subjected to pope—Remained subject three hundred years—Deplorable condition of the people—Henry VIII. asserts supremacy—George Brown made archbishop of Dublin—Opposition of Romish clergy—Edward VI.—Resistance to the liturgy—English

ministers unwilling to occupy Irish sees—Bishop Bale—
His firmness—Queen Mary—Elizabeth—Ireland a place of
shelter for Protestants—Distracted state of country unfavorable to religion—Want of Reformed ministers—Description of the Irish Church—Dublin College established—Its
purpose—Slow progress of the Reformation—Accession of
James I.—His pacific and wise measures—Province of Ulster—Colonizing schemes—Prosperity of these plantations—
Confession of faith for the Irish Church—Its liberal character—Efficiency of Scotch clergy—Price, Hubbard, Glendenning, Blair and Hamilton—Their reception by Bishop Echlin—Revival of religion—Many converts—Welsh, Stewart,
Dunbar and Livingston come over from Scotland—Liberality of Bishop Knox—Labor of Scotch clergy greatly blessed
—Presbyterian worship and discipline maintained—Romanists and Bishop Echlin oppose the revival—The latter perse-
cute Blair and others—They appeal to Archbishop Usher—
Restored—Again suspended—Apply in vain to the lord-
deputy of Ireland............................................................ 147

## CHAPTER VII.

### From the Accession of Charles I. to the Irish Re-bellion.

Romanism rather than the Reformed faith encouraged—Some
Protestants think of emigrating to the New World—King
needs funds for his Irish army—Concessions to Romanists—
Protest of Irish prelates—Laud and Wentworth favor Roman
ritual—Bramhall and Leslie promoted—Bedell—Alterations
in Dublin University—Convocation of the clergy, 1634—
Adopt the Thirty-nine Articles of the English Church—People deceived—High Commission court erected—Condition of
Presbyterians deplorable—The four ministers that were restored again deposed—Death of Echlin—The bigot Leslie
his successor—Suspends five ministers—Sailing of the Eaglewing — Returns — Wentworth's persecutions — Many clergy
fly to Scotland—Remain there—Discontent in Ulster alarms
Wentworth—The Black Oath—Cruel imposition of it—
Sufferings of the Presbyterians—Henry Stewart—Wentworth's cruel proceedings—Bishop Adair—Deposed—Op-

posed by Bishop Bedell—Wentworth created an earl—Raises an Irish army to suppress the people of Ulster—Opposition—Remonstrance sent to the king—Meeting of the Long Parliament—Earl of Strafford impeached imprisoned and beheaded—Presbyterians petition Parliament—Their requests granted—Change in administration—Two Puritan lords-justices appointed—High Commission court abolished—Peace in Ireland .................................................................................. 181

## CHAPTER VIII.
### From the Irish Insurrection to the Death of Charles I.

The rebellion incited by Romish priests—Object to destroy Protestantism — Plot discovered — Important towns saved from capture—Places of refuge—Rebels master of most of Ulster—Their cruelties—Universal massacre—Famine and pestilence—Sufferings of Protestant clergy—Death of Bishop Bedell—As many Presbyterians fled to Scotland, they suffered less than Episcopalians—Charles sends commissions to Irish Protestant leaders—Lords-justices furnish arms—English and Scotch Parliaments send relief—Arrival of regiments—Severe engagements—Insurrection subdued—Re-establishment of the Presbyterian Church—Ministers and people return from Scotland—Army chaplains—Presbytery revived—Congregations gathered—Petition to the Scotch Assembly—Ministers arrive from Scotland—The Church grows rapidly—Many Episcopalians join the Presbyterian Church—Giving evidence of repentance—Overruling Providence—Peaceful and prosperous state of the Church—Ecclesiastical reform in England—Westminster Assembly called—Commissioners sent to Scotland—Solemn League and Covenant—Taken in Ireland, Scotland and England—Its effects—Growth of the Church—Thirty settled ministers in 1647.

### From the Death of Charles to the Accession of James II.

Ulster Presbyterians protest against his murder—Assent, under protest, to Cromwell's government—His judicious measures in Ireland—Baptist and Independent ministers—Parliament favors education and religion—Endowments and salaries—Engagement oath—Presbyterian clergy opposed—Oath enforced—Sufferings of ministers—Council of Independents and Presbyterians—A public debate—Change of Irish commissioners—Baptists in favor—Forcing Presbyterians to take the oath—Appeal to Fleetwood—Appear before the council—**Dismissed with favor—Cromwell dissolves Parliament—His** accession to **power** favorable to **Presbyterians—Ministers** allowed to pursue their calling—Danger from **dissensions in** Church of Scotland—Did not extend to **Ulster—Increase of ministers—Presbytery** divided—Church **prosperous—Death** of Cromwell—Charles **II. restored—His efforts to restore prelacy—Bramhall and** Leslie restored—Measures employed **to crush out Presbyterianism—Proclamation against** presbytery—**Unavailing** appeal to the Irish privy-council—Jeremy Taylor's intolerant spirit—Ejects thirty-six ministers from their churches—Their privations—Meeting of the Irish **Parliament—**Solemn **League and** Covenant **burned—Duke of** Ormond's **leniency—Ministers** for a time not molested—Blood's plot—Conspirators **apprehended—Presbyterians not** implicated—Leniency shown them—Ministers **return from** Scotland—Growth **of the Church—Presbyteries again organized—**Lord Robart's administration—Jealousy of Episcopal bishops **and clergy—Boyle bishop of Down—Sir Arthur** Forbes **shields** Presbyterians **from persecution—Revival** of religious worship—Regium Donum—Schools **and a theological seminary established—Insurrection in** Scotland—Injurious to Ulster Presbyterians—Ormond **presses the oath** of supremacy—Persecution—The **prelates active persecutors**—The condition of Presbyterians such they think of removing to America.

## From James II. to Emigration of Presbyterians to America, 1725.

James II.'s policy favors Romanists—Tyrconnel lord-deputy—Papists restored to power—Protestants depressed—Act of Toleration—Presbyterians enjoy a brief freedom—Calm followed by a storm—Alarm in Ulster—Council appointed—Tyrconnel's army seizes the principal towns—Gates of **Derry** and Enniskillen shut—The former a great barrier to James' army—Landing of Prince of Orange in England—Promises aid to Protestants in Ireland—Numerous battles—Siege of Derry—City relieved—Defence of Enniskillen—Retreat of the Irish army—King William leads his army—Battle of Boyne—Total defeat of Irish army—Different conduct of Episcopal and Presbyterian clergy—The king favors Presbyterians—Presbyterianism restored in Ulster—Presbyteries and synods again held—Losses by the war—Ulster Presbyterians hospitably received in Scotland—Jealousy of Irish bishops—King William secures the abolition of the oath of supremacy—Its effects—Meeting of the Irish Parliament—Act of Toleration defeated—Controversy of Bishop King with Boyse and Craighead—Results—Increased hostility of Episcopalians—Oppressive measures—Oath of abjuration—Sacramental test—Its effects—Futile efforts to obtain legal toleration—Half century of civil disabilities—Brief periods of relief—Still the Presbyterian Church grows—Two synods formed, and become a delegated body—An educated ministry—Missions—Church extended—Presbyterians excluded from office—Desire to emigrate to America—Causes which led to a large emigration of Ulster Presbyterians to America............................................................................ 199

# EMIGRATION OF SCOTCH AND SCOTCH-IRISH.

## CHAPTER IX.

### EMIGRATION TO AMERICA.

Character of the Scotch emigrants—Causes which led to their emigration—The colonists in South Carolina—Virginia, Maryland and Delaware—North Carolina—Their sympathy for the Presbyterian Church—Scotch-Irish emigration—Causes—Religious bigotry, commercial jealousy and oppressive landlords—Emigration so great as to alarm the Irish magistrates—Reasons assigned by the magistrates for the emigration—Ports of entry—New England Presbyterians—

## CONTENTS.

Largest number came to Philadelphia—States in which they principally settled—Character of the colonists—Protestants and Presbyterians—Rapid growth of the Presbyterian Church—The emigrants retain their modes of worship and system of church government—The Catechism—Lord's Supper, how administered—Influence of this emigration on the Presbyterian Church in America.................................................. 265

# FOREIGN MINISTERS OF THE PRESBYTERIAN CHURCH IN AMERICA.

## CHAPTER X.

### FOREIGN MINISTERS IN AMERICA.

Larger number from Ireland—Difficulty to determine the nationality of some ministers—Francis Makemie the first minister—MacNish and Hampton his associates—Other clergymen from 1685 to 1715—William Tennent and his sons—Robert Cross—James Macgregor—Samuel Blair—Alexander Craighead—Francis Alison—John Elder—John Craig—Charles Beatty—Samuel Finley—Robert Smith—Other ministers previous to 1758—At union of synods nearly one-half of the clergy foreign-born—Formative period of the Church—Great indebtedness of the American Presbyterian Church to the Scotch and Irish churches .................................... 286

# EARLY EDUCATIONAL INSTITUTIONS.

## CHAPTER XI.

### PRESBYTERIANS AND EDUCATION.

Presbyterians patrons of learning—Public schools in Scotland—Early provision for education in America—Action of the synod of the Carolinas—Numerous classical schools and academies—The Log College—Synod's school at New London—Fagg's Manor school—Nottingham academy—Classical academy at Pequa—Upper Buffalo academy—Schools at

Elizabethtown, Pencader, Baskinridge, Mendham and Philadelphia—Schools in Virginia—At Guilford, Thyatira, Wilmington, **Sugar Creek, Rocky** Hill, Poplar Tent, Bethany, and Liberty Hall academy, North Carolina—Schools in Tennessee—Principal object of these to educate ministers—**Higher educational** institutions—College of New Jersey—**Jefferson, Dickinson,** Hampden-Sidney and Washington Colleges.................................................................... 299

## PATRIOTISM OF PRESBYTERIANS.

### CHAPTER XII.

Essential principles of liberty—The creed of republics—The Scotch and Irish exiles foes to arbitrary power—Reasons why the latter distrusted England—Had governed Ireland for her own selfish ends—Would do the same with her American colonies—Friends of civil and religious freedom—Dread of Episcopal supremacy—Efforts to establish Episcopacy—Religious freedom sought—Civil and religious liberty inseparable—Presbyterians first to combine in resistance—Testimony of Mr. Adolphus—Union with New England against the Stamp law—Testimony of Messrs. Reed and Galloway—Action of Synod of New York and Philadelphia—North Carolina Presbyterians and **Mecklenburg** Declaration—Presbyterians of Western **Pennsylvania—Memorial from Cumberland** county, Pa.—Action of Hanover presbytery, Virginia—Presbyterian ministers **active and earnest** patriots—Efficient as statesmen, soldiers, chaplains, etc.—Dr. Witherspoon's services and other ministry—Patriotism of elders and members of the Presbyterian Church—Many of them officers—Worthy of their lineage—Presbyterians in the civil service—Introduced elements of their system into the government—Proper founders of new States—Not anarchists—Favored constitutional freedom—Church and State separate—Prized their principles—Ready to defend them at every sacrifice.......... 314

# SCOTCH AND IRISH SEEDS IN AMERICAN SOIL.

## HISTORY OF THE SCOTCH CHURCH.

### CHAPTER I.

FROM THE INTRODUCTION OF CHRISTIANITY TO THE ESTABLISHMENT OF THE GREAT CHARTER OF THE CHURCH.

THE Scotch was one of the most important elements which entered into the composition of the early Presbyterian churches of America. It possessed characteristics which were peculiar to itself, and which left a deep impress upon the new communities, of which it formed no inconsiderable part. Its piety was stern and uncompromising, for it had learned, through centuries of persecution, to dread both papal and prelatic error and usurpation. It had been forced to contend, in a hand-to-hand conflict, with these alternately dominant powers for the maintenance of the distinctive principles of its faith and order. Out of this protracted struggle it finally emerged with the three cardinal principles inscribed on its banner of loyalty to Christ as the true and only Head of the Church, the parity of the clergy, and the right of every congregation to a voice in the election of its officers. Of the truth and importance of these fundamental principles the Scottish Christians were so fully and firmly convinced that when necessity was laid upon them they did not shrink from sufferings, and even death itself, rather than renounce or betray their faith.

It is impossible now to determine when Christianity was first introduced into Scotland. The best authorities favor the belief that it was not later than the close of the second century, and that the first Christian ministers were men of singularly pure and holy lives. They mingled freely with the people, instructed them in the doctrines of God's word, inculcated the duties of morality and virtue, endeavored to check all forms of vice and to soften the rough manners which then prevailed.

This condition of things, however, was not permitted to continue, even in a country so insulated as Scotland. The Church of Rome, which at an early period corrupted the simplicity of the Christian religion in the other countries of Europe, at length cast its baneful influence over the Scotch Church. There is reason to believe that as early as the fifth century the pope had taken measures to regulate the policy of the Scottish Church, and there is evidence that the inhabitants from this date acknowledged him as the head of the Church.

Popery, with its false doctrine, its superstitious rites and its persecuting spirit, with a wealthy and powerful hierarchy that had corrupted the whole spirit of religion, and with the people sunk in ignorance and debased by slavery, presented no ordinary difficulties to be surmounted by the Reformation, which began in Scotland in the sixteenth century. Germany and England had preceded it in a successful effort to free themselves from the oppression of the papal yoke. But when the doctrines of the Reformers were at length made known in Scotland, there were not wanting noble-minded men, who proved valiant defenders of the fundamental truths of the gospel, and who, in the contest with a corrupt and persecuting Church, were honored with the glorious crown of martyrdom.

Of these Patrick Hamilton, abbot of Ferne, was the first sufferer. Descended from an illustrious family and of noble blood, he had before him all the prospects of church preferment which could excite the ambition of an aspiring youth. He prosecuted his studies at St. Andrews, and subsequently visited Wittenberg and Marbourg, in Germany. There he held intercourse with Luther, Melanchthon and other German Reformers, and became convinced of the truth of their opinions and of the errors of the Church to whose ministry he had been destined by his parents. With the conviction that the Reformed doctrines were in accordance with the word of God, he felt it to be his duty to impart to his countrymen the knowledge he had acquired. Returning from the Continent in 1527, he entered with great zeal upon the duties of his ministry. He began at once to expose and to reprove the superstitious practices of the Romish Church in Scotland, and to preach the doctrine of free and complete justification by faith in Christ alone. His ministry drew multitudes around him, impressed by the power of his fervid appeals, while many embraced the truth to the saving of their souls. The message was not only new to them, but the earnestness and spirituality of the preacher contrasted powerfully with the carelessness and the vices of the mass of the priesthood.

Alarmed at the great success of the abbot's preaching, the priests determined to silence him, if possible, by falsely accusing him of teaching heresy. Accordingly, the charge of "Lutheranism" was preferred against him and the entire enginery of their Church employed for his overthrow. Under pretence that the archbishop wished to consult him, Hamilton was enticed to visit St. Andrews, where Alexander Campbell, a Dominican friar, was appointed to insinuate himself into his confidence and to learn the real nature of the opinions which he entertained. These were immediately communicated to other prelates with every aggravation which malice could suggest. As soon as a tribunal of the clergy could be assembled they pronounced his views heretical; and having ineffectually exhorted him to abandon them, they condemned him to be burnt at the stake. With a cruelty having scarcely a parallel, on the same day upon which he had been condemned he was led forth to execution, and with true Christian heroism he suffered death before the gate of St. Salvator's College.

The effects produced by this martyr's death were very different from those which his persecutors desired. The terrible retribution that befell Campbell for his treachery and hypocrisy deepened greatly the impression made upon the people by the intrepid conduct of Hamilton as he was fastened to the stake and while the flames were kindling around him. Calling to his betrayer, he said, "O thou most iniquitous of men! who condemnest those things which thou knowest, and didst a few days before confess, to be true,\* I summon thee to the tribunal of God!" These words never ceased to ring in the ears of the perfidious man, and he died a raving maniac. Fearing the influence upon the people of the severe and unjust execution of Hamilton, the prelates secured the subscription of those in authority as a sanction of the sentence. But all was in vain. The heart of the Scottish nation was deeply stirred. Men began to inquire as to the nature of the crime for

---

\* In his conference with Hamilton he had acknowledged the truth of the Reformed doctrines.

which such punishment had been inflicted upon so noble a man, and they were led by a consideration of the doctrines fully to embrace them. Not a few persons began to question many things which they had never before doubted. Inquiry and discussion could not be excluded even from the University of St. Andrews, and impressions then made were never obliterated. Several of the friars began to hold and to preach doctrines savoring strongly of the Reformation, nor did they hesitate to expose the licentious and ungodly lives of the bishops and of the clergy.

All this very naturally alarmed and irritated Archbishop Beaton and his satellites, and they again resolved to try the effect of persecution to silence all opposers. A servant of the archbishop sagaciously advised him that if he burned any more to burn them in cellars; "for the smoke," said he, "of Mr. Patrick Hamilton hath infected as many as it blew upon." This advice, however, was not heeded. Other victims were imprisoned, and perished at the stake exhibiting a Christian heroism that scorned the flames. The mistaken and wicked policy of the prelates multiplied rather than repressed the number of those who adhered to the reform. Their corruption as well as their violence excited disgust and opposition. The vices of the clergy were not only a scandal to religion, but an outrage on common decency. Even the bishops were not ashamed to confess their ignorance of the Bible,* save what they had learned from their missals.

These persecutions under Archbishop Beaton were mainly instigated by his nephew, David Beaton, who, after his uncle's death, in 1539, succeeded him in the office, and at the request of the king of France was raised by the pope to the rank of a cardinal. He was a man of talents, of unbounded ambition and of a cruel disposition. No sooner had he attained to his office than he began to employ the most rigorous measures to exterminate the Reformers and their doctrines. The better to accomplish his purpose, he endeavored in every way to ingratiate himself with King James V. and to secure for his favorites stations of dignity and power. And so far had he succeeded in his plans that at the death of the king, in 1542, it was found that he had already prepared and presented for his approval a list of some hundreds of persons of various ranks—not a few of them nobles and barons—who were suspected of heresy, and the confiscation of whose estates was urged as the means of replenishing the king's coffers.

Defeated in this scheme by the king's death and by the appointment of the earl of Arran as regent, the baffled cardinal only thirsted the more for vengeance upon the Reformers. An act of Parliament declaring it lawful for all persons to read

---

* Spottiswood, p. 66.

the Scriptures in their native language, and by which thousands of copies of the sacred volume were brought into circulation, called forth his bitter hostility. He at once bent all his energies to acquire an ascendency over the weak and fickle regent, who was known to be favorable to the Reformed religion. With the aid of two other able and designing men, he succeeded only too well in his purpose, and the wily cardinal soon had all the authority he wished to imprison and put to death those suspected of sympathy with the Reformed faith. Like a chafed tiger thirsting for blood, he entered at once upon his murderous work. With barbarous cruelty he put five men and one woman to death at Perth. In company with the regent, to give the appearance of his sanction to the crimes, he made a bloody circuit through the kingdom, inflicting fines upon some, imprisoning others, and persecuting not a few unto death.

His most distinguished victim was the gentle, learned and pious George Wishart. Having been banished by the bishop of Brechin, Wishart resided for some years at the University of Cambridge. Returning from England in the year 1544, he commenced to preach the doctrines of the evangelical faith, and with such persuasive eloquence that he made a profound impression upon his large audiences. This was an unpardonable offence in the estimation of Beaton. Such a bold heretic could not be permitted to live in peace. Hunted from place to place as if he were a wild beast, he was finally betrayed into the hands of his persecutor by the earl of Bothwell. The cardinal summoned his prelatical council, and with much ostentation proceeded to the trial and condemnation of his victim. After a mock trial, which was but a series of insults, Wishart was sentenced to be burned on the following day as a heretic. The martyr met death with fortitude and holy boldness, forgiving his enemies and persecutors; but before he died he turned toward the cardinal, who was witnessing the execution from a window of the tower, and said, "He who in such state from that high place feedeth his eyes with my torments within a few days shall be hanged out at the same window, to be seen with as much ignominy as he now leaneth there in pride." Only a few months passed before this prediction was fulfilled. Thus a death which seemed at the time the triumph of the cardinal's power proved to be the knell summoning him to judgment. John Leslie, a brother of the earl of Rothes, headed a conspiracy, which surprised Beaton in the castle of St. Andrews and slew him in his own bed-chamber while pleading for mercy and crying, "I am a priest! I am a priest!" and without one word of repentance or prayer. And to allay a tumult caused by the attendants of the castle, and to assure the populace of his death, the cardinal's dead body was exposed at the very window from which he had witnessed Wishart's execution. So perished David Beaton, one of the most unscrupulous, treacherous, licentious and cruel prelates that ever cursed any country.

Though the destruction of this bold, bad man was regarded by a large part of the community as necessary in order to preserve civil and religious liberty, yet upon no Christian principle could such an act be justified. Its perpetrators were guilty of an infringement of the laws of the kingdom. But convinced as they were that the illegality of Wishart's sentence had converted his death into murder, and that the civil power was unable or unwilling to punish the crime, they believed that they were doing God's service and performing a patriotic deed in ridding their country of one of its worst enemies.

This misjudged act was calculated to keep alive the fierce spirit of the age, and to impede the progress of the cause it was intended to promote. While it was a warning to the persecutors of the Reformers, it alienated many good men, who were shocked at the illegal manner and the circumstances of the cardinal's death. The warning, however, was disregarded by his successor, John Hamilton, who, when installed in office, adopted Beaton's policy. Unable to wreak his vengeance upon the more prominent preachers of the Reformed faith, he seized an old priest of fourscore years, Walter Mill, who had been accused of heresy in the days of his predecessor, but at the time had escaped. Being discovered by one of the archbishop's spies, he was apprehended, brought to trial, and burnt at the stake. So great was the compassion felt for this venerable man, and such the horror awakened by this great outrage, that the archbishop was compelled to employ one of his own domestics, a dissolute fellow, as the executioner. As he expired in the flames the aged sufferer uttered these prophetic words: "I trust in God I shall be the last that shall suffer death in Scotland for this cause." And he *was* the last victim the archbishop was permitted to sacrifice. "His death," says Spottiswood, "was the death of popery in the realm."

In the mean time events rapidly culminated. The lords and chief gentry who were devoted to Protestantism resolved to meet at Edinburgh, and there determine what was best to be done in the present crisis. On assembling they resolved to stand steadfast in the defence of the Reformed religion, and entered into a common bond or covenant for the support of each other and to maintain the gospel. This league was formed December 3, 1557, and was subscribed by the earls of Argyle, Glencairn and Morton, and by a great number of other distinguished men among the barons and influential country gentlemen.

This is truly a remarkable document, especially

when we consider the times and circumstances in which it was drawn up. The demands made in it upon the queen-regent were few and moderate, showing both their loyalty and their desire to avoid all conflict with the civil power. The subscribers insisted, however, that the curates and pastors should discard the use of Latin in their services and perform them in the English language, which the people understood, and they promised to apply their "whole power, substance and their very lives," to maintain "faithful ministers who would purely and truly minister Christ's evangel and sacraments to his people." Subsequently, they claimed that the election of ministers should be made by the people, according to the custom of the primitive Church, and that great diligence should be exercised by those who presided at such elections, so that men of unholy lives or holding erroneous doctrines should not be retained in the sacred office. It was also afterward provided by act of council that "it should be lawful for every one that could read, to use the English version of the Bible until the prelates should publish a more correct one." Continued and strenuous efforts also were made by the nobility and gentry to suppress all superstitious rites and practices—including the *mass*—which seek "to destroy the evangel of Christ and his congregation."

The time of conflict now drew nigh when these

principles would be subjected to the severest test in the persons of their adherents. The queen, under the influence of her brothers, the princes of the French house of Lorraine, was to be used as the instrument for the suppression of the Reformation, not only in Scotland, but throughout Europe. As Mary was also the nearest heir to the English crown, it was thought that the best method to secure their design would be first to suppress the Reformation and establish the French and papal powers in her realm, and from thence assail England. In order to accomplish this, it was necessary that the crown-matrimonial of Scotland should be secured to Mary's husband, the son of the king of France and heir to the throne. The queen employed every artifice in her power to induce the Protestant nobility to consent to recognize her husband Francis and herself as king and queen of Scotland. By her solemn promise that she would " protect their preachers and themselves from the malice and hatred of the bishops and promote the reformation of religion," she succeeded only too well in her scheme.

But the mask she wore was thrown aside so soon as she had gained her purpose. At once she adopted measures to banish or silence the Protestant ministers. Though overawed in her plans for a time by the resolute attitude of the nobility, she only awaited a more favorable opportunity to renew the attempt. Four of the preachers of the Reformed doctrines, distinguished for their eloquence and boldness, were summoned to appear before the court at Stirling, May 10, 1558, to stand trial for "usurping the ministerial office and exciting seditions and tumults among the people."

At this critical period the Protestant cause received a most important accession of strength in the person of John Knox, who had returned from the Continent at the earnest entreaty of the Scotch nobility, they promising to jeopardize their lives in the cause of true religion. His arrival at this opportune moment produced consternation in the hearts of the prelates. Already they had felt the keenness of his blade, and their corrupt system still reeled under the terrible blows he had dealt it. Instead of attacking the outposts, Knox had turned his heavy artillery on the very citadel of the enemy, boldly maintaining that the papal Church of Rome was Antichrist. Disdaining all compromises with the apostate Church, rejecting everything in doctrine and government which had no higher authority than was derived from its teaching or practice, his final and sole appeal was to the word of God. From Knox's appearance on the scene we may date the real beginning of the Reformation in Scotland.

After the death of Wishart, Knox had gone to England, and finally to the Continent, where he found a welcome refuge in the little republic of Geneva. Here he formed an intimacy with Calvin, a kindred spirit to his own, and in friendly conference and Scripture study matured his views of Church reform. Here, too, he found a system of order and discipline combined with pure doctrine which excited his greatest admiration. The more he studied it, the more enthusiastic was his approval of it, and from this period he became convinced that the Presbyterian form of church government was the one best adapted to his own country. And all the lessons which he learned by observation and through intercourse with the Genevan Reformers were garnered up for the service of the Church in his native land.

It was but the week previous to the trial of the ministers at Stirling that Knox landed at Leith. From the hour of his arrival he became the ruling spirit in the councils of the Lords of the Congregation. His presence encouraged his friends, and his words inspired them with his own zeal and firmness. Their antagonists could scarcely have been more disconcerted by the news of an invading army; for, while the papal fraternity were engaged in their deliberations in the monastery of Grayfriars, one of their number rushed in pale with terror, exclaiming in broken words, "John Knox! John Knox is come! he is come! He slept last night at Edinburgh!" They ceased to deliberate, broke up the council, and dispersed in confusion.

It was in vain that the queen-regent proclaimed him an outlaw and a rebel. His voice could neither be silenced nor his influence suppressed. Communicating his own courage in a large degree to the Protestant nobility, they resolved to defend their right of liberty of worship and to protect their pastors who had been put on trial. For this purpose they assembled at Perth *with arms* to enforce their just demands. But again were they deceived by the false promise of the queen-regent, who agreed that "if they would quietly disperse no steps should be taken against their ministers." No sooner, however, had the Protestants returned to their homes than their pastors were denounced as rebels for not appearing for trial on the day originally named in the summons, and all persons were prohibited, "under pain of rebellion, to assist, comfort, receive or maintain them in any sort."

The duplicity of the queen excited in the minds of Protestants the utmost contempt, and in that of the people at large a total loss of confidence. The prior of St. Andrews and the earl of Argyle retired in disgust from her councils and joined themselves to the Protestant cause. Strengthened by these and other valuable accessions, the Lords of the Congregation "framed and subscribed another bond, pledging them to mutual support and defence in the cause of religion." They resolved, also, to abolish the idolatrous rites of popery, and to establish Protestant worship wherever the authority of the nobility or the favor of the people sanctioned it. Lord James Stewart, the prior of St. Andrews, who had recently joined the Reformers, invited Knox to preach publicly in the abbey on a certain day. The invitation was eagerly accepted, and on the 9th of June the preacher arrived at St. Andrews. The archbishop was enraged. He threatened that if John Knox should dare to appear in the pulpit of the cathedral "he should be saluted with a dozen of culverings, whereof the most part should light on his nose." Fearing to expose the life of the preacher, as well as their own lives, to such imminent peril, some were disposed to retreat. But when Knox was consulted, he entreated them not to hinder him from preaching, for this was an opportunity for which he had longed and prayed and hoped; and "as for the fear of danger that may come to me, let no man be solicitous, for my life is in the custody of Him whose glory I seek. I desire the hand and weapon of no man to defend me. I only crave audience."

This language was becoming him "who never feared the face of man." The call he regarded as one of sacred duty, and his dauntless courage so inspired the lords that they ceased to think of danger. On the appointed day Knox appeared in the pulpit and preached to a large audience, including the archbishop and many of the inferior clergy, and no "culverings" were fired at him, for God restrained the fury of his enemies, while his Spirit subdued the hearts of the people. His subject was our Lord's driving the traders from the temple, which he applied to the duty of Christians to purify the Church and remove from it all the corruptions of papacy. For three days he preached in the same place, and the result was that the Reformed worship was established in the city, and the magistracy and people stripped the church of images and pictures.

Information of what had taken place not only at St. Andrews, but in the other parts of the kingdom, led the queen-regent to adopt vigorous measures to suppress the Lords of the Congregation. She raised an army, which was met by armed resistance on the part of the Protestants. After alternate reverses of both parties and a long war of diplomacy, the Protestants applied to Queen Elizabeth of England for aid, and with the assistance afforded by her army and fleet the French troops were driven from Scotland. In the treaty which followed it was stipulated that a free Parliament should be convened, which assembled in August, 1560. Both the circumstances in which they met and the subjects on which they were called to deliberate, constitute this the most important meeting of the estates of the kingdom that had as yet been held in Scotland. A petition by a number of Protestants was presented to this body, praying "that the anti-Christian doctrine maintained in the Popish Church should be discarded;

that means should be used to restore purity of worship and primitive discipline; and that the ecclesiastical revenues should be applied to the support of a pious and active ministry, to the promotion of learning and to the relief of the poor." In this petition we have the assertion of several great principles—purity of worship, return to primitive discipline and the proper support of a pious and devoted ministry—which subsequently were put into operation in the Scottish Church and made it a blessing and a power in the kingdom.

With respect to the first request of the petitioners, that of purity of worship, the Parliament required the Reformed ministers to lay before them a summary of doctrines agreeable to the Scriptures and which they wished established. This they did in a confession of twenty-five articles. It was read first before the lords of articles and then before the whole Parliament, and after due examination it was formally ratified by the Parliament, only three noblemen voting against it. This body also, August 24th, abolished the papal jurisdiction, prohibited the celebration of mass, and rescinded all the laws against the Reformed faith.

Thus, by the act of the State, the Protestant religion became the national religion of Scotland. But Parliament, though it had annulled the papal jurisdiction, created no ecclesiastical authority in its stead. During these distracted times little comparatively had been done to organize even local churches. Converted priests and laymen taught the doctrines which they had received as opportunity offered. There were very few stationed preachers. Most of those capable of presenting the Reformed faith in a suitable manner to the people itinerated in different parts of the kingdom. But the circumstances had so changed that all felt there was a pressing necessity to adopt measures for a national ecclesiastical organization. The vacant field was in need of diligent and wise cultivation; it was plainly their duty to secure the vantage-ground gained for the Reformation.

To this end the first General Assembly of Scotland was convened at Edinburgh, December 20, 1560. It owed its authority to no earthly power, and hence was free to adopt a system of doctrines and a form of government which it considered most consonant to the Scriptures. Scotland escaped for the present the evil under which the English Church had long suffered—the forced acknowledgment of the supremacy of the civil power as her spiritual head. But the principle which was now conceded was afterward to become an object of fierce and protracted conflict.

The Assembly consisted of but forty members, and only six of these were ministers. While few in number, however, the clergy were men of ability and piety and raised up by God for the work given them to do. Great simplicity and unanimity characterized the proceedings. Seven different meetings were held without a moderator or president. The Assembly in many of its features resembled a missionary organization, having been called into being by the exigences of the occasion. The papal organization had been abolished, and they were under the necessity of making immediate provision for the spiritual instruction of the people. And as the *purity* of the Church was essential to its well-being, and as this could in their view only be maintained by the power of discipline, their first work was to draw up a complete system of ecclesiastical government. This task was devolved upon the same eminent men who had framed the Confession of Faith which had been ratified by Parliament—John Knox, John Mirriam, John Spottiswood, John Douglas, John Row and John Willock. The work they divided among themselves; and having finished their several parts and examined the whole together, they laid it before the General Assembly, by whom it was approved. Whether it was formally adopted, as opposition was made by some of the nobility with whose selfish schemes it interfered, there is some reason to doubt. The probabilities are that it *was* adopted at a meeting held in the following January. This much we do know—that this, the FIRST BOOK OF DISCIPLINE, was afterward referred to and regarded as the standard book of the Church, regulating her practice and guiding her decisions.

As this is the constitution of the Church of Scotland and contains the matured opinions of the Scotch Reformers, it is very desirable that we have clear views respecting its provisions. The leading ideas of the book of discipline were suggested by Knox, who was at the head of the commission, and the principles of church government embodied in it bore a striking resemblance to those of the Genevan Reformers. Nor is this surprising. For years Knox and Calvin had been intimately associated, and we have before seen that their views were remarkably accordant in doctrine, as they were now respecting the polity of the Church. These two great men, in common with the early Puritans, recognized four classes of church officers—pastors, who were to preach the gospel and administer the sacraments; doctors or teachers, whose province it was to interpret Scripture and refute error and to teach theology in schools and universities; ruling elders, who assisted the pastor in exercising discipline; and deacons, who had special charge of the revenue of the church and of the poor. But in the Scottish as in other Presbyterian and Congregational churches, the distinct office of teacher fell into disuse. As merely academical or theological, or of the nature of an aid to the pastor, as in the Congregational churches of New England, it lacked the position and prominence which were essential to its permanent recognition.

The session, consisting of the pastor, elders and deacons, managed the affairs of the individual congregation. They were chosen by the people, and met weekly or oftener for the transaction of business. There was also held in every principal town a meeting, called the "weekly exercise," composed of ministers, teachers and educated men in the vicinity. This was subsequently converted into the presbytery and had the oversight of the neighboring churches. The provincial synod discharged kindred duties, only on a wider field. The General Assembly, which was composed of ministers and elders commissioned for the purpose, and meeting twice or thrice a year, attended to the general interests of the national Church.

Two great objects were sought to be secured by these arrangements—the one the freedom and vigor of the individual congregation, the other a system of order and discipline common to all the churches. The first was vindicated by declaring it as a principle founded upon the word of God that "it appertaineth to the people and to every several congregation to elect their minister." The last was promoted through the influence exerted by synods and the General Assembly, constituting as they did the missionary and aggressive organization for all the churches. Public worship was held twice on the Sabbath, and in every town a sermon was preached also on one other day of the week. Baptism, when administered, was accompanied with preaching, and the Lord's Supper was observed four times a year with appropriate sermons and instruction. A school was to be established in every parish, and in every "notable town" it was proposed to erect a college for the higher education of the youth. Measures were adopted to secure the instruction of all classes, those who were able being obliged to do it at their own expense, while a fund was provided to educate the children of the poor. To carry all these important measures into effect, the patrimony of the former ecclesiastical establishment was divided between the ministry, the schools and the poor.

These were the principal features of the government and discipline of the Church of Scotland as set forth in the book of discipline. As thus constituted, the Church was purely Presbyterian. It had, it is true, one peculiar feature—that of a system of *superintendence*, which some have claimed favored a modified form of episcopacy. But the office of a superintendent had little if anything in common with that of a bishop. Superintendents were required to be preachers and to remain in a particular place for months, exercising the pastoral office, and were subject to the *censure* and *control* of the clergy. While visiting the churches they were to preach not less than three times weekly, were not to relax their efforts until all the churches were supplied with ministers, and if condemned for any offence they were deprived of their office like any ordinary pastor. All these restrictions are inconsistent with the privileges and the dignity of the office of a prelatic bishop.

Their duties more nearly resembled those of a synodical missionary than of any other officer in the Church of the present day. They exercised a general supervision over extended districts—a provision greatly needed at that time, owing to the want of properly qualified ministers and the destitute condition of the congregations. The superintendents were not a separate order of the clergy, and their authority was carefully guarded, so as not to infringe upon the parity of the ministry. Yet their own usurpations of power and authority, together with the intrigues of certain of the nobility, who wished to use them for their selfish purposes, and with this object in view conceded to them episcopal titles, soon rendered the office very obnoxious with the people. By way of derision they were called *tulchan bishops,* and a more contemptuous term than this could scarcely have been devised. The "tulchan" was a calf's skin stuffed with straw, which was laid beside the cow to induce her to give her milk more freely. "The bishop," it was said, "had the title, but my lord had the milk."

The plan to make them bishops was not owing

to any zeal for episcopacy on the part of the people, but, as before stated, grew out of the avarice of the nobility, who were anxious to get hold of the episcopal revenues. At the period when the attempt was made to invest the superintendents with the title and authority of bishops Knox was on his deathbed, and his last hours were embittered by a knowledge of the proposed innovation. He gave his "dead hand and dying voice" against it. Like Calvin, he was willing to allow expediency a large place in the outward constitution of the Church, and he saw nothing unscriptural in the appointment of superintendents who should supervise large districts in the capacity of missionaries in order to provide the means of grace to destitute congregations, and to organize churches where they were needed, but to the very last he steadfastly refused to acknowledge them as a distinct order of the ministry, and would never give his consent to their ordination as such.

On the 5th of December, 1560, her young husband, Francis II., who occupied the throne but for a few months, died, and Mary returned to her native country from France. She landed at Leith, and was conducted to Holyrood House with many demonstrations of joy by a people who were ready to be loyal to their queen, provided they could at the same time maintain their higher allegiance to the King of kings. From motives of policy, and with the design to secure the confidence of the Protestants, she was led to make many concessions to them, since they were the predominant party in the kingdom. But in all these measures the queen was insincere, and was distrusted by the Protestant party. It was known that she still adhered to the tenets of the Romish faith and was at heart a bigoted papist, and her subsequent conduct confirmed the worst fears of Knox and the other Reformers. She refused to ratify the acts of Parliament that had established the Reformation, she repeatedly attempted to restore to the papal prelates their civil jurisdiction, and in 1563 she sent a letter to the Council of Trent, professing her submission to its authority, and expressing the hope that she would succeed in time in bringing both England and Scotland under the dominion of the Roman see. To the petition of her Protestant subjects for the suppression of the superstitious rites and worship of the papal Church she in great anger replied that "she hoped before another year to restore the mass throughout Scotland." But her crowning act of perfidy was her subscribing the treaty of Bayonne, formed between the queen-regent of France, the queen of Spain and the duke of Alva, which contemplated the total and universal extermination of the Protestants by fire and sword.\* Thus, with a duplicity characteristic of Romanism in all ages, Mary, by proclamations and acts of councils, wished to be re-

\* Hume.

garded as favoring the Reformed ministers, while she was secretly negotiating for the subversion of the Protestant religion throughout Europe.

A determined resistance was made against these and all other measures intended to restore the spiritual domination of Rome. At the same time the Scottish Reformers displayed equal zeal in maintaining their religious liberties. Foremost among these was John Knox, who launched his fiercest invectives against the queen for her deceptive conduct, and against certain of the nobility, who, through the bribes of power and the loose manners to which they had become accustomed at a licentious court, were ready to betray the interests of Protestantism. Wherever the contest was the fiercest, wherever the assault was most determined and persistent, and wherever boldness and inflexible courage, combined with prudence and great wisdom, were needed, there stood the intrepid Reformer, ready to resist successfully all the attacks of the enemy, until, worn out by anxiety of mind and his long and arduous labors, he died on the 29th day of October, 1572.

To the very last he evinced the same faithful intrepidity to truth and principle. Addressing the wicked regent, Morton, he boldly told him: "God has beautified you with many benefits which he has not given to every man, and therefore, in the name of God, I charge you to use all these benefits aright, and better in time to come than ye have done in times by the past. If ye shall do so, God bless you and honor you; but if ye do not, God shall spoil you of these benefits, and your end shall be ignominy and shame." How prophetic these words! and how forcibly must they have recurred to the regent's mind as he lay in prison and was subsequently led to the scaffold!

Scarcely could a higher or more just eulogy have been uttered than was pronounced by Morton when Knox's body was lowered into the grave: "*There lies he who never feared the face of man.*" "He was the greatest living Scotchman," says the historian Froude, "and the full measure of his greatness no man in his day could estimate. The spirit of Knox created and saved Scotland; and if Scotland had been Catholic again, neither the wisdom of Elizabeth's ministers, nor the teachings of her bishops, nor her own chicaneries, would have preserved England from revolution." Carlyle calls him "the bravest of all Scotchmen"— "the one Scotchman to whom, of all others, his country and the world owe a debt."

While his age and his contemporaries may not have been able to measure his greatness, his countrymen were not insensible of their indebtedness to him. Sincere and heartfelt grief was felt at his death by every Protestant throughout the kingdom, for they were painfully conscious that a grievous calamity had fallen upon the Church of Scotland.

Notwithstanding the Church had been obliged

for the last quarter of a century to maintain an incessant struggle with the court, which was anxious to establish a spurious prelacy and to make the spiritual subordinate to and a vassal of the civil power, yet was it a period of great prosperity to the Church. Though encountering either direct persecution or the secret stratagems of insidious foes, its General Assemblies were convened frequently, by means of which its ecclesiastical organization was speedily perfected, purity of doctrine maintained, a suitable ministry provided, the destitute parishes supplied with pastors, and its forms of divine worship established. When the first Assembly met, in 1560, it is stated that there were but *twelve* Protestant ministers in Scotland; while in 1567, just seven years afterward, there were two hundred and fifty-two, and in addition to these there were six hundred and twenty-one readers and exhorters. The order of supplying destitute congregations was first the reader, then the exhorter, and lastly the minister; and at the beginning the cases were rare, except in the larger towns, where more than one of these agents were employed. But the fact that in 1576, only nine years after this, one hundred and sixteen out of the two hundred and eighty-nine Presbyterian parishes were supplied with both a minister and a reader is a clear indication of the wonderful growth of the Church. The rapid and general diffusion of the truths of the Scriptures by means of these several church officers led the people speedily to abandon the superstitions of the papacy. That this was wellnigh universal throughout the kingdom may be inferred from the language of the complaint presented to the General Assembly in 1588, which stated that there were still "twelve papists in Dumfries and its neighborhood, ten in Angus and Mearns, three in the Lothians," etc. How shall we account for so great an external growth, accompanied as it was by an equally remarkable improvement in doctrine and discipline? Such energy as was shown and such wondrous deeds as were achieved by the Church of Scotland can only be accounted for on the supposition that the ministry was largely imbued with the Spirit of their divine Master, and that their exertions to enlighten and save the people were accompanied by the Holy Ghost. "Not by might, nor by power, but by my Spirit, saith the Lord of hosts;" and thus only could so great and so gracious a change have been wrought throughout an entire kingdom.

It should be borne in mind, too, that this great progress of the Church was achieved in the face of strong opposition. The ill-timed pretensions of Mary to the crown of England and her bigoted attachment to popery had kept the kingdom in a state of constant disturbance; and when her power to annoy and harass the ministers had ceased and the regent Morton succeeded to the civil authority, their trials and difficulties were by no means at an end. The latter—a bold, wicked man and an adept in all manner of intrigue—was more to be dreaded than an open enemy. As direct violence had proven ineffectual to suppress the Reformed faith, he resolved to try what could be accomplished by more subtle and insidious measures. His efforts were directed to these two things—first, to change the constitution of the Church of Scotland, making it prelatic, like that of England, and subject to the civil power; and second, to impoverish the Church in order to enrich himself. The former was to be reached by exalting and confirming the power of his "tulchan" bishops and placing the most sycophantic and unprincipled of them in influential positions; the latter, by gaining control of the thirds of the benefices, under pretence that the stipends of the ministers should be paid more regularly and satisfactorily. But no sooner had he obtained the money than he joined several parishes together and appointed over them one of his tulchan bishops, paying him as if he had only a single charge and retaining for his own the balance of the funds.

It was against such hindrances and such opposition as this that the Protestant ministry had constantly to contend. The struggle knew no intermission and it was for the right of existence. The clear judgment and intrepid spirit of John Knox were at this period greatly missed in their councils. Had that skillful pilot been at the wheel, the storm-tossed vessel would have been spared from encountering many of those tumultous waves which frequently threatened to engulph it. True, there were not wanting many excellent men sincerely attached to the principles of the Reformation and capable in more peaceful times of defending them, but they were unable successfully to surmount the new difficulties against which they had to contend at the hands of the subtle and stern regent.

At this juncture (1574) Andrew Melville returned from Geneva to his native land. During his residence of ten years on the Continent he enjoyed the acquaintance and counsels of Beza, the successor of Calvin. With the firmness, courage and integrity of Knox, and with more than his learning, being a distinguished Oriental scholar and familiar with law and the great principles of civil government, Melville was the man for the crisis. His presence infused a new life and vigor into the Protestant cause. He at once began a spirited opposition to the machinations of Morton, and in the Assembly of 1575 discussed freely and fearlessly the question of the *lawfulness of episcopacy,* affirming " that none ought to be office-bearers in the Church whose titles were not found in the book of God; that, though the appellation of bishop was used in Scripture, it was not to be understood in the sense usually affixed to it, there being no superiority amongst ministers al'owed by Christ; that Jesus was the only Lord of the Church, all his servants being equal in degree and power; and that the corruptions which had crept into the state of bishops (tulchan bishops) were so great that, unless they were removed, it could neither go well with the Church, nor could religion be preserved in purity."

The question respecting the lawfulness of episcopacy continued to agitate the Church for several years. In 1576 the Assembly had advanced in its solution so far as to declare, with a good degree of unanimity, "that the name of bishop is common to all who are appointed to take charge of a particular flock, and that preaching the word, administering the sacraments and exercising discipline with the consent of their elders, are their chief duties according to the word of God." The contest between Morton and the Church knew no abatement in 1577, the former being determined to retain and extend his favorite tulchan system, and the latter as fully resolved to put an end to it. Even after Morton had resigned and King James had assumed the reins of government, this subject was the chief topic of dispute in the succeeding Assemblies, until in 1580 it was declared "that the office of a bishop, as it was then used and commonly understood, was destitute of warrant and authority from the word of God, *was of mere human invention*, introduced by folly and corruption, and tended to the great injury of the Church." It was further ordained "that all such persons as were in possession of said pretended office should be charged *to demit it.*"

In this long and important conflict Melville was the most distinguished opponent of the civil power, which had sought first to corrupt and then to destroy the influence and authority of the ministry of the Church. The sagacious Morton early discerned his great abilities and that he was destined to wield an extensive influence, and accordingly had attempted to secure him as his agent to prosecute his own designs. With this object in view, he requested him to act as domestic instructor to the regent, and promised him advancement whenever a vacancy should occur. His next bribe was the living of Govan, and finally he offered him the archbishopric of St. Andrews upon the death of Douglass. But all his bribes were alike ineffectual, and Melville remained the most strenuous, as he was the ablest, opponent of the regent's wicked policy.

He next attempted to *intimidate* him. In defending from the Scriptures their right to meet as an Assembly in 1577, to frame a system of faith and to exercise discipline in the Church of Christ without asking permission of the civil magistrate, he incurred the bitter anger of Morton, who told him that "there will never be quietness in this country till half a dozen of you be hanged or banished." "Tush, sir!" replied Melville; "threaten your courtiers after that manner. It is the same to me whether I rot in the air or in the ground. The earth is the Lord's. My country is wherever goodness is. I have been ready to give my life where it would not have been half so well expended, at the pleasure of my God. Let God be glorified; it will not be in your power to hang or exile his truth." The regent was greatly incensed, but did not dare to put his threats into execution. The seizure of the bold Reformer would only have ensured his own defeat.

The previous discussions, growing out of certain inconsistencies in the constitution of the Church, made it desirable that its powers should be more accurately defined. A committee had been engaged in this work for some years; and when the Assembly met in 1578, it proceeded to consider the system of ecclesiastical polity which this committee reported. The articles were read one by one, and after long and deliberate discussion were approved and adopted by the Assembly, and the system thus formally ratified is known as the SECOND BOOK OF DISCIPLINE. It defines the government of the Church more precisely than did the first book of discipline, which was hastily drawn up. It makes the line of distinction clear between civil and ecclesiastical power, vindicates the rights of church courts as independent of the civil magistrate, asserts the parity of the ministry, the right of congregations to select their own officers, protests against the intrusion of laymen into the ministerial office, and defines the proper courts of the Church, as sessions, presbyteries, synods and General Assemblies. It thus presents the order and principles to which the Presbyterian Church has since adhered. Although not at first contended for as *jure divino*, the assaults made upon them by kingcraft and by Episcopal prelates led their defenders to maintain their scriptural authority, and their superiority in this respect to any other system taken, not "from the pure fountains of God's holy word," but from "the systems of men's invention."

Even those who most earnestly dissent from the claim of divine authority for the system are foremost in their praise of its wisdom and its exceeding usefulness. As it is "the great design of every ecclesiastical establishment to disseminate the doctrines and the precepts of religion, and to afford the most effectual aid for the formation of a pious and virtuous character, it provides an efficient and resident clergy, unites them with the people, whom they are to instruct and comfort and for whose welfare they are bound to labor, devoting their time and their talents to advance the moral and religious improvement of all classes of the community, and guards the office of the ministry from being assumed by men who had not received a liberal education and attained that proficiency in human science which is necessary for explaining and defending the records of revelation. Moreover, it does not leave the absolute decision of any important point to one man or to one society of men; but constituting a regular gradation of judicatories, to which all had access, it gives every security which could be afforded for the examination of whatever affects the character or the happiness of those who acknowledge its authority. And it is most favorable to the prevalence of that political liberty and that independence of mind which cannot be too highly valued."* Referring to this same system, another writer says: "It has ultimately proved itself eminently adapted for preserving political freedom, for defending the truths of religion, and for conveying in a most impressive manner to the great part of the community that interesting instruction which all ecclesiastical orders and systems were intended to impart."

The Church of Scotland continued to have many severe struggles with the king and his Parliament up to the year 1585, when the papal influence was finally destroyed by the expulsion of the earl of Arran from the councils of the young king, James VI. Through the influence of Morton, who had once more gained an ascendency in the councils of the nation and a large influence with the king, the latter had scarcely agreed to the *National Covenant*,

* Cook's *History of the Church of Scotland*, p. 289.

abjuring popery and solemnly engaging to support the Protestant religion, before he turned back and attempted to revive the policy of the former regent. As the Assembly claimed and exercised the right to control the "tulchan" bishops manufactured by Morton, the king was persuaded to arrest the execution of its acts by means of orders in council. If the bishops were amenable to the authority of the Assembly, then one of the easiest and best methods of subjecting the Church to the civil power would not be available. And it was to prevent this that the king and his courtiers bent all their energies. If, on the other hand, bishops were created by the king and allowed a place in Parliament, they being his favorites and cringing sycophants, the task of at least indirectly controlling the Church would be comparatively easy. Through the prelatic element he could manage the Assembly and at the same time gratify the avarice of the nobility, who were anxious to grasp the revenues of the Church. This attempt upon their rights the Assembly boldly withstood. It forbade any one to accept the office of bishop under the penalty of excommunication. There was, of course, an immediate collision between the jurisdictions, civil and ecclesiastical. The question was a vital one to the Church, being nothing more or less than whether it would surrender its spiritual independence. To force it to yield, all the terrors as well as all the bribes the court could offer were brought into requisition. But the Assembly was firm and equal to the emergency. A spirited remonstrance was drawn up, and a deputation appointed, with Andrew Melville at its head, to present it to the king. In this remarkable paper they address him in these bold and courageous words: "Your Majesty, by device of some councillors, is caused to take upon you a spiritual power and authority which properly belongeth unto Christ as only King and Head of the Church, the ministry and the execution whereof is only given unto such as bear office in the ecclesiastical government in the same, so that in Your Highness' person some men press to erect a new popedom." When the remonstrance was presented and read to the king in council, the earl of Arran, with a threatening countenance, asked, "Who dares subscribe these treasonable articles?" "WE DARE!" replied Melville; and advancing to the table, he took the pen from the clerk and subscribed. The other commissioners followed his example.

This was a bold deed, and it provoked the vengeance of the court. Though the deputation escaped personal violence, the matter was not allowed to rest. The chief offender was summoned to appear before the privy-council to answer for seditious and treasonable speeches, which it was charged he had uttered in his sermon and prayers on a fast-day; and although declining the jurisdiction of the court because his judges were not capable of deciding according to Scripture upon his ministerial conduct, he was found guilty in the absence of all criminating evidence, and sentenced to be imprisoned in Blackness castle and punished in his person and goods at His Majesty's pleasure. By the importunity of his friends Melville was induced to fly to Berwick, and thus escape punishment.

The ensuing Parliament, May, 1584, proceeded by a series of acts to destroy altogether the independence of the Church. By these it was made treasonable to impugn the power and authority of the three estates of the kingdom, by which all that the Assemblies had done to abolish prelacy was condemned; no ecclesiastical court could be held without the special command and license of the king, thus rendering unlawful the meetings of presbyteries, synods and General Assemblies; and it was forbidden, under the severest penalties, that any one, either in public or private, should presume to censure the conduct of the king or his council. These despotic acts, generally spoken of as the BLACK ACTS, struck a blow at once at civil and ecclesiastical freedom. Yet were they basely submitted to by the nobility, barons and gentry. Not so, however, were they treated by the ministers. They denounced them and protested against them in the name of the Church of Scotland. Presbyterianism in this sad crisis, as afterward, was the standard-bearer of the liberties of the nation.

The danger to the State, as well as the Church,

was imminent. Such was the violence of those in power that more than twenty ministers were obliged to save their lives by flight. And when direct persecution ceased, the king still proceeded in his measures to establish episcopacy. But the tide of popular feeling was against him; and when this was reinforced by the patriotism shown by the ministers and members of the Church at the appearance of the Spanish Armada in 1588, and by the prudent administration of the affairs of the kingdom by Robert Bruce, one of the Edinburgh ministers, who had been made an extraordinary member of the privy-council, the king was induced to desist from the rash and foolish project of restoring prelacy.

At this period James was very favorably disposed toward the Presbyterian system and ready to adopt wiser and more moderate views. He attended one of the sessions of the Assembly (1590), and in reply to the request that he would confirm the liberties of the Church, banish the papists and provide a proper support for all parish ministers, he said, "The first were confirmed by Parliament, the second had ever been his endeavor, and he wished a committee appointed to meet with his council to devise a plan by which the third object might be secured." In answer to an English divine who expressed great surprise that the Church of Scotland was never troubled with heresy, he is said to have replied in substance that it was owing entirely to the fact of that Church having well-defined and regularly-graded courts for the trial of all offenders; and if not discovered and punished by the session, presbytery or synod, the General Assembly, "I'll warrant you, will not spare him." It was also in response to overtures of the Assembly of 1590 that he pronounced his well-known panegyric of the Church of Scotland: "I praise God that I was born in such a time, to such a place, as to be king of such a Kirk, the sincerest Kirk of the world;" and then, declaring it to be superior to either the churches of Geneva or England, he exhorts ministers and people to preserve its purity, and closes with pledging himself, "so long as he brooked his life and crown, to maintain the same against all deadly."\*

In consequence of the friendly disposition of the king, Presbyterians, through their Assembly, were emboldened to ask, and Parliament at once passed, an act ratifying the form of government as then administered by General Assemblies, synods, presbyteries and sessions, defining the powers of these judicatories and reversing all acts inconsistent with this polity. Thus was Presbytery legally declared to be the CONSTITUTION OF THE CHURCH OF SCOTLAND. This parliamentary sanction was in the highest degree satisfactory and valuable to the ministers. Secured against

\* Cook, vol. i., p. 456.

opposition, they were in a much better position to promote the public welfare, and could now devote themselves to the spiritual interests of the people.

# CHAPTER II.

## From the Charter of the Church to the Renewing of the Covenant.

The state of tranquillity arising from the establishment of the Presbyterian Church was of short duration, owing to the vacillating policy of the king. The principles, spirit and discipline of the Protestant Church just established were too pure and sacred to suit the crafty and despotic monarch or his avaricious and dissolute courtiers. His past experience had taught him that he could neither deceive by his arts nor overawe by his threatenings the high-souled ministers of the Presbyterian Church. Their freedom, therefore, must be circumscribed as far as possible, and their influence diminished, even if it periled the safety of the kingdom. Accordingly, papists were again restored to favor at court, and priests and Jesuits became once more active in the government. Soon another conspiracy was formed, under the lead of certain popish earls, who were promised assistance in their efforts to suppress Protestantism and establish the Romish religion in Scotland. An army furnished by the king of Spain was relied upon as their efficient ally.

The ministers, as usual, were the first to apprehend the danger, the most forward in their loyalty to the king and most valiant in the defence of the kingdom against the threatened invasion. But notwithstanding that the conspiracy was detected and exposed and the popish noblemen apprehended, the king exerted his powerful influence to shield them from merited punishment; and when the General Assembly proceeded to excommunicate two of the conspirators, who by a former subscription to the Confession of Faith were amenable to its jurisdiction, the act was highly displeasing to the monarch. His resentment to these and other measures proposed was so great that he threatened to call a Parliament for the purpose of overthrowing Presbyterianism and restoring prelacy. He was shrewd enough to perceive that he could more readily bend to his crafty design prelates upon whom he had conferred wealth and titles than ministers who derived nothing from him, and who owed him only natural allegiance.

In 1596 the design was seriously entertained of recalling the popish earls who had been compelled to fly the country for being concerned in the late conspiracy. The Protestant ministers earnestly remonstrated "against receiving into favor convicted traitors and popish apostates, enemies at once of their country and of the gospel." Their boldness and persistence offended the king. At one of their conferences with him he charged them with holding seditious meetings and unreasonably alarming the country. At this juncture Andrew Melville stepped to the front and boldly confronted the king. Seizing him by the sleeve of his robe and calling him "God's silly vassal," he addressed him in a tone such as rarely salutes a royal ear from the lips of a loyal subject. "Sir," said he, "as divers times before I have told you, so now again I must tell you, there are two kings and two kingdoms in Scotland: there is King James, the head of the commonwealth, and there is Christ Jesus, the King of the Church, whose subject James VI. is, and of whose kingdom he is not a king nor a lord nor a head, but a member. Sir, those whom Christ has called and commanded to watch over his Church have power and authority from Him to govern his spiritual kingdom, the which no Christian king or prince should control and discharge, but fortify and assist. We will yield to you your place and give you all due obedience, but again I say you are not the head of the Church; you cannot give us that eternal life which we seek for even in this world, and you cannot deprive us of it. Permit us, then, freely to meet in the name of Christ and attend to the interests of that Church of which you are chief member."

These were certainly very plain as well as bold

sentiments to address to a monarch. But the occasion rendered the language justifiable. Under their power the king's passion cooled; his heart was awed and he showed that he felt the influence of the truth which had been so clearly and forcibly presented. He did not attempt to dispute the principle to which he had just listened, but declared that the popish earls had returned to Scotland without his knowledge, and finally dismissed the ministers with fair promises. The Church was once more proving itself the guardian of civil while contending for religious liberty. The latter cannot long exist without producing the former, and civil freedom cannot long survive spiritual bondage.

The promises of the king were soon found unreliable. Measures were adopted to restore the popish conspirators and to admit Romish adherents to royal favor. These were strongly protested against by the Assembly, which appointed a day of humiliation and prayer in view of the imminent danger, and summoned an extraordinary council of the Church to consult as to what was needed to avert the peril. The contest soon became an avowed one on the part of the king, who perceived that *deceit* could not secure his design; and as the freedom of ecclesiastical meetings was becoming more and more offensive to him, he determined to make an open assault upon this privilege of the Church. In an interview with some of the ministers he told them plainly that there could be no agreement between them and him "till the marches of their jurisdiction were rid," and he claimed that no Assembly should be convened except by his special command, and that nothing that was done should be valid until ratified by him. Nor were they left in doubt as to his ultimate purpose. In his work entitled *Free Law of Free Monarchies* he distinctly claimed that "a king was free to do what he pleases," that his will "is above all law with a parliament," whose duty it is to execute his commands and for the people passively to obey; and in his *Basilicon Doron*, wherein he gives instructions to his son Henry, James asserts "that the office of a king is of a mixed kind, civil and ecclesiastical, and that a principal part of his function consists in ruling the Church." To these claims the Presbyterians of Scotland would not for a single moment yield. With protestations of loyalty as civil subjects, they repudiated the iniquitous claim of the monarch to ecclesiastical control. They stood ready to sacrifice all else before the supreme headship of Christ.

The contest which was now fairly entered upon, was a long and arduous one. At first the king and his council endeavored to carry their ends by violence. One of the most zealous of the Presbyterian clergy was put on trial for treasonable words said to have been used in a sermon, and, by order of the court, was banished. The ministers of Edinburgh were obliged to withdraw from their parishes to avoid punishment for the stand they had taken. All these things, however, were unavailing, and were, besides, not in accordance with the king's taste. He much preferred to accomplish his designs by the use of kingcraft. Accordingly, he caused to be drawn up fifty-five questions concerning the government and discipline of the Church and published them in his name, and called a convention of estates and a meeting of the General Assembly in Perth to consider these questions. Having no hope of securing an acquiescence in his scheme on the part of men who had shown a willingness to suffer and die rather than violate their duty to God, he brought into requisition his kingcraft, and sought to gain his ends by the introduction of ambitious and unprincipled men into the Assembly.

A messenger from the court was sent to the northern part of the kingdom to induce the ministers from these remote districts to meet at Perth on the day appointed by the king. By artful misrepresentations, by flatteries and by exciting a spirit of jealousy against their brethren in the south, the royal emissary succeeded in gaining a majority of the members of the Assembly. Was this a lawful body? This question was decided, after a three days' debate, in the affirmative, and then answers were given to the leading propositions submitted to them by His Majesty, which he was pleased to regard as the sanction of the Church to his measures. In this way he partly accomplished by stratagem what force and persecution could not effect.

His next step was to induce the Assembly to appoint a committee of fourteen ministers, with whom he might advise " in all affairs concerning the weal of the Church." Through this, his ecclesiastical council, he was able more leisurely to mature his devices and introduce them into the Church. Nor was he slow to use this advantage. At the very next meeting of the Assembly he induced this council to petition Parliament, requesting that the Church might be represented in that body and have a voice in its decisions. The petition, through the king's influence, was granted by Parliament, and *prelacy* was declared the third estate of the kingdom. The spiritual power of the prelates who were raised to this dignity was subsequently to be arranged by the king and the General Assembly. In this insidious way episcopacy was introduced, "a wedge being taken out of the Church to rend her with her own forces." \*

The more clear-sighted of the ministers saw through the artful measure and protested against it. The venerable Ferguson denounced it as the *Trojan horse*, and Davidson, making use of this

\* Calderwood.

illustration, said, "Busk, busk him as bonilie as ye can, and bring him in as fairly as ye will, we see him well enough; we see the horns of his mitre." Bruce and James Melville also strenuously opposed the royal scheme, Andrew Melville having been prohibited by the king from taking his seat in the Assembly. But by menaces and by bribes, and by the removal of the Assembly to Dundee for the convenience of the northern ministers, a bare majority was secured in favor of the project to make the clergy the third estate in the kingdom.

The permission of the Assembly, which had been secured chiefly through the votes of the elders, was guarded by many wise restrictions, but the king disregarded them whenever it was his interest so to do. These restrictions were designed to protect the liberties of the Church, especially against the encroachments of prelacy. The title of bishop was not to be applied to those holding a seat in Parliament, but that of commissioner. Six were to be nominated by the Assembly in each province, one of whom should be chosen by the king, as its ecclesiastical representative, and it was provided that they were not to propose anything to Parliament without the Church's express warrant and direction. They were also to render an account of their work to the Assembly, and in all parts of ecclesiastical government and discipline they were not to claim any more power than what belonged to other ministers. All these restrictions, however, availed nothing. At a meeting of the commissioners in the following October, while certain of the most decided opponents of the king's scheme were absent from the house, James summarily nominated David Lindsay, Peter Blackburn and George Gladstanes to the vacant bishoprics of Ross, Aberdeen and Caithness. These men afterward took their place in Parliament, and voted in direct violation of the "caveats" or cautions to which they had but recently consented. Still, the free spirit of the Assembly was a great check upon them. The struggle went on for the next twenty years with scarcely an intermission. Leading ministers were either banished or imprisoned, many others were intimidated or bribed, until, by the aid of the nobility and a subservient Parliament, the king won a victory disgraceful alike to the vanquished and to the victor.

One of the first measures of the monarch in this long tissue of trickery was to summon and dismiss Assemblies by virtue of his royal prerogative. This was a plain infringement of the rights of the Church, for the act of 1592 stipulated that the Assembly should meet at least once a year, and that the commissioners were annually to render to it an account of their conduct. After proroguing and altering the times of Assemblies at pleasure, James at last ventured to prorogue indefinitely the one which should have met at Aberdeen in 1605.

To all persons it was now clear that the king was resolved to suppress the Presbyterian Church and to set up prelacy in its place. But a few faithful men were determined that the liberties of the Church should not be surrendered without one more struggle, and accordingly they met at Aberdeen at the time appointed. When the king heard of the meeting, he ordered his commissioner to dissolve it. But the Assembly resolved to constitute itself before reading the communication. A moderator was chosen, and the message was then listened to. But while the reading was going on a messenger-at-arms arrived and ordered the Assembly to disperse on pain of rebellion. The members consented to do so if the commissioner would name a place for the next meeting of the Assembly. This he refused to do. The reason was obvious, and the Assembly itself made an appointment.

When informed of their action, His Majesty was greatly incensed. Such a bold measure could not be overlooked. By his orders fourteen of the ministers, including John Forbes, the moderator, and John Welsh, son-in-law of Knox, were apprehended, cast into prison, and put on trial before the privy-council for high treason. A packed jury, by a majority of three, found six of them guilty, who, after suffering fourteen months' confinement in the castle of Blackness, were banished to France. The others, by a like perversion of law and justice would have shared their fate had not public sympathy for the sufferers made it evident that it was unsafe to proceed with their trial. For most of them, however, the respite was very brief. Before the next Parliament six of the most distinguished of them, including both the Melvilles, were commanded to meet the king in London (for James was now king both of England and Scotland), on the pretext that he wished to treat with them "respecting such things as would settle the peace of the Church." When admitted to an audience, they were questioned about the Aberdeen Assembly, and such a construction put upon their replies as furnished the desired pretence for instituting judicial proceedings. On a despicable charge Andrew Melville was arraigned for trial; and, notwithstanding his able and eloquent defence, he was committed to the Tower of London. After four years' imprisonment he was banished to France, where he remained until his death. His nephew, James Melville, was prohibited from returning to Scotland, and the remaining four ministers to their parishes. In this way the perfidious monarch was enabled to secure the triumph of his scheme by striking down the free-spirited men who had resisted it. Surely nothing more is needed to form a correct judgment between the two systems of presbytery and prelacy than the methods which it was found necessary to employ to establish each in Scotland. The former won the hearts of the people by the faithful preaching of the word and by the pure, pious and self-sacrificing lives of its ministers; the latter was forced upon them by arbitrary power, by treachery, by corruption and by persecution.

Other steps in this succession of intrigue, intimidation and bribery were to appoint the bishops *constant moderators* in all meetings of presbyteries and synods, to restore to the bishops the civil jurisdiction formerly held by the popish prelates; and that they might exercise the power thus conferred, the COURT OF HIGH COMMISSION was instituted.

This court was composed of prelates, noblemen, knights and ministers. It was regulated by no fixed laws or forms of justice, and was armed with all the power of civil and ecclesiastical despotism. It could receive appeals from church courts, depose and excommunicate, fine and imprison. But such was the public feeling excited by these measures of the prelates that for several years the court prudently did but little business. Thus one right of the Church after another was trampled under foot by the imperious monarch and his obsequious retainers. The bishops acknowledged themselves his creatures. Archbishop Gladstanes crouched before the king with all the menial servility of an Eastern slave. He repaired, he said, to His Majesty's most gracious face, "that so unworthy a creature might both see, bless and thank *my earthly creator.*"

In 1617 the king indulged what he called his "natural and salmon-like affection to see the place of his breeding" by a visit to his native and ancient kingdom. The chapel of Holyrood House was repaired, an organ was sent down from London, and English carpenters began to set up carved and gilded statues of the apostles. The people murmured, the bishops were alarmed, and at their solicitation the apostles were dispensed with. The liturgy, however, was daily read, and the purpose was openly avowed that the royal example should be imitated throughout the kingdom. An obsequious Parliament, aided and abetted by venal bishops, gave him full authority to enact ecclesiastical laws for the government of the Church. With this sanction of his power, he no longer concealed his plans. He declared he would never more consent to have matters ruled as they had been in General Assemblies. "The bishops," he said, "must rule the ministers, and the king rule both."

Against all these usurpations a large body of ministers protested. The cowardice of one, however, prevented their petition from being placed in the hands of the king. But meeting with a copy of it, he flew into a great passion and denounced the petitioners. Some of the ministers were subsequently treated with great cruelty, and even the bishops were severely reprimanded and called *dolts* and *deceivers* for inducing him to believe that the people of Scotland were in favor of prelacy.

In the Assembly which met at Aberdeen in 1616 the prelatical party presented a new *Confession of Faith*. The articles were afterward put into form and submitted for adoption to the Assembly of Perth, 1618, which was ordered to meet by royal mandate. Every possible device which a despot could employ was brought into requisition to ensure a majority of commissioners favorable to his scheme. The prelates addressed the Assembly in a domineering tone, and in the name of their master threatened those who should refuse to adopt the articles, that their names would be marked and sent to His Majesty for punishment. Though thus menaced, there were forty-five ministers who stood true to their principles, and the *Five Articles of Perth*, as they are called, were adopted by but a small majority. These articles were kneeling at the communion, the observance of holidays, episcopal confirmation and the private dispensation of the Lord's Supper. Parliament three years after sanctioned these rites, and thus by its vote was the constitution of the Presbyterian Church of Scotland subverted. This day, the 25th of July, 1621, was marked by lowering clouds, deepening gloom, hail and tempest, and was long known as the *Black Saturday*— "black," says Calderwood, "with man's guilt and with the frowns of Heaven."

The ratification of the five articles of Perth by Parliament gave the bishops the constitutional sanction they desired. They at once began to enforce the obnoxious rites. But civil and ecclesiastical authority combined were unequal to impose them on an unwilling people, as the unavailing contest for the next twenty years proved. The court of High Commission, urged by the king, proceeded against those ministers who refused to conform to the recent acts of Parliament. The cruel treatment of John Welsh and Robert Bruce indicated the spirit with which submission would be enforced. It was not the fathers alone, but every eminent minister in the kingdom was persecuted. If they could be induced to subscribe the Perth articles, the prelates hoped their people would either yield to their example or become alienated from them. Pursuing their cruel plan, they summoned before them Messrs. Dickson, Dunbar, Row, Murray and Johnstone—men eminent for their piety and talents, and greatly beloved in their parishes. At first entreaty and then threats were used to induce them to submit, and their refusal was followed by banishment to different parts of the kingdom. Attention was next directed to the universities, and the principal of Edinburgh College, the celebrated Robert Boyd, was forced to resign, and Robert Blair was deprived of his professorship in Glasgow and obliged to retire to Ireland. Students, moreover, were constrained to take an oath to submit to the prelatic form of church government before they were allowed to preach. Nonconforming ministers continued to be displaced, congregations were compelled to do without the ordinances unless they would receive them conjoined with superstitious rites, and all the oppressive enactments of previous years were enforced during the remainder of James' reign.

After his death, which took place 1625, ministers and people had a brief respite from persecution. This they owed to the fact that the court of High Commission expired with the king who had created it. But his successor, Charles I., began almost immediately to carry out the policy of his father. He directed that the affairs of the Church should proceed as in the previous reign, and, inspired by that despicable creature Laud, he instituted new measures to harass Protestants and to restore the prelates to their possession of church property, while to all the just grievances of a suffering people he turned a deaf ear.

Being refused relief and redress by their earthly monarch, the more fervent were the supplications of the persecuted to the King of kings. As very many of the best and most pious ministers were prohibited from laboring in their own parishes, they went from one district to another throughout the kingdom, kindling the sacred fire that burned so brightly on the altar of their own hearts. Soon a powerful revival of religion began under the preaching of such men as Bruce, Dickson and Livingstone, which continued for several years and extended over a wide region and to all classes of society. While the latter was preaching at the kirk of Shotts the converting power of the Spirit was so graciously displayed that nearly five hundred persons were born again. This fresh baptism of the Spirit was what the people needed to confirm their resolution and inspire them with courage for the impending conflict with prelacy and despotism.

The struggle was near at hand. It was precipitated by the infatuation of the enemies of the Church. Though unable to enforce obedience to the Perth articles, except to a very limited extent, the more ardent and least wise of the prelatists urged that a book of canons and a liturgy should be prepared for the government and worship of the Church. This was done; and after *Laud's* supervision and amendment, the canons were confirmed under the great seal in 1635. Among other things, the canons pronounced excommunication upon all who denied the king's supremacy in ecclesiastical matters, or who asserted that the prelatic form of church government was unscriptural. Every minister was obliged to adhere to the forms prescribed in the liturgy under penalty of deposition; which liturgy was not at the time *in existence*. No General Assembly could be called except by the king, and no private meetings could be held by the ministers for expounding the Scriptures. Thus was it attempted, at one and the same time, by this book of canons, to subvert the entire constitution of the Church of Scotland. The despotic acts were unsparingly denounced by all Presbyterians, and the nobility were pleased to see the offensive measures adopted, knowing well that all attempts to enforce the provisions of the book of canons would react upon the prelates, whose power they wished diminished, as they had usurped so many of the highest offices in the State.

A liturgy or book of public worship was completed in 1636, which all faithful subjects were commanded by the king to receive and observe, and an order was obtained from the privy-council requiring ministers in every parish to provide two copies of the *Service-Book* for the use of their people. Edinburgh was the place chosen where the public use of the book was to be commenced. On the 23d day of July, 1637, the perilous experiment was made by the dean of that city in the cathedral church of St. Giles. The church was crowded, and "a deep melancholy calm brooded over the congregation," presaging the fierce tempest which was about to sweep away every barrier. At length the dean, attired in his surplice, began to read the liturgy, but his voice was speedily drowned in tumultuous clamor. An old woman, Jenny Geddes, was the heroine of the occasion. "Villain!"

she cried; "dost thou say mass at my lug?" and with these words hurled the stool on which she had been sitting at the dean's head. Others quickly followed her example. Missiles of every kind flew, while some of the more impetuous rushed toward the desk to seize the offender. Terrified by this sudden outburst of popular anger, the dean threw off his surplice and fled. The bishop attempted to allay the tumult, but was greeted with shouts of "A pope! a pope! Antichrist! Stone him! Pull him down!" and he was with great difficulty rescued by the magistrates. This unexpected storm of public indignation surprised and terrified the court-party. They were prepared for and expected resistance from some ministers, and these they intended to crush into the dust, but they were stupefied by the exhibition of the violence of the pent-up feelings of the populace. And great as were their fears, they did not exaggerate the danger. This unlooked-for tumult was the *deathblow* to the liturgy in Scotland. Intelligence of what had transpired in Edinburgh soon spread through the kingdom, and was the signal of open resistance in other towns and cities. At Glasgow, Ayr and other places it was found absolutely necessary to suspend the use of the service. The people would no longer tamely submit to see the institutions of their fathers wantonly violated and overthrown.

Petitions from ministers and letters from noblemen and gentlemen from all parts of the country were addressed to the privy-council, requesting that the reading of the liturgy might not be forcibly imposed. To these a favorable reply was received, which very much enraged the prelates, as they felt that the nobility were about to desert them. Through false representations and the influence of Laud they induced the king to write a sharp, reproving letter to the privy-council. This " acted like a spark thrown upon a train of gunpowder." It roused all who had the welfare of the country at heart. Crowds of noblemen and gentlemen, as well as ministers, flocked to Edinburgh, where they awaited the king's answer to their petition to suspend the use of the liturgy. The answer was delayed, but when it did come it showed that the king meant to support the prelates in their demands. It enjoined obedience to the canons and the instant reception of the service-book, condemning all dissent under pain of treason. The crisis was upon them, and they recognized the fact that they must prepare to defend their rights or bow their necks to the despotism of Church and State.

Their resolution was taken at once. The National Covenant was renewed, with a mutual bond on the part of The Four Tables to resist all innovations, and by all lawful means recover the purity and liberty of the gospel. The Covenant consisted of three parts—the old covenant of 1581, the acts of Parliament condemning popery, and an application of the whole to the present circumstances. This proved to be the MAGNA CHARTA of Scottish liberties. It set up an effectual barrier to the encroachments of royal and prelatical prerogative.

The day appointed for renewing the Covenant was the 28th of February, and the place Grayfriars' church, Edinburgh. Here, at daybreak, the commissioners met; the covenant was read over and all parts of it deliberately examined. As the hour approached for signing the bond of union the church and churchyard were packed with the wisest and best of Scotland's men and women. Henderson opened the meeting with an earnest prayer, and the earl of Loudon explained and vindicated the object of their assembling. Johnstone then in a clear and distinct manner read the covenant, while the vast multitude listened with deep yet subdued feelings difficult of restraint. A solemn stillness followed, which was finally broken by the earl of Rothes announcing that if any had objections to offer, if they would state them, the commissioners would then and there endeavor to remove them. Another pause ensued. Was it from any lack of resolution? Having gone so far, did they hesitate to put their names to the bond? Far from it. They modestly deferred to each other the high honor of being the first to subscribe. At last the venerable earl of

Sutherland slowly and reverentially came forward, and with trembling hand put his signature to the Covenant. Then name followed name in rapid succession, until all within the church had signed. It was then removed to the churchyard and spread out on a gravestone, where a still more impressive scene was witnessed. Some as they subscribed wept aloud, others added the words "*till death*" to their names, others opened a vein in their arms and wrote their subscription with their blood. The signatures were added while there was space left for even the initial letters to be subscribed; and this being no longer possible, the people, with faces bathed in tears and moved as by one impulse, lifted up their right hands to heaven and solemnly appealed to God as to the sincerity of their motives and their future fidelity to the cause of Christ.

On the next day the Covenant was again read, when three hundred ministers at once added their names to the large numbers that had previously subscribed. It was then carried to different parts of the city for signature, and wherever it appeared it was received with great joy. Copies were afterward sent to every part of the kingdom, and before the first of May there were few parishes in which the Covenant had not been signed by nearly all of competent age and character. No compulsion was required or permitted, the subscribers regarding it a high honor and a solemn duty. The subscription was frequently accompanied by evident tokens of the Spirit's presence and power. "I was present," says the celebrated Livingstone, "at Lanark and at several other parishes when on Sunday, after the forenoon sermon, the Covenant was read and sworn, and I may truly say that in all my lifetime, excepting at the kirk of Schotts, I never saw such motions from the Spirit of God." The sacred pledge thus mutually given to be faithful to their country and their God awed and hallowed the souls of the signers. From the subscription to this renewed Covenant, we may date the Second Reformation in Scotland.

# CHAPTER III.

### From the Signing of the National Covenant to the Restoration of Charles II., 1660.

The unanimity and cordiality with which the Covenant had been received by the Scottish people led the prelates almost to despair of their cherished schemes. Spotiswood, who better than any other understood those with whom they had to deal, exclaimed: "Now all that we have been doing these thirty years past is thrown down at once." All parties—the privy-council, the prelates and the Presbyterians—sent deputations to the king in London to acquaint him with the real state of affairs in the kingdom. But, as usual, he heeded only the partial and false statements of the bishops. Their pernicious advice induced him to enter upon measures which finally involved his kingdom in the miseries of revolution, and cost the monarch his life.

Satisfied that it was too dangerous at present to attempt to compel obedience by force of arms, the king abandoned all such measures. His resort was to negotiation, whereby he hoped to divide the Covenanters; and failing in this, he would gain time to make the requisite preparations for war. He appointed, therefore, a commissioner to treat with his Scottish subjects, selecting for this purpose the marquis of Hamilton. He was authorized to employ every method, however base, even to pretend friendship and compassion for the Covenanters, only that he might better deceive, circumvent and overpower them. On June 19, 1638, the commissioner made his public entry into Edinburgh in great state. Approaching the city, sixty thousand people received him, ranged for miles in ranks along the seaside. These were in large part composed of nobles and gentry from all parts of the country, and the ministers and people who had signed the Covenant; and while thus showing their loyalty to their king in things temporal, they besought Hamilton with tears to persuade him to grant a redress of their grievances. But Charles and his bishops were not to be dissuaded. The Covenanters demanded that a free General Assembly should be called, where the conduct of the prelates should be investigated, and a Parliament, by which all unconstitutional acts might be rescinded. Then began a long series of measures by the monarch and his commissioner, designed to outwit, intimidate, divide or gain over the adherents to the Covenant. All their efforts, however, proved a failure. The Presbyterians remained united and stood firmly by their principles. The king was most reluctantly constrained to allow the convening of "a free

General Assembly" at Glasgow, and the meeting of a Parliament at Edinburgh, "for settling and confirming peace in Church and State." In the mean time, he prohibited the enforcement of the Book of Canons, the Liturgy and the Five Articles of Perth, and abolished the court of High Commission. These were indeed great concessions; and had the Covenanters been able to place any reliance upon the king's sincerity, they would have been generally satisfactory. But the act itself convening the Assembly was open to suspicion, in that the religion to be maintained was what was "at present professed;" and besides, the bishops whose conduct was to be investigated were made constituent members of the very court that was to try them.

Care was taken by the Presbyterians to have the Assembly constituted according to the principles of their Church. Deputations were sent to the presbyteries with instructions how to act in the emergency. They were successful in securing the return as commissioners of the ablest of the ministers, and the most influential of the nobility and gentry as ruling elders.

The Assembly met November 21, 1638, in Glasgow, and consisted of two hundred and thirty-eight members, of whom three-fifths were ministers. Alexander Henderson, acknowledged to be the fittest man by reason of his self-command and sound judgment, was chosen moderator. The king's commissioner appeared, and contested every step of the Assembly's proceedings. Among other things he wished to have the paper from the prelates declining the jurisdiction of the Assembly read before the body was properly constituted. But this was negatived, as had been his other proposals. As soon as the commissions of the members were examined and the integrity of the court rendered sure, the declinature of the bishops was presented by their procurator, Dr. Hamilton. To this a committee made answer, and the Assembly by a vote declared itself competent to judge the bishops. The commissioner at once forbade the Assembly to proceed, and in the name of the king required it to dissolve.

It was a critical moment. Should the Assembly recede from the position which it had just taken or surrender its rights to the dictate of the royal commissioner? If the members receded, they might just as well admit all the claims of the monarch to control the Church. Against this act of Hamilton, Henderson, Loudon and Rothes, all ably reasoned and expressed their regret; and while the commissioner was retiring, having once more declared the Assembly dissolved, a protest was read by the clerk against his proceedings, the protestors maintaining it to be their duty to remain in session until the important duties were done for which they had been called together.

And when the question came to a vote, it was carried almost unanimously in the Assembly.

With the exception of one or two, all the members remained at their posts. With great promptitude the Assembly nullified the six corrupt Assemblies from 1606–1618, by which prelacy had been introduced, and declared all the changes and innovations made by them illegal; condemned the Five Articles of Perth, the Canons, Liturgy and Book of Ordination, and the High Commission; declared prelacy abjured by the National Covenant and contrary to the principles of the Church of Scotland; and finally, in the name of the Church, voted its removal and the substitution of the Presbyterian government and worship to their former integrity. The prelates' conduct, after a full and impartial investigation, was declared to be of a character to render them worthy of censure, and eight of them were deposed and excommunicated, four simply deposed, and two deposed from the prelatic station, but permitted to hold the office of pastor over a single parish. Having finished its business, this memorable Assembly closed its labors on the twentieth day of December. In pronouncing the Assembly dissolved the moderator added these words: "We have now cast down the walls of Jericho. Let him that rebuildeth them beware of the curse of Hiel the Bethelite."

Thus by a single month's work was swept away

the whole fabric of prelacy, which had been laboriously erected by the king and his ecclesiastical minions, and on which more than thirty years of kingcraft and priestcraft had been expended. Not a vestige remained. The General Assembly was reinstated in the exercise of its legitimate authority, and everything moved forward in as orderly a manner "as if the thirty years' suppression had been only a semi-annual adjournment." "No Church, except one constituted on the Presbyterian model, could have borne such a testimony or gained such a triumph." It should not, therefore, be a matter of surprise that a Church which had maintained a successful struggle against the despotic claims of kings and prelates for more than half a century, and had vindicated its scriptural simplicity of church order and worship, should be regarded by not a few as possessing *jure divino* authority. Some of the principles which had been so boldly and successfully vindicated were unquestionably vital to spiritual freedom and the progress of the gospel. The independence of church courts of civil control, the right of the congregation to the choice of its own officers and the parity of the ministry, were too essential to the freedom, if not the very life of the Church, to allow them to be regarded as of secondary importance; and these fundamental principles of the Presbyterian system invest it with claims which, in no offensive sense, confer upon it the peculiar distinction of being most accordant with the Scriptures and the genius of civil and religious liberty.

While the Covenanters had calmly and firmly taken their position, from which they could not be driven, they were anxious to avoid any conflict with the monarch. Before the marquis of Hamilton left Edinburgh several of their leading men waited upon him to solicit his friendly mediation. This failing, they sent a supplication to the king himself, in reading which he indignantly said, "When they have broken my head, they will put on my cowl." He was greatly enraged at what he considered an insult to his royal prerogative, and immediately resolved upon the suppression of the offenders. He began at once his preparations for war, receiving his chief supply of money from the liberal contributions of the English bishops. Most reluctantly the Presbyterians engaged in the conflict which they saw was inevitable, for the king would not pardon the offence of the Assembly, and Scotland would not recede from the stand which had been taken in the name of the nation. In the minds of many Christians there were grave doubts concerning the propriety of even a defensive war. But when the question was clearly seen to be, as it really was, whether, in obeying the monarch, they must disobey God, they soon arrived at the conclusion "that a Christian people were entitled to take up arms in defence of their religious liberties against any assailant." They did not hesitate—nay, were forward—to yield obedience to the king in all things pertaining to the State, and even to submit to civil wrongs after a simple protest or remonstrance, but they were convinced that religious liberty could not be yielded without committing grievous sin.

Having thus concluded, they began their preparations to defend their rights. Full executive powers were given to the committee in Edinburgh, arms and ammunition were collected, and experienced officers were employed to instruct those who were willing to serve in the army; and as the forces of Charles were already assembling at York, the precaution was taken to seize the strong fortresses of Edinburgh and Dumbarton. Dalkeith was also taken possession of, and Leith fortified to protect the capital from assault by sea. All attempts at compromise having failed, the infatuated monarch demanded the renunciation of the Covenant and the Glasgow Assembly, and an unconditional submission to his royal will. Orders were issued by the committee for the Scottish army to march to headquarters. The chief command was entrusted to the experienced and veteran soldier, General Leslie, and the army moved forward in two divisions to Dunse Law, where it encamped within sight of Charles' forces. The level summit of the hill on which the Scottish troops had taken up their position bristled with cannon. Around it were pitched the tents of the soldiers, and at the door of each captain's tent a staff was planted, from which floated a banner with the inscription in golden letters, "For Christ's Crown and Covenant." Attached to each regiment was an able and honored minister, who regularly, morning and evening, conducted devotional services in the presence of the assembled troops. The army was composed mainly of peasants, to whom religious liberty was dear, and who were ready to sacrifice their lives in its defence. These were led by their time-honored nobility, encouraged by their beloved pastors, and rendered invincible in their own estimation by the righteous cause for which they contended. Fearing God, they feared not the face of man.

No wonder that the king hesitated before risking battle with so formidable and resolute an enemy, particularly as he must have known that the English had little heart to engage in what was justly regarded as the bishops' war. Accordingly, he made it known that he was ready and anxious to receive proposals for peace from his aggrieved subjects. These were promptly made, since the Covenanters were not moved by pride and were only desirous to have their religious freedom assured. After protracted negotiations the king acceded to articles of peace, in which the requests of the aggrieved party were virtually granted. Then followed the signing of a treaty, the disbanding of the armies, and the restoring to the king of the castles that had been seized.

Short-lived was the peace thus inaugurated. Kingcraft was again invoked, and was employed in every possible manner to thwart the wishes of the loyal subjects of the realm. The Assembly that met in Edinburgh that same year abolished all the prelatic innovations which again had been forced upon the Church, and made provision for the annual meeting of Assemblies and the regular meeting of synods, presbyteries, and kirk sessions. The National Covenant was also renewed, and the privy-council petitioned to sanction it and to require all subjects to subscribe it. This was done, the whole council subscribing as well as the king's commissioner.

These acts of the Assembly and the council incensed the monarch, who resolved once more on war. By great exertions his exhausted treasury was replenished, and he took the field with an army of over twenty thousand men. As usual, the Covenanters tried every pacific measure before engaging even in a defensive war. But convinced of the uselessness of all their efforts, the alarm was again sounded, and was answered by the mustering to their former station, Dunse Law, of thousands of the nobility and ministers and brave peasantry. After remaining inactive for a time, no enemy appearing, they resolved to advance in a peaceful manner toward the royal army. Disclaiming all hostile intentions against the English nation, they marched to the Tweed, and then, crossing the Tyne, took possession of Newcastle after a feeble resistance on the part of the royal forces. The latter were allowed to retire unmolested to show their pacific intentions, and a petition was presented to the king urging him to grant their just requests and thus restore peace to his distracted kingdom. The treaty of Ripon was the result of the decisive stand taken by the Covenanters, and was succeeded by the meeting of the Long Parliament, so memorable in the annals of the nation, and which continued its sessions until English episcopacy was overthrown.

The English nation had become weary of the despotic rule of their prelates. The residence of the commissioners in Scotland while the treaty of Ripon was being concluded, and the free intercourse which some of the principal ministers of Scotland enjoyed with all classes of society in London while acting as chaplains to the Scottish commissioners, had a powerful influence in recommending the Presbyterian form of church government. Petitions began to be presented to Parliament. Some of these prayed for the total abolition of the prelatic system, others only for a reformation in the liturgy, discipline and government. The desire was widespread for a change, and the hope was general that uniformity of worship might be established in the three kingdoms. Following out this idea, which had been first suggested by the commissioners in London, the Assembly of 1641 appointed its moderator, Henderson, to the duty of framing a confession of faith, a catechism and a directory for public worship, that might meet all the requirements of a regularly constituted national Church. But before much progress had been made in this matter, the breach between the king and his Parliament took place. The Scotch commissioners attempted an amicable adjustment of the points in dispute, but their mediation was rejected by the king, who regarded them as the chief cause of all his troubles, from the example they had set of successful resistance to his despotic measures.

The position was a difficult one for the Covenanters. They were disposed to remain neutral in the contest. Loyalty to their sovereign kept them from all overt acts of hostility to him, while all their sympathies were naturally with those who were striving to maintain civil and religious liberty. But the progress of events soon rendered neutrality impossible. A common sense of danger compelled them to take sides with their English brethren, that conjointly they might avert the perils of their country. When, therefore, the English commissioners sought a conference with the members of the Edinburgh Assembly, August, 1643, it was granted, and as the result of their deliberations that ever memorable and remarkable document was adopted styled "THE SOLEMN

League and Covenant." This bound the united kingdoms to preserve the Reformed religion in the Church of Scotland; to labor for the reformation of religion in England and Ireland according to the word of God and the example of the best Reformed churches; and for the extirpation of popery and prelacy, while the king's person, authority and honor were to be carefully guarded. This document was first approved by the Assembly, in which it originated, afterward unanimously ratified by the Convention of Estates, and then carried to London, where it was accepted and subscribed by the English Parliament and the Westminster Assembly of Divines.

This latter body deserves very special mention in this connection. It was convened by an ordinance of Parliament issued on the 12th of June, 1643, to devise some method whereby uniformity might be secured in faith, discipline and worship in the two kingdoms. It numbered one hundred and fifty-one members, of which one hundred and twenty-five were divines, the others being lords and commoners. Of this list about twenty-five never met with the Assembly, having either died before the meeting, or absented themselves through fear of the displeasure of the king, or from preference for episcopacy. To supply the vacancies thus caused the Parliament summoned twenty-one additional members, and requested the Church of Scotland to send commissioners to assist them in their deliberations. Upon this commission the General Assembly of that Church placed four of its most eminent ministers, and two elders. Of the thirty-two lay assessors and the one hundred and fifty-two divines, including those sent by Scotland, but sixty-nine appeared the first day, and generally the attendance ranged between sixty and eighty. They met July 1st in the Abbey church, Westminster, and organized by appointing Dr. Twisse prolocutor, who opened the meeting with an able sermon.

The Assembly was peculiar in many respects. It was neither a Convocation called to meet by episcopal authority, nor a General Assembly convened according to the rules in force among Presbyterians. The prelatic form of church government had been abolished, and there was no other yet in existence. The Church was in a transition state, and the civil power, recognizing Christianity as it did, called together a large number of Christian men to deliberate respecting those questions of faith and order which were essential to the highest welfare of the people. The problem to be solved was: On what terms could a national Church be formed so as neither to encroach upon civil liberty, nor surrender those inherent spiritual rights and privileges essential to a Church of Christ?

That the Parliament wished to act with fairness and impartiality in this important matter, is evident from the fact that they named men of all shades of opinion in matters of church government. Their intention was to have the whole subject fully discussed, and with this in view four bishops were selected, besides many others well known for their talents and their attachment to Independency. Though the purpose was a laudable one, yet this was the chief element of weakness in the Assembly. The great diversity of opinions prevented that unity of action which was necessary to accomplish the work given them to do. From the very beginning of the Assembly three parties appeared. The first held that it was the province of the civil magistrate alone to inflict church censure, and that he is the proper head and source of all power, ecclesiastical as well as civil. The second held that every congregation of Christians has entire and complete authority over its members in all religious matters. The third, the Presbyterians, who formed the majority of the Assembly, held firmly to the opinions and principles which were in practice in the Scottish Church.

The first difference arose respecting the headship of the Church, the majority contending that Christ was the Head, and having ascended from the earth committed the rule of his Church to properly designated officers. This proposition was opposed by those who claimed that the infliction of church censure belonged to the king, by reason of his civil magistracy. Though overruled in the Assembly, they triumphed in Parliament, which refused to sanction the proposition. The struggle with the Independents was more protracted, as they derived much of their strength from active friends and sympathizers in Parliament and in the army. With their aid "they contrived to embarrass, retard and overreach the Assembly, till they were able to subvert all its labors, so far as England was concerned; they kept the Parliament in a state of confusion and indecision with their intrigues till they had power to suppress it; and they contrived to paralyze both king and Parliament until the opportunity occurred of putting to death their monarch, and placing the sceptre in the iron grasp of military despotism."

The uniformity in religious worship in England and Scotland which had been attempted was thus indefinitely postponed. While the *jure divino* claims urged in behalf of Presbyterianism may have had some influence in preventing an agreement, yet to those who claimed for the civil magistrate ecclesiastical control likewise, and to the policy of Cromwell, who encouraged the Independents in their factious opposition, the principal share of the blame must be attributed.

For nearly twenty years from the time of the revival of the General Assemblies, and embracing the period of the flight of Charles I. in disguise to Scotland, the defeat of his army by Cromwell, his death and the steps taken to secure a successor to the vacant throne, the Presbyterian system was left for the most part unmolested. The General Assembly of 1647 ratified the Confession of Faith of the Westminster divines, and in 1649 passed an act defining the method of electing ministers, and their installation over parishes. These measures were necessary to perfect the organization of the Church and prepare it for the protracted and terrible conflict which it had to encounter upon the restoration, May, 1660, of Charles II. to the throne of his father.

## CHAPTER IV.

### From the Restoration of Charles II. to his Death, in 1685.

After the death of Oliver Cromwell a "strange frenzy of extravagant royalty seized upon the whole kingdom like some uncontrollable epidemic," and Charles was placed upon the throne without the exaction from him of any of the promises or conditions that had been demanded of his predecessors. Against this fatal error the Church of Scotland could make no successful resistance, owing to its weakness, caused by internal dissensions. The power most dreaded by politicians being thus paralyzed, measures were almost immediately taken to establish an arbitrary government. A Council of State was formed for Scotland, composed of men hostile to Presbyterianism and in favor of the prelatic system. As preparatory to its attempted introduction, some of the most powerful supporters of the Covenant had to be removed out of the way; and orders were therefore given for the imprisonment of certain of the chief nobles and ministers. Proclamations were issued against the holding of what were designated as unlawful meetings, and the people were commanded to bring all seditious books in their possession that they might be burned. Those who were suffering from any grievance whatever were prohibited from presenting addresses or petitions to any source for redress, but to the Parliament or the Committee of Estates.

A new but clearly an illegal Parliament was held in 1661, and its members took an oath of allegiance which acknowledged the king's supremacy in ecclesiastical as well as civil affairs. Having accorded this, they proceeded at once with their despotic acts. Among these it was declared to be the prerogative of the king to choose all officers of the State, to call and dissolve all Parliaments and meetings, and that no convocations or leagues could be made without the sovereign. And to remove every obstruction, so that absolute despotism might have unimpeded sway, the members of Parliament were absolved from the obligation to subscribe the Solemn League and Covenant, and were required, if they filled any public office, to take the oath of allegiance and acknowledge the king's prerogative. As if this were not sufficient to bind the yoke upon the necks of submissive subjects, these minions of arbitrary power annulled all the proceedings of the Parliaments held since 1633; thus by a single stroke abolishing not only all the laws made in favor of the Church of Scotland, but also those in favor of civil liberty, which had been passed during the late reign.

Should it seem impossible that acts like these could be passed by any Parliament composed of men not themselves *slaves*, the solution is to be sought in what Burnet has to say of the morals of the people: "Vices of all sorts were the open practices of those about the earl of Middleton.* Drinking was the most notorious of all, which was often continued through the whole night till the next morning. This extravagant act was only fit to be concluded after a drunken bout." The purpose was to destroy the Presbyterian Church, but in attempting this they were compelled to destroy all the existing laws of the land, as well as all the security which law itself can give. It is no wonder that such vile creatures as these were the active enemies of religious freedom, and stood ready to sacrifice civil liberty also at the bidding of a despot, and the fact that it was necessary to make use of such agencies to introduce prelacy into Scotland, places the stamp of infamy upon the system itself.

The next step was to inflict the extreme penalty of these destructive acts upon some of the most honored of the Presbyterians. The marquis of Argyle and James Guthrie, minister of Stirling, were the first victims. The first, when he received his sentence, said, "I had the honor to set the crown upon the king's head, and now he hastens me to a better crown than his own;" and on taking leave of his friends on the day of execution,

---

* The commissioner for holding the Parliament.

with a calm courage that justified his words, he said, "I could die like a Roman, but choose rather to die as a Christian." The second, when condemned to die as a traitor, said to the judge, "My conscience I cannot submit, but this old crazy body and mortal flesh I do submit to do with it whatsoever you will; only I beseech you to ponder well what profit there is in my blood. My blood will contribute more for the propagation of the Covenant and the work of reformation than my life or liberty could do;" and when standing on the scaffold and about to yield to the axe of the executioner, he lifted the napkin from his face, and cried, "The covenants, the covenants shall yet be Scotland's reviving."

The next victim marked for slaughter was "the heavenly-minded Rutherford." But death cheated his enemies. In answer to their summons to appear at Edinburgh and stand trial for high treason, he replied: "I have received a summons already to appear before a superior Judge and judicatory, and I behove to answer my first summons; and ere your day arrive I will be where few kings and great folks come." Other ministers distinguished for their piety and talents were apprehended and imprisoned by the order of Parliament, and finally banished.

In the judgment of many persons, the time had now fully come when it would be safe to attempt to introduce episcopacy into Scotland. They pressed the king to proceed with the intended change, and he, disregarding his many oaths and declarations to maintain and defend the Presbyterian Church of Scotland, sent a letter to the privy-council, in which he declared it "his firm resolution to interpose his royal authority for restoring the Church of Scotland to its rightful government by bishops." Four men were consecrated to the episcopal office, at the head of whom was James Sharp, a renegade Presbyterian. Following this was a letter from the king to his council, prohibiting the meeting of synods, presbyteries and sessions, unless authorized by the bishops, and requiring all persons to respect their office and the authority entrusted to them. On the arrival of the bishops at Edinburgh a deputation from Parliament was sent to invite them to take their seats as the third estate of the realm, and the first act passed—and that on the very next day—restored them to their ancient prerogatives, spiritual and temporal. Other acts of Parliament made all covenants and leagues for reformation treasonable, and prohibited any person to teach in universities or to preach, keep schools or to be tutors to persons of quality, who did not admit the prelatic government and obtain a license from the bishops.

Notwithstanding these grievous oppressions, the ministers continued to occupy their pulpits, and refused to acknowledge the authority of the bishops. An act was passed at the instigation of the archbishop of Glasgow requiring them to attend the bishops' courts under pain of being held contemners of royal authority, and the council enforced the order by decreeing banishment against all ministers who refused to comply. The latter, rather than violate their conscience, submitted to the cruel penalty. Nearly four hundred resigned their livings and bade farewell to their congregations, who, in parting with their loved pastors, could not repress their feelings, but wept aloud. A third part of the pulpits of Scotland were in the course of a few months vacated.

To supply the place of these exiled ministers was an impossibility. The attempt to do so, resulted in bringing into the parishes many persons who were a reproach to the profession. "They were the worst preachers I ever heard," says Bishop Burnet. "They were ignorant to a reproach, and many of them were openly vicious. They were a disgrace to their orders and the sacred functions, and indeed were the dregs and refuse." These were not the men to reconcile the people to the loss of their beloved pastors. It is not strange that their entrance to the churches should have been resisted, or that they were very soon left without hearers. The bishops, in forcing them upon the unwilling people, only made themselves more odious. At Edinburgh only a single pulpit continued to be occupied by the former incumbent. Large numbers of the pastors retired to the most secluded parts of the country, while not a few fled to Holland.

Since the Glasgow act, as it was called, included only those ministers who had succeeded to charges since 1649, a number of aged pastors were for a time left in possession of their churches. To these the people, who had been deprived of the services of their own ministers, flocked from great distances; and as some of the ejected clergy were allowed to remain in their parishes, though not permitted to discharge the duties of their office, their former parishioners were accustomed to collect in large numbers in their houses at the hour for family worship, in order that they might enjoy their private expositions and prayers. Frequently such numbers assembled that no room was large enough to hold the worshipers, and necessity constrained them to hold the meeting in the open air. This was the origin of the field-meetings—or *conventicles*, as they were derisively called—which were first held in 1663. But even those who sought in this quiet way to worship God were subjected to the rage of their persecutors. The rude soldiery, instigated by the vile curates, intercepted the people on their way to these private meetings, and imposed a fine upon them for not attending the prelatic church.

As before stated, others of the ejected ministers, when banished from their homes, took refuge in the wilder and less accessible parts of Scotland, where they met many of their own people, who had fled from their homes, and at their earnest desire they instructed them in the word of God. To meet this new phase of affairs an act was passed called the bishops' *drag-net*. It punished as seditious all who ventured to preach without the permission of the bishops, and fined those who neglected to attend the parish church. Proclamations were also issued *against conventicles*, prohibiting ministers from preaching or holding even private meetings for worship, and magistrates were obliged to sign a bond to pay a certain sum if a conventicle should be held within their jurisdiction. Another act was passed, which provided that those who refused to sign the declaration condemning the Covenanters should "forfeit all the privileges of merchandising and trading." And, as if this was not sufficient, the court of High Commission was again erected, and the perjured apostate Archbishop Sharp put at its head. Power was given to it to summon before it and punish with fines and imprisonment all deposed ministers who presumed to preach, and all persons who attended conventicles, or who kept meetings at fasts and the sacrament of the Lord's Supper, and to employ magistrates and military force for seizing their victims. *The curates were organized spies*[*] to give informa-

---

[*] If any one supposes that I have used stronger terms than the truth of history will warrant, I would refer him to Hallam's *Constitutional History of England.* Speaking of the prel-

tion to the Commission of all sincere, and therefore obnoxious, Presbyterians. These were summoned to appear before the Court, and, generally without the formality of calling witnesses or hearing evidence, they were sentenced to pay a ruinous fine or were sent to prison. Some were reduced to abject poverty, some died of loathsome diseases contracted in their prisons, some were banished the kingdom, and some were sold as slaves. And as a refinement of the other cruel deeds, all persons were forbidden to extend any assistance to those actually starving for want of food, under the pain of being regarded as movers of sedition.

In the enforcement of these iniquitous measures the army was actively employed. The soldiers were encouraged by the prelates in their work of plunder and death, and their conduct was rather that of fiends than of men. James Turner, a selfish, cruel, military adventurer, and his "lambs," as his troops were called, were sent to the west and south of Scotland to levy fines and compel submission to

ates and their efforts to crush out dissenters, he says: "It was very possible that episcopacy might be of apostolical institution; but for this institution houses had been burned and fields laid waste, and the gospel had been preached in the wilderness, and its ministers had been shot in their prayers, and husbands had been murdered before their wives, and virgins had been defiled, and many had died by the executioner and by massacre; it was a religion of the boot and the thumb-screw, which a good man must be very cold-blooded indeed if he did not hate."—*Hallam*, vol. iii., p. 442.

the bishops and curates. If a Presbyterian refused to pay the imposed fine, they at once quartered themselves in his house, where they reveled in riot and drunkenness and inflicted every species of outrage, without distinction of age or sex. Stationing themselves at the doors of churches, when the congregation came out they demanded of each person upon oath whether he belonged to that parish. Those who did not were at once fined; and if the fine was not promptly paid, the soldiers seized upon their Bibles, hats, plaids, or any part of their clothing which could be readily carried away and sold. Thus the soldiers robbed the poor people, devoured or wasted their provisions and reduced them to starvation. Complaints but served to increase their abuse. The extent of this robbery may be judged from the historical statement that "in the course of a few weeks the sum of fifty thousand pounds Scots was raised in the west" by the joint efforts of the curates and soldiers.

These intolerable wrongs could not longer be endured, and a spark kindled the flame of insurrection. The attempt, by four wandering countrymen, to rescue a poor old man from the barbarous abuse of the soldiers brought on a conflict. This being considered an act of rebellion, they knew they had no mercy to expect from the civil authorities. To yield was certain death to them; to act in self-defence could but be death. They preferred the latter course, and were joined by many of their persecuted countrymen. The rising was unpremeditated and ill-timed, and in an enterprise of so much importance should not have been undertaken without consultation and without well-matured plans, to secure a general movement throughout the country. For this reason the band of insurgents did not receive the encouragement they expected; and after marching from place to place, they encamped in the vicinity of the Pentland Hills, where they were met by the enemy's army, at least thrice as numerous as their own. A sharp and bloody encounter followed. Fifty of the Covenanters were slain in battle, as many more taken prisoners, and the remainder driven from the well-fought field by Dalziel's cavalry. Though so summarily suppressed, the rising showed the feelings of an oppressed people, and should have been a significant warning to those whose wicked policy had produced these evil results.

The prisoners were dragged to Edinburgh for trial, where sixteen of them were summarily condemned to be hanged, and to have their heads and right hands cut off and exposed to public gaze in different parts of the kingdom. Among the sufferers were several distinguished citizens. John Neilson of Corsack was a gentleman of property, fine talents and unblemished character, who had been exposed to the malice and exactions of the curates and Turner's "lambs," and who had saved Turner's life when he was captured by the insurgents. He was put to the torture of the *boot*, with the hope to extract from him a confession of a widespread conspiracy, in order that the number of victims whose estates could be confiscated and whose lives should be forfeited might be increased.

Another of these sufferers was the eloquent and eminently pious preacher Hugh M'Kail, who said as he mounted the ladder, "I care no more to go up this ladder and over it than if I were going to my father's house." "Friends," said he, turning to the multitude before him, "be not afraid; every step in the ladder is a degree nearer heaven." "Welcome, God and Father; welcome, sweet Jesus, the Mediator of the new covenant; welcome, blessed Spirit of grace and God of all consolation; welcome, glory; welcome, eternal life; welcome, death." Thus died, with these sublime words on his lips, one of the purest and noblest of Scotland's sons, a victim to prelatic tyranny. Thus, too, did judicial vengeance revel in the blood of these defenceless prisoners. But their cruel execution only exasperated the feelings of their sympathizing countrymen, and increased the detestation in which the bishops and curates were held by the people. The dying speeches of these Christian martyrs, and particularly of M'Kail, were remembered with fervent admiration by every true Scottish Presbyterian.

Wherever the people refused to attend the

churches of the prelates or to acknowledge their authority, there the soldiery were sent with full powers to perpetrate whatever barbarities they pleased. Suspicion was all that was required for the infliction of any punishment which caprice or cruelty might dictate. From some money was extorted, others were reduced to starvation, and many more crowded into dungeons, where they could only stand upright day and night, though sick and dying from the fetid and pestilential vapors. The recital, even, of such deeds as were committed in the name of religion stirs the blood with horror, and we cannot dwell upon them.

Through many more years and with slight intermissions and unimportant alleviations, the persecutions against the Covenanters continued. Conventicles were still more sternly repressed, and it was made a capital offence for ministers to attend them. Gentlemen were held responsible if their wives, children, servants or tenantry were found in attendance upon them, and were ruined by the exorbitant fines exacted. But all these unjust and cruel measures, as well as the vigilance of the curates and dragoons, failed to suppress the assemblages. As a necessary precaution those who attended them went armed, and their numbers were frequently large enough to overawe the soldiers sent to disperse them. Yet wherever vengeance could be exercised it was unsparingly indulged. Fiends in human shape like Dalziel and Claverhouse were the ready tools of the cruel policy of which Archbishop Sharp was the ruling spirit. At the solicitation of the latter, repeated orders were issued by the council against field-meetings, each one more oppressive and cruel than the preceding. At length war was virtually declared against the ministers and all who should attend their meetings and protect them, and the barbarities attendant upon the execution of these orders drove the people to desperation. Nine gentlemen took it upon themselves to rid the country of this arch-enemy. Meeting him unexpectedly—for they were looking for his tool, Carmichael—they made him leave his coach; and notwithstanding his offers of money, his promise to abandon his prelatic office and his cries for mercy, they first shot him and then pierced him with their swords. So perished the guilty apostate who, by his repeated acts of perjury, and by eighteen years of bloodshed, had brought untold woe and ruin upon his country, and who finally fell a victim to the indignation which his merciless proceedings had aroused in the breasts of his countrymen.

Large but ineffectual rewards were offered for the apprehension of the murderers. The king was greatly incensed, and sent a proclamation to his council expressing regret for his past *clemency*, and a determination to wage a war of extermination in future against conventicles. He and his council, for their own purposes, chose to represent the persecuted Presbyterians as approving of the death of Sharp, while they could not but know that their oft-avowed principles would never sanction private individuals in taking the law into their own hands even to redress the greatest wrongs. But the time when endurance ceased to be a virtue had nearly come. The persecuted had either to submit to live as abject slaves or to rise up in defence of civil and religious liberty. Some of the more impetuous, judging themselves entitled by the laws of God and nature to defend their own lives when assailed, banded themselves together for this purpose. In their declaration of principles, however, they not only asserted this *right*, but censured the conduct of those who had brought the great evils upon the country. This was construed into an act of rebellion against the government, and an armed force was dispatched to apprehend those who had made the manifesto. Claverhouse was in command of the king's troops; and meeting two hundred Covenanters, who were protecting a field-meeting near Loudon hill, he ordered his men to fire upon them. The fire was returned with vigor by the Presbyterian party, who at last rushed upon their assailants, putting them to flight and leaving forty of the soldiers dead upon the field of battle. This spirited and successful contest is known in history as the battle of DRUMCLOG.

With the victors the question to be decided was whether to disperse, or to remain together in order to protect each other. The latter course was decided upon, and the insurgents were joined by large numbers. Unhappily, however, there had been no previous plans or concert of action agreed upon, and differences of opinion paralyzed the assembled forces. One party was for asserting their loyalty to the king, although such oppressive tyranny had been practiced in his name; the other declared that when kings violate their solemn engagements with their subjects and become tyrants, the people are released from their obligations to support and defend those who thus oppress them. Neither party would submit to the other, and the scenes of contention which arose discouraged those already in arms, prevented many from joining the army, and led others to abandon the cause. After seizing Glasgow the insurgents marched toward Edinburgh, then returned to their former camp on Hamilton Moor, near Bothwell Bridge. Here they were met by the royal army in command of the duke of Monmouth, who ordered them to lay down their arms and submit themselves to the king's clemency. The half hour given them for consultation having passed, and they not yielding, their position was charged by a detachment, which attempted to wrest the bridge from them. It was defended with great bravery, but want of proper support and a superior force obliged them at last to yield this, the key of the position. The enemy, crossing the bridge and charging the undisciplined and poorly commanded army of Covenanters, put them to flight, hewing down large numbers of them in the defenceless rout. While but few fell during the conflict, *four hundred* were slain in their flight, and twelve hundred were taken prisoners, many of whom afterward perished upon the scaffold. Such was the result of the battle of BOTHWELL BRIDGE.

The Presbyterians owed their defeat mainly to their divided councils. Some of their clergy were among the "indulged," and had been restored to their pulpits by a defection from their principles, as some of their brethren understood it. Others had consented, under protest, to pay the tax levied for the support of the troops engaged in plundering the adherents of the Covenant, while many persistently refused to pay it. These irreconcilable opinions, not to say dissensions, rendered their overthrow inevitable.

But disastrous as was the battle, it was followed by still more terrible horrors. The prisoners, bound together two and two, were driven to Edinburgh as cattle to the slaughter. Arriving there, they were confined for five months in Grayfriars' churchyard, half naked and half starved, without any protection from the cold and rain except the tombstones, and at the best a few rude huts. Some of them were hanged, others kept a long time in vile prisons, while two hundred of them were crowded into a small vessel to be transported to Barbadoes and sold for slaves. Upon the western and southern counties "the bloody Claverhouse" and his cruel soldiers were let loose to fine, imprison, torture and murder all suspected of aiding or approving of the late rising. Indiscriminate carnage followed. The country was put under martial law, and unparalleled atrocities were committed by the licentious soldiery. The people who fled from their homes were shot down in the fields, while their houses were pillaged and burnt; aged men of threescore and ten were dashed to the ground and trampled under foot; the sick were dragged from their beds and murdered; women were subjected to brutal violence worse than death itself; and tender youth were tortured with the hope to wring from them the place of concealment of their parents. In a word, complete desolation reigned wherever the fierce exterminators went.

Even yet the persecutors were not weary of their merciless but fruitless work. The following year they were allowed to glut their vengeance upon such distinguished victims as Richard Cameron, Donald Cargill and Hackson of Rathillet, whose heads and hands were cut off, and the former fixed on spikes above two of the gates of Edinburgh. In 1681 a new engine of tyranny was devised. This was the infamous *Test Act*—a long, complex oath, which bound those who took it to acknowledge the supremacy of the king in all cases, ecclesiastical as well as civil, to renounce the Covenants, and to promise that under no circumstances they would attempt the alteration of the government of either Church or State. This last of necessity implied on the part of Presbyterians a complete abandonment of the principles for which they had so long contended. Portions of the oath, moreover, were inconsistent with other parts, and a compliance with it was therefore impracticable. But it was required to be taken by all, *papists* alone excepted. Some of the prelatic clergy—to their credit be it said—refused to take the test, and resigned their livings rather than perjure themselves. Large numbers of the nobility, and some of the bishops even, had to take it with explanations. But these were not in all cases allowed. The oath was designed originally only for persons occupying places of public trust, but it was discovered to be so comprehensive, and so convenient a tool of persecution, that it was determined to impose it upon all. The earl of Argyle, who had become suspected by the duke of York and the Scottish council of being too friendly to the Covenanters, was the first victim of the test act, and only escaped the vengeance of his enemies by flying in disguise to Holland. All his past services to his country, his high rank and that of his distinguished ancestors, availed nothing with those who sought his ruin. His offer to relinquish his hereditary possessions and evince his loyalty as a private citizen would not satisfy his enemies. His declinature to take the absurd and impious bond was sufficient ground to proceed against him as a criminal, and to compel him to seek refuge in a foreign land.

Notwithstanding the espionage of the curates, who continued to be diligently employed as informers, and the activity of the civil magistrates, who were equally zealous in inflicting punishment upon all violators of the unjust and absurd acts of the king and council, field-meetings and meetings for consultation were occasionally held in the more secluded parts of the country. The holding of such a meeting in 1682 was made the occasion for issuing a violent proclamation, making the failure to give information of such assemblages a crime equal in magnitude to that of those who took part in them. As most persons objected to be employed as spies and informers, military officers were commissioned, on whom was conferred both judicial and executive authority. They could call before them any suspected person and pass sentence upon him, and even execute those whom they chose. Here we have the very *essence* of despotism. And our abhorrence is increased when we learn the nature of the offences which these military judges punished. By them it was adjudged a crime for any person not to attend on the ministry of the persecuting prelates, or to speak in terms of respect or pity of those who had suffered for their religion, or to be seen reading the

Bible in private, or heard conducting family worship in one's own house. For these and similar offences great numbers were impoverished by exorbitant fines, or thrown into prison, or banished. The estates of others were confiscated under the false charge of constructive treason, which latter proceeding caused such dismay among landholders that many of them seriously thought of abandoning their native land. The threat of the popish duke of York, that "Scotland would never have peace till the whole country south of the Forth was turned into a hunting-field," was yet, they feared, to be put into execution.

An event occurred in 1684 which deserves special mention. It was a warning to all "intelligencers and informers," by the persecuted and outlawed Covenanters, that the limits of Christian endurance had at last been reached, and that retaliation would follow any further acts of persecution. Having been hunted like wild beasts and obliged to make their abodes in caves upon the mountains, or in rocky glens and impenetrable thickets—and even in these their wild retreats they were not secure from the keen scent of the bloodhound informer—it is no wonder that they had finally, "like a stag at bay," turned upon their pursuers. Their very remarkable paper, or "apologetical declaration," they caused to be affixed on the market-crosses of the chief towns of Scotland.

The effect of this declaration upon the informers, curates and others was most salutary. These base emissaries showed a wholesome fear of men rendered desperate by long and intolerable oppression. They dared not follow them to their desolate retreats and furnish lists of them to the military judges. But the fury of the council knew no bounds, and it hastened to forge and put in operation another terrible weapon of persecution. This is known as "*the Bloody Act*," which ordained that every person should be put to death "who owns or does not disown the late traitorous declaration." Commissions were issued to several noblemen, gentlemen and military officers, requiring them to assemble all the inhabitants, men and women, above fourteen years of age; and if any owned the late declaration, they were to be immediately executed; while those who were absent were to have their houses burned and their goods seized. The "abjuration oath" was also framed and put in force, and a proclamation issued forbidding any one to travel without having a certificate of his loyalty, which was based on his taking the last-named oath. All indulgences were recalled, and ministers were obliged to give bonds not to preach or teach in Scotland.

Nothing was now wanting, as it would seem, to ensure the work of exterminating the Presbyterians. If a minister preached the gospel, he was either imprisoned, exiled or hanged. Those who refused to take the impious and contradictory oath were visited with instant death by the lawless military commissions. Those who, on calls of duty or business, were obliged to travel, were in danger of being shot down by the soldiers, without even the formality of an inquiry as to whether they had the required pass. This may well be called, as it has been designated in the history of the period, "the killing-time." Without a recital of individual instances of cruelty and slaughter, we will summarize what is needed to be said, and that in the words of another: "All the terrible enginery of persecution was now brought into full operation, and the practiced hands and callous hearts of the oppressors wielded their murderous weapons without remorse. When disappointed in one instance, their savage spirits thirsted the more intensely for a deeper draught of blood from some less protected source. Public judicial murders gave sanction and encouragement to that indiscriminate slaughter perpetrated by the soldiery throughout the country, till the entire west and south of Scotland was one field of blood."

# CHAPTER V.

## From the Accession of James II. to the Revolution Settlement and the Emigration to America.

The death of Charles II., February 6, 1685, occasioned a brief pause in the dreadful persecution which the Presbyterians endured. His death was attributed to apoplexy, but it was strongly suspected that he died of poison. Thus perished a monarch ungrateful, unprincipled and treacherous, and whose reign was mean, disgraceful and tyrannical. So soon as the intelligence of the king's death reached Scotland, his brother, the duke of York, was proclaimed sovereign, and in terms which recognized him as the source of all law, civil and sacred. Nor was he reluctant to use the despotic power thus acknowledged to be his by divine right. A prelatic, and consequently an obsequious, Parliament was called, which at his royal bidding passed a number of the most infamous acts imaginable. By these the giving or taking the National Covenant, or owning that it or the Solemn League and Covenant was lawful or obligatory, was a treasonable proceeding. So also was the giving food to, or concealing those who had been declared traitors, and the punishment of death was to be extended to hearers as well as preachers at conventicles. It was an act of treason, also, if at family worship five individuals more than the members of the household were present, and the test oath was imposed upon all, *papists* alone excepted.

It was apparent that James was determined to remove all limits to the royal prerogative and to force upon Scotland his own religion. But the time had not yet come for an avowal of his design to root out the established faith; for though many were ready to promise abject submission to the king's will, he knew the nation was at heart decidedly Protestant and that his throne would be endangered if he openly attacked the Church. The better to conceal his real and ultimate purpose, an *indemnity* was published, which was, however, so framed as to shut out all nonconformists from the advantages of the indulgence. The bishops and magistrates were instigated to employ still harsher measures toward the Presbyterians, and the same murderous system which, before the death of his brother, had excited the greatest horror, was continued. Drummond, one of the most cruel of the generals, was given a commission authorizing him to hold courts at his pleasure, to exact fines, and to inflict summary punishment upon all persons who had performed any of the most common acts of humanity for the proscribed, and to call to his assistance the "Highland Host"—soldiers composed of the very refuse of society in that uncivilized region. This part of Scotland, being now put under military law, was exposed to all the excesses and to the devastation which would naturally be committed by undisciplined and savage men, guided by passion and stimulated by love of plunder.

While this infamous persecution was in progress, intelligence was received that the earl of Argyle had left Holland, and had entered the kingdom "for the purpose of recovering the religion, rights and liberties" of the people. This dangerous enterprise was undertaken without proper consultation or preparation, the earl expecting that his rank and personal influence, combined with the justice of the cause, would induce the disaffected to flock to his standard. He soon found that he had greatly erred in his estimate of the assistance expected. He was distrusted by the Covenanters, both as to his principles and his military talents, and they refused to unite with him. His own forces, few in number and much dispirited, were soon dispersed, and their leader, having been taken prisoner, was brought in triumph to Edinburgh, where he was afterward executed. The intrepidity and tranquillity of spirit with which the earl met his fate served to deepen the impression in the public mind of his patriotism and his personal piety, and to cause him to be regarded as a noble martyr in the sacred cause of civil and religious liberty.

When the apprehension occasioned by the rebellion had passed away, the persecution against the Presbyterians was renewed with merciless severity, for the king believed that they were secretly friendly to Argyle, though they had declined to join his standard. Multitudes were forced into banishment, many of them after their persons had been disfigured by torture; others were put into dark subterranean dungeons full of mire and filth, where they were denied every comfort, and where many of them died for want of food and air; others still were wantonly murdered in the fields and their families stripped of all their possessions. But there was soon to be an end to these fiend-like outrages, and we are to be spared the recital of horrors that make humanity shudder. Although some instances of cruelty occurred in the two following years, a change in the government took place which happily brought immediate relief to those who had endured all things, not even "counting their lives dear unto them," in order to uphold constitutional liberty and the right to worship their Maker as their enlightened consciences dictated.

The king, through his exterminating process with the Covenanters, had so far reduced the number of his victims, and had succeeded in so enlarging his prerogative by means of a purely prelatic Parliament, that he believed the time had come when he could with safety enter upon his schemes in favor of popery. Having already, as we have seen, exempted the papists from the operation of the *Test* oath, his next step was to remove all their civil disabilities. But the English Parliament refused to repeal the penal statutes against them, believing that if tolerated they would subvert the religion of the kingdom. Foiled in England, James had recourse to the Parliament of Scotland. At last, however, some of this obsequious body saw the danger which threatened. Even the subservient prelates who had been most forward in offering the incense of non-resistance to the royal nostrils when the king's enemies were theirs, were now convinced that if the penal statutes against Roman Catholics should be repealed, and all offices of trust and authority be opened to them, the Church of Rome, with all its intolerance and superstitions, would soon be restored. Laying aside, therefore, their animosities to the Presbyterians, they joined them in resisting the demands of a popish ruler. The most that could be wrung from the Parliament by the king's commissioner was that His Majesty's commands would be taken into "serious and dutiful consideration," all being agreed that papists should be protected in their civil rights and should be free from punishment for privately exercising their religion. No compromise was proposed or made that could endanger the Protestant faith, and it was, moreover, enacted that the statutes which the king wished set aside "should continue in full force, strength and effect." The Parliament, proving unyielding, was prorogued, and King James sent a letter to the council, in which he claimed "his undoubted right and prerogative" to "take the Roman Catholics under his royal protection, allowing to them the free exercise of their religion and giving to them the chapel of Holyrood House for a place of public worship." He thus wielded in behalf of popery the formidable weapon which had been placed in his hands by the prelatic party, who had so repeatedly declared that the *will of the sovereign* was the *fountain of all law*, which no subject could *question* or *resist*.

The monarch was undoubtedly much surprised at the opposition his scheme encountered from Episcopalians. He supposed—and not without good reason—from their passive obedience to the royal will heretofore, that they would not resist a change which simply made the pope instead of the king the head of the Church. In this he was greatly mistaken, for the Episcopal Church was still Protestant, though prelatic. The resistance of the prelates, joined with that of Parliament, determined James to make a total change in his mode of procedure. Instead of continuing a fierce persecutor of nonconformists, he adopted the policy of universal toleration. He was forced to this course as the only available way in which he could extend the protection he desired to those of his own faith. Three acts of indulgence were published, avowedly to relieve dissenters from the disabilities they were under, and to allow liberty of conscience to all, but evidently to render papists eligible to places of public trust; and hence care was taken, in the very first of these acts, to annul all laws that had been passed in Parliament against Roman Catholics. Each of these acts, too, affirmed in behalf of the king a dispensing and absolute power, at direct variance with all civil and religious liberty. Their language was, "By his sovereign authority, prerogative royal and absolute power" these favors were granted. The purpose was so plain that it would seem no one could be deceived by the king's pretences. The despotic authority assumed in these acts of toleration should have induced their rejection by all who were unwilling to surrender the liberty of their country, and the favor shown to the papists should have led all true Protestants to combine in order to prevent the triumph of popery, and to save themselves from the thralldom of the papal yoke.

The last act of indulgence was framed with the intention of pleasing, and possibly winning over, the less scrupulous Presbyterians. Hence it suspended all penal laws made against nonconformity to the established religion, and allowed Presbyterians "to meet and serve God after their own way and manner, be it in private houses, chapels, or places purposely hired or built for that purpose." The only limitation was that of field-preaching, against which the laws were left in full force. It should not surprise any one that this sudden deliverance from persecution, and the granting of these unusual privileges, made a deep impression upon those to whom they were extended, or that in the vehemence of their feelings, caused by the longing desire once more to preach the blessed gospel to their former congregations, some ministers overlooked the dangerous exertion of power to which they were indebted. A large portion of the Presbyterian ministers in Scotland embraced the opportunity to resume public worship and to collect again their scattered flocks. Several who had fled to Holland came back and renewed their labors in their former parishes. Many of the people, released from prison or coming from their places of concealment, returned to their former homes, and engaged anew in their work of building up the Presbyterian Church. And while, in accepting this clemency, they made at least a partial acknowledgment of the royal supremacy in matters spiritual, "they refused to make the slightest compliance which could give any advantage to popery, and they were even charged with ingratitude for the boldness and the success with which they warned their hearers against its introduction."

But the strict Covenanters were more consistent in their course, and adhered more resolutely to Presbyterian principles. They promptly rejected every indulgence or toleration of "man's inalienable right to worship God according to his revealed will and the dictates of an enlightened conscience," especially when such indulgence is founded upon "the unlimited prerogative and absolute power of the monarch—a principle equally inconsistent with the laws of God and the liberties of mankind." Defying the king's threats and spurning his favors, they kept on their course. Their field-preaching was continued, and they disregarded the laws which were still in force against conventicles. Renwick, one of their most revered and courageous preachers, was apprehended and publicly executed—a man of heroic mould, "inflexible as Knox and vehement as Melville"—closing by his death that long list of martyrs who sealed with their blood their testimony in behalf of civil and religious liberty in Scotland.

While James was persecuting in Scotland all who dared oppose his wishes to introduce the Roman Catholic religion, whether Covenanters, the indulged ministers, or the seven prelatic bishops, whom he confined in the Tower for petitioning against being compelled to read one of his arbitrary indulgences from the pulpit, he was at the same time, by his despotic acts in England, alienating the feelings of the people and inciting them to resist his arbitrary rule. The nation was ready for a change, and the great majority of those who still loved freedom instinctively turned to William, prince of Orange, the son-in-law of James, as the defender of the Protestant faith and of constitutional law and liberty. That prince, having closely watched the state of affairs in Britain, was convinced that the favorable moment had come when it was his duty to attempt to save the nation.

Making his preparations as speedily as was possible, William set sail for England, and landed at Torbay, November 5, 1688, without opposition. He issued a proclamation which contained the reasons that had induced him to appear in arms. These were, in brief, his desire to preserve the Protestant religion and restore the laws and the liberties of the kingdom. At first few joined him and there seemed but little desire for the change which he sought to accomplish. The prospect, however, soon brightened. The proclamation was spread throughout the length and breadth of the land by the zealous Covenanters, and made a deep impression upon the public mind. Most of the nobility and gentlemen of Scotland declared for the prince, and these were followed by the army and navy of the kingdom. The king, after some feeble attempts to assert his authority and to regain the affection of his people, fled, an exile from his throne and kingdom, and the prince of Orange became the successful vindicator of the liberties of England. Thus the REVOLUTION was accomplished, and the Presbyterian Church was again established in Scotland. The formidable structure which the two tyrants, Charles and James, with the willing assistance of the prelates, had spent twenty-eight years in erecting, and which had been cemented with the blood of *ten thousand victims*, was thus overthrown almost in a moment.

During all this stormy period of persecution the exertions of the bishops and the mandates and violence of despotic power had failed to make any real progress in bringing over the people of Scotland to the episcopal Church. For nearly thirty years *prelacy* had had almost unlimited sway, with its hard task lightened by governmental aid. It had been armed with influence and dignity, the offices of trust and honor in the kingdom had been largely filled by prelates, and the civil and military power of the nation had been employed to do its bidding. With this power and prestige, is it not a remarkable fact that during all this period it never ventured to attempt to introduce the ceremonies of the English Church? It instinctively knew that this would have been a perilous undertaking. As a matter of fact, the form of worship differed little from the Presbyterian. There was no liturgy, no ceremonies, no surplice, no altars, no crossing in baptism. Even the Perth articles were very generally ignored. Nor was there any new confession of faith introduced, nor any new standard of doctrine or discipline, except the will of the bishops, themselves the *creatures* of the will of the king. It was truly, as some one has said, a "nondescript" Church—as much so as is possible to be conceived; for it was neither popery, prelacy nor presbytery, but a strange jumble of all three, with the king for pope, his council for cardinals, the bishops for moderators, and the dragoons of Dalziel, Turner and Claverhouse (as Makenzie called them) for "ruling elders." Not less absurd were some of the statutes enacted by this great politico-ecclesiastical authority. During its supreme reign a law was passed forbidding ministers lecturing, in which method of instruction it was discovered Presbyterian divines excelled. A preacher might speak all day or all night, provided he selected but a single verse of Scripture for a text; but if he chose two or more verses, he exposed himself to the penalties of treason.

Prelacy in Scotland showed itself to the very last to be a slavish, intolerant, irreligious and persecuting system as well as a foe to civil and religious freedom. When the fortunes of the prince of Orange were for a brief time obscured by disaster, the Scottish prelates, with the exception of two, hastened to send the tyrant James a letter containing the most extravagant eulogiums of him and his government; avowing their steadfast allegiance to him, they concluded by wishing him "the hearts of his subjects and the necks of his enemies." When we remember that this letter was addressed to a sovereign who had clearly shown his intention to subvert the freedom and the religion of the kingdom, and was designed to defeat a prince who had inscribed upon his banners, "The Protestant religion and the liberties of England," and who had come to put an end to the system of tyranny which had deluged the country with blood, it is difficult to conceive anything more base and servile. It was followed, too, by resistance to the rightful authority of William, by maintaining a secret correspondence with the exiled tyrant, and by furnishing him information and supplies of men and money. It was only the inflexible adherence to right principles on the part of Presbyterians, their fortitude in enduring every extremity of suffering under long and relentless persecution, and their united and earnest support of a Protestant prince, that prevented Scotland from being reduced to a state of abject slavery.

Looking, then, upon prelacy as the enemy of civil and religious freedom, as they were forced to do, it would have been strange indeed if Presbyterians had not refused to fellowship the prelates when restored to their former rights and privileges. It was to be expected also that when they had the power they would embrace the opportunity to expel the prelatic curates from the positions into which they had intruded, and deprive them of the parish property which they had unlawfully seized. Some of these merciless persecutors, they turned out of their usurped residences, and, taking them to the boundaries of their parishes, sent them away, without offering them further violence. The wonder is that many of these wretched men had not to atone with their lives for the system of espionage which they had employed, and the cruelties they had been instrumental in having inflicted upon their defenceless Protestant brethren. The clemency of the Presbyterians toward their enemies, in this the hour of their triumph, is one of the strongest evidences that can be adduced of their humane disposition and that they possessed the true spirit of the gospel—a gospel of peace and brotherly kindness.

The English people united with those of Scotland, in declaring that James had violated the fundamental laws of the kingdom and had forfeited his right to the government, and in placing the prince of Orange on the vacant throne. William lost no time in calling together the leading Scottish noblemen and gentlemen who were in London, to counsel with them as to the best method to secure the civil and religious liberties of the country. They advised that a representative convention should be held in Edinburgh, and that in the selection of members all Protestants should have the right of ballot and of serving as members. The convention met on the 14th of March, 1689, when it ratified the acts of the English legislature and adopted measures for settling the government. In the Claim of Right, which forms the basis of the settlement to which they gave their assent, it is asserted " that prelacy and the superiority of any office in the Church above presbyters is and hath been a great and insupportable grievance and trouble to this nation, and contrary to the inclinations of the generality of the people ever since the Reformation, they having been reformed from popery by presbyters, and therefore ought to be abolished." And when the convention assumed the status of a Parliament by permission of the king, they passed an act "abolishing prelacy and all superiority of any office in the Church above presbyters," and rescinded all acts of previous Parliaments by which prelacy had been established. Through the desire of the king, who favored, for State reasons, a union of the prelatic clergy and the Presbyterian ministers in one and the same Church, the complete settlement of the question of church government was deferred until the next Parliament.

This met in April, 1690, and was chiefly occupied with ecclesiastical matters. The act of supremacy, the fruitful source of persecution in previous reigns, and against which the Presbyterian Church steadily and uniformly protested, was formally repealed. The ejected Presbyterian ministers who yet survived were restored to their churches, and the prelatic incumbents were ordered to be removed from the usurped parishes. Sixty of those who had been compelled to give up their parishes in 1661 were still living, and were by this act allowed to enter upon their duties and receive their salaries. The fines and forfeitures of the persecuted were removed, and the laws against conventicles and non-conformity, as well as all the tests and oaths, with their fearful penalties, were repealed. On the 7th of June, 1690, the memorable act was passed "ratifying the Confession of Faith and settling Presbyterian church government." The Presbyterian government is characterized in this act as "the government of Christ's Church within this nation agreeable to the word of God, and most conducive to the advancement of true piety and godliness;" and taking the statute of 1592 as the model, the different courts, sessions, presbyteries, synods and General Assemblies were restored. The members of these courts were declared to be the Presbyterian ministers who had been ejected and who were now restored to their livings, and such ministers and elders as they have or may hereafter admit.

By the ratification of the Confession of Faith the great principle that Christ is the sole Head of the Church, and—its direct consequence—the Church's spiritual independence of an earthly sovereign, were affirmed. This was one of the chief principles for which the Presbyterian Church had so long contended, and no settlement could be satisfactory to Presbyterians that did not secure the Church her freedom. It was now necessary, as the next most important legislative measure, to protect, as far as possible, the religious rights and privileges of the members of the churches. This was done by an act which made void the power of presenting ministers to vacant churches, and transferred to the people the right of selecting their pastors. By this it was intended to abolish patronage entirely, and to permit the voice of the people to be supreme in the choice of ministers. Thus the independence of the Church and State, in their respective spheres, was clearly defined and asserted, while the many causes for jealousy between them, and which had produced so much friction in past times, were now happily removed.

To give effect to these legislative enactments, a General Assembly was called, to meet in Edinburgh in October. Many and formidable were the difficulties it had to face and overcome. Within the Assembly were many jarring and discordant elements, scarcely possible to be reconciled; while without, and pressing for consideration, were the well-known wishes of the king for a union between the prelatic clergy and the restored Presbyterian ministers, under the same form of church government. Within the Church were three parties—the ejected ministers, numbering about sixty;

the Cameronians, only three in number; and the indulged ministers, who had conformed more or less to prelacy, and whose numbers were more than twice that of both the other classes combined. It was evident, therefore, that no measure could be carried in the Assembly by the more strict and faithful ministers if the latter party should resolve to oppose it; and it was too much to expect that men who had submitted to the tyrannous acts of the preceding reigns would forfeit the favor of William, by opposing his desire to have the prelatic clergy included in the established Church.

We have referred to these things, not to excuse the weak policy of those who temporized at this important juncture, but to show the causes which were in operation, and which led to the compromise finally made. It was the duty of the Assembly to see that none of the inherent and essential principles of the Presbyterian Church should be overborne or sacrificed through any plea of expediency. By yielding to the policy of William, and adopting measures of comprehension that retained large numbers of the prelatic clergy within the national Church, a grievous error was committed, and its disastrous influence was long felt in Scotland. These Episcopalians were not overscrupulous. They did not hesitate to subscribe with alacrity the Confession of Faith in order to retain their positions. But their presence in the Church and their influence acted as a poison in the Presbyterian system. It was the noxious seed of "moderatism," which proved in the succeeding century the upas tree of the Church of Scotland. Her *jure divino* Presbyterianism on one hand, and her Arminian, if not worldly, moderatism on the other, were most disastrous to her peace and purity. But while we regret that the revolution settlement was imperfect in this respect, we must never cease to be grateful to the persecuted Presbyterian Church of Scotland, which maintained the great principle of the spiritual independence of the Church of Christ and the right of Christian people to choose their own spiritual advisers, and in this way secured an amount of civil and religious freedom, in both the Church and the kingdom, far greater than had ever before been enjoyed.

In tracing this history from the introduction of the Reformation in Scotland to the revolution, where we now leave it, we have constantly been reminded of the intimate connection between civil and religious liberty, and that the latter not only influenced, but produced, the former. It is true that the resistance of the Scottish Church proceeded from a higher principle than simply to assert and maintain the civil liberties of the country. The contest, on its part, was waged in defence of the central principle of religious freedom—that the Lord Jesus Christ is the sole Head and King of the Church, and that, within its domain, the civil magistrate has no right to intrude with his authority. This great principle, when fully recognized by the civil ruler, preserves the consciences of men free from the control of external power; and where the conscience is free, the subject cannot be made a slave. This fact was most clearly perceived by the brother tyrants Charles and James, and they employed the *oath of supremacy* as their chief weapon to destroy this grand and fundamental principle of religious liberty. If it could be overthrown, it would be easy to build upon its ruins a despotic government. But our Presbyterian fathers, recognizing the fact that civil and religious liberty exist or perish together, were constrained to contend equally for both; and what the world to-day enjoys of both, it owes very largely to the unconquerable fortitude with which they encountered the perils and endured the sufferings which cruel, persecuting and despotic rulers inflicted.

With such a history and with such a providential training, it would indeed have been strange if the descendants of these heroic defenders of the faith should not manifest a strong attachment to the Presbyterian form of doctrine and government wherever they made their homes in America. Past experience had shown their fathers, even if they themselves had not learned it by personal experience, that prelacy and Romanism were the natural allies of the despot—that they had always been ready to bend their supple knees to secure royal favor, and to submit their necks to the yoke of bondage which the oath of supremacy imposed upon the subject—and consequently both were to be distrusted and opposed. With a zeal, therefore, born of knowledge, they not only made very strenuous efforts, but endured many privations, in order to successfully establish Presbyterianism in the New World, for they felt assured that in its extension, all could enjoy freedom of conscience and constitutional liberty. The principles which moulded their characters, and the spirit which actuated those who came from Scotland to this country, made them not only an important element in the Presbyterian Church, but a tower of strength to the young nation when it was compelled to resist the exercise of arbitrary power by England.

# HISTORY OF THE IRISH CHURCH.

## CHAPTER VI.

### From the Introduction of the Reformed Religion to the Great Revival of 1625.

During the first half century of its history, American Presbyterianism was largely indebted for its growth and efficiency to the pious and worthy immigrants who sought refuge in this country. Holland, France, England, Scotland and Ireland all made liberal contributions of their very best people. These colonists, while diverse in their origin, were singularly harmonious in their political principles and their religious faith. Doubtless this was owing to the fact that they were persecuted heroes who had suffered in common for their resistance to despotic power; and as exiles for conscience' sake, they were agreed in their wishes to found a commonwealth where civil and religious freedom could be enjoyed.

To no one of these countries was the Presbyterian Church in America, in its origin and its rapid growth, so largely indebted as to the north of Ireland. A large proportion of those who composed its membership, and of those who occupied its pulpits, were previously connected with the Presbyterian Church of Ireland. To form a just estimate of their character, their spirit and their influence—a work which it is here proposed to do—it will be requisite to pass in review the prominent circumstances and features in the history of the Irish Church.

It would appear from the most ancient records that Ireland was visited with the gospel as early as the second century. Nor was it planted there by the agents of the Romish Church, as is commonly claimed. On the contrary, the evidence is abundant and clear that the Irish people for ages resisted all the encroachments of the papacy. The forms of Christianity that prevailed in Ireland were those of the Eastern churches, and were introduced, it is probable, by Greek, and not Roman, missionaries. "I strongly suspect," says Dr. O'Halloran, a Roman Catholic historian of high authority, "that by Asiatic or African missionaries, or, through them, by Spanish ones, were our ancestors instructed in Christianity, because they rigidly adhered to their customs as to the tonsure and the time of Easter. *Certain it is that Patrick found a hierarchy established in Ireland.*" So much for the claim that St. Patrick was the first gospel missionary in Ireland.

Archbishop Usher has adduced convincing evidence that until the twelfth century, when popery was first introduced, the bishops and clergy of the Irish Church were married men; that the communion service of Rome was not in its liturgy, and that the Lord's Supper was received by it in both kinds; that auricular confession and the doctrine of transubstantiation were unknown to it; that image-worship was not permitted; that it neither prayed *to* dead men nor *for* them, and had no fixed service for the dead; and that it refused to pay tithes to the Romish see.

History assigns the first place among the early propagators of a pure faith, in the ancient Irish Church, to Columba, who died at Iona, Scotland, in 597, a distinguished missionary of the gospel in Scotland and England as well as in his own country. The people were simple in their mode of life and evangelical in their religious faith and methods of worship. For nearly seven hundred years more, and until the twelfth century, in the reign of Henry II., the Irish Church remained independent.\* It was by the latter sovereign, and by the aid of a council of clergy assembled at Cashel in 1172, that the Church of Ireland was brought into obedience to the Roman pontiff—a disastrous day for that country, followed by a series of calamities rendered only the more painful by

---

\* "Celtic Ireland was neither papal nor inclined to submit to the papacy till Henry II. riveted the Roman yoke upon it."—*Froude*, vol. i., p. 30.

contrast with its prosperous career from the days of St. Patrick to the council of Cashel. Most of its members continued to practice the rites of their ancient religion, and to resist as best they could the bondage of Rome. But the latter, with the help of English money and English arms, finally succeeded in making Ireland a chief stronghold of "the man of sin," and for three centuries Rome there maintained an almost undisputed dominion. Large numbers of monasteries were erected and liberally endowed, and nothing was left undone that power and money could effect, to obliterate the cherished associations of the people for their more simple faith and worship, and to reconcile them to the spiritual supremacy of the pope. This state of things continued to the period when Henry VIII., with the consent of its nobles, was proclaimed "king of Ireland and *supreme head of the Church.*"

Most deplorable was the condition of the entire country at this time. It is described by Froude "as shared out between sixty Irish chiefs of the old blood and thirty great captains of the English noble folk, who lived by the sword and obeyed no temporal power, but only himself that was strong. The cattle and human beings lived herded together, even in the latter half of the sixteenth century." Without education and but partially civilized, enslaved by error and debased by superstition, the dupes of designing monks and the slaves of bigoted priests, the people were in the grossest ignorance and irreligion. Even the heads of clans and the feudal lords were raised but little, if at all, above the common level of the community. They were turbulent, irreligious, vicious, and constantly engaged in scenes of violence or dishonorable conspiracies. If it suited their purposes, or in any way was conducive to their personal ambitions, they did not hesitate to destroy the temples of Religion, or to gratify their revenge upon those who ministered at her altars. The unsettled and distracted state of the island was, of course, very unfavorable to anything like a reformation in religion.

Such was the social and religious condition of the people when Henry VIII. sent his commissioners to Ireland to proclaim the royal supremacy and demand the subjection of the Irish prelates to his own ecclesiastical control. In this he was not influenced by any love that he cherished for the doctrines of the Reformation, but by a desire to overthrow the power of the pope. Hence but little was accomplished for Protestantism besides the establishment of English supremacy and the suppression of some of the numerous monasteries. The chief agent employed by the king was an Augustinian monk, George Browne, on whom the king, in 1535, had conferred the title of archbishop of Dublin. His selection for this delicate and important work was due to his previous opposition to some of the doctrinal errors of the Romish Church while provincial of his order in England. His zeal against popery seems to have been fervent and sincere. Charged with the royal commission, he repaired at once to Dublin, where, in a conference with the principal nobility and clergy, and in obedience to his royal instructions, he demanded that the Roman Catholic prelates should acknowledge the king's supremacy. Cromer, archbishop of Armagh, and his suffragan clergy, met this demand with prompt and spirited opposition. Thus matters remained for nearly a year, until the calling of a Parliament in 1537. In the mean time, the vigorous means adopted by the clergy to excite the nobility to resist the attempted usurpation were so far successful that the question was with great difficulty carried in the Irish Parliament. The laws necessary for the required alteration of the national faith were, however, passed. Among these were enactments declaring the king supreme head of the Church; renouncing the authority of the pope and declaring his supporters guilty of high treason; forbidding all appeals to Rome, together with the payment of dues and the purchasing of dispensations; also, several of the religious houses were dissolved and their revenues vested in the Crown.

The exercise of this authority had but little influence on the advancement of the great truths of the Reformation. While public opposition was silenced wherever British power prevailed, the attachment of the Romish clergy to their Church continued as strong as ever. Acting under injunctions from Rome, they steadfastly resisted the claims of the king, and the archbishop declared those accursed who should acknowledge any power superior to that of the pope. The change was merely nominal, and the order sent from England to the archbishop of Dublin, to purge the churches of his province of their images, relics and superstitious rites, was successfully evaded. As new bishops were elevated to the vacant sees they were prompt to promise obedience to the king, but were powerless to carry out the views of the new government. The people and the inferior clergy continued ignorant and bigoted in their religion, and were indignant at the orders of Lord Cromwell, whom they called, in derision, "the blacksmith's son."

The accession of Edward VI., while it was favorable for the advancement of the reform in England, accomplished very little for Ireland. In the former it was diligently fostered, and, meeting with only slight opposition, made rapid progress. A book of homilies was composed for the use of the clergy, English Bibles were placed in every parish church, the mass was changed for the communion in both elements, tables were substituted for altars, divine worship was conducted in English, and a book of common prayer compiled. But a single one of these various methods of promoting the Reformation was adopted in Ireland, and this was accompanied by an inexcusable artifice, designed to impose upon the ignorance of the clergy and people. A proclamation was issued in 1551, requiring the English common prayer-book to be used throughout the kingdom in the celebration of divine worship. Anticipating resistance to the order on the part of the Romish clergy, the council represented the new liturgy as "a mere translation of the Romish service," thus attempting to conceal its real character. It was in vain that the priests were commanded to use it. Dowdal, the primate, contended earnestly against the proposed innovation; the lord-deputy was firm, and on Easter-day the new liturgy was read in the cathedral of Christ church, Dublin, in the presence of the civil and ecclesiastical authorities.

Little advantage, however, resulted to the truth from this change in public worship brought about by civil power. Only four of the bishops adopted the liturgy, and their example had but slight influence upon their own suffragans. Even though more conciliatory measures were subsequently employed, they were not successful. The primate refusing to yield, harsher methods were at last brought into requisition. In order to mortify him and his partisans, the primacy of Ireland was transferred from Armagh to Dublin. This deprived the popish party of its most influential leader, but the want of Reformed preachers, even in the metropolis, prevented the Reformation from making any marked progress.

Several of the Irish sees, as well as the primacy, becoming vacant, efforts were made in England to find proper persons to fill these important places. Richard Turner, of Canterbury, on the recommendation of Archbishop Cranmer, was selected by the king for archbishop of Armagh. He, however, declined to accept the honorable situation, giving as the chief reason that his ignorance of the Irish language, which he was not disposed to learn, would forbid him access to the minds of the native population and compel him to preach "to the walls and stalls." Nor could Cranmer overcome his reluctance to accept the office. If it was so difficult to fill an archbishopric, it was more hopeless to provide gospel-preachers for humbler stations.

Two of the vacant sees were at length filled by men in every way qualified for the office, and who were willing to make the needed sacrifices for the gospel's sake. These were Hugh Goodacre and John Bale. The first was raised to the see of Armagh, but within three months was poisoned at Dublin, "by procurement of certain priests of his diocese, for preaching God's verity and rebuking their common vices." Of Bale, who occupied the see of Ossory, we have honorable testimony. He is said to have been learned and pious as a reformer, energetic and courageous as a champion of the truth. For his honest boldness in exposing the errors of popery he had been twice imprisoned in England by the ruling clergy. Released by Lord Cromwell, he fled to the Continent upon the death of his patron, where for eight years he enjoyed opportunities of converse and intimate friendship with Luther, Calvin and other distinguished Reformers.

His firmness was put to the trial on the occasion of his consecration to his office. The dean of the cathedral insisted upon using the popish form, and even Goodacre, the primate-elect, was disposed to acquiesce for the sake of peace, as were also the other assembled prelates. But Bale was decided in his opposition, and would not consent to adopt the ritual of so corrupt a Church, and his firmness secured the adoption of the Reformed ritual. The apprehended tumult did not follow, and the people were permitted for the first time to make the acquaintance of a man whose consistent course won respect for the doctrines which he preached. His views and his conduct on this memorable occasion had doubtless been somewhat shaped by his long and familiar intercourse with the Genevan Reformers. His zeal was untiring and his labors in his diocese abundant. He abolished the service of the mass and sought to lead the clergy and the people to a knowledge of the true religion.

The death of Edward VI. and the accession of

Queen Mary drove him from Ireland. Five of his servants were murdered before the doors of his residence, and it was only from the fact that a large escort of his affectionate people gathered around him and protected him from violence that he escaped with his life from the hands of his persecutors. After many perils he reached the Continent; but when he returned to England on the accession of Elizabeth, nothing could induce him to accept a bishopric. His sympathies were on the side of the nonconformists.

Under Mary the Roman Catholic religion was formally restored by Parliament, and the pope's supremacy acknowledged. Eight prelates who had professed the Reformed doctrines returned at once to the Church of Rome. Others were prevented from a similar apostasy for the reason that they were married. The people speedily relapsed into their former condition, and scarce a trace of the Reformation could be seen in Ireland.

Indeed, the general adherence of the people to the Romish faith made Ireland a place of shelter for some of the persecuted Protestants of England. The bigotry of the queen was not directed against them, owing to their limited numbers, and for the same reason they did not excite the suspicion of the papal clergy. Several small colonies of English Protestants, accompanied by their ministers, consequently found an asylum for years on Irish soil; and when at length Dean Cole, in 1558, was dispatched by the queen with a persecuting commission to punish these Protestants, the brief respite secured through the substitution of a pack of cards in place of his commission by a friend of the persecuted people deferred all hostile measures until the accession of Elizabeth. The dean, much to his surprise and dismay, on presenting to the council of Dublin the box which was supposed to contain his commission, that it might be formally read, found in place of it only *a pack of cards with the knave of clubs faced upward.* Evidently not displeased at being thus relieved from the discharge of his invidious office, he humorously replied, "Let us have a new commission, and we will shuffle the cards in the mean time." Another commission was procured, but unfavorable winds prevented the sailing of the vessel from England until after the death of the queen, and thus God preserved the Protestants.

The reign of Elizabeth was favorable to the spread of the truth in Ireland, but owing to the distracted state of the kingdom its beneficial effects were not apparent at once. Many of the ecclesiastical arrangements adopted by Bloody Mary were reversed, and an order was sent to the dean of Christ's church, Dublin, to remove from the walls of his cathedral all relics, images, pictures, and other memorials of Romanism, and to substitute in their place appropriate texts of Scripture. The credulous multitude were more readily reconciled to this change owing to the exposure of a gross imposition that had long been practiced by the priests of the cathedral—that of making an image of our Saviour sweat drops of blood by means of a sponge saturated with blood concealed in the head of the image. Soon after this change was made, Heath, archbishop of York, sent over two large English Bibles to be fixed in the centre of the choirs of the cathedral, to be read not only in divine service, but to be accessible at all times to the people. They came in crowds to hear the word of God read, and eagerly availed themselves of the opportunity to peruse it after the congregations were dismissed. In this way knowledge was increased, and a large demand for Bibles sprung up. One bookseller, in less than two years, disposed of more than seven thousand copies, to which the progress of the Reformation in Ireland was largely due.

Much less, however, was accomplished than might have been had the government adopted a wiser policy. In removing the sanction of the law from the Romish faith, as was done by the Parliament of 1560, and substituting the prayer-book for the missal, provision should have been made for that large class of persons who were ignorant of the English language. The first necessity was to have divine service conducted in a language understood by the worshipers. In the place, however, of providing for the translation of the prayer-book into Irish, the absurd order was given that the public service should be conducted in Latin, which neither English nor Irish understood. Surely, prudent and wise rulers who had the welfare of the community at heart, and who wished to promote the truth, would not have kept the masses in ignorance and cut them off from the benefits of public worship. Nor was it of much service to Protestantism that of the nineteen prelates who had conformed to popery under Queen Mary only two adhered to their Romish profession. All the others took the oath of supremacy in order to retain their places. But their adherence to the doctrines of the Reformation was merely nominal, and their conformity in worship was but to escape the penalties that were inflicted for neglecting to attend the Established Church. And so indifferent were the civil authorities to the spiritual condition of the native population that even the prominent sees, including the primacy, were left vacant for years, and those who controlled the more remote offices cultivated intimacy with the pope rather than with the English Church. So that, between shameful neglect on the one hand and harsh and violent measures to secure external conformity on the part of a prejudiced and ignorant people on the other, the Irish Establishment only alienated those whose confidence and affection it should have endeavored to win. Even if Elizabeth and her ministers had had the religious welfare of Ireland at heart—which they did not have—their time was almost exclusively occupied with measures of defence against Irish chiefs instigated to rebellion by the Holy See. As fear and interest were the chief agents in effecting the changes in favor of Protestantism, no sooner did the queen's political power begin to be menaced by Spain than the priests became bold and active in their opposition, and in every possible manner fomented the discord which had always existed between the natives and the English. A few zealous and benevolent individuals did what they could to remedy this deplorable condition of things. A translation of the New Testament was partly completed and the translation of the Liturgy in the Irish tongue commenced, but neither was rendered available during Elizabeth's reign. The greatest of all hindrances to the Reformation was the want of learned and pious ministers, since nothing short of sound scriptural teaching could overcome the deep-rooted errors and superstitions of more than three hundred years.

We have a description of the deplorable state of the Irish Church in 1576 by Sir Henry Sidney in a letter sent to Queen Elizabeth on the subject of an evangelical ministry, wherein he proposes that she shall adopt the means which he suggests for the removal of this great evil. In a diocese of two hundred and twenty-four parish churches, only eighteen of the curates were found able to speak English; "the rest are Irish priests, or rather

Irish rogues, having very little Latin, and less learning and civility, and were wont to live upon the gain of masses, dirges, shriving, and such-like trumpery." Nearly all the parish churches were in a ruinous condition, and many of them were necessarily abandoned. Earnest and pressing were Sir Henry's recommendations to have these sad deficiencies supplied; especially did he insist upon the necessity of repairing the neglected churches and supplying the parishes with Reformed ministers. But though coming from so influential a quarter, no attention was given to these recommendations, and the religious condition of Ireland was altogether neglected. How could the gospel be expected to prevail against prejudice and ignorance without the presence of ministers to make known its doctrines and illustrate the excellency of its principles?

At a subsequent date, 1590, a measure of much importance to Ireland was carried into effect. This was the establishment of the University of Dublin. Its chief object was to educate ministers for the national Church, the want of which, as we have seen, had been the main obstacle in the advance of the Reformed doctrines. It was founded on very liberal principles. Those questions which had divided the Church in England into conformists and nonconformists were suffered to rest in Ireland, and whatever preacher of the gospel made his appearance in the latter kingdom was gladly received and left unmolested in his work. He might verge almost to Romanism or he might be a zealous Puritan, and yet be undisturbed by any authoritative imposition of terms of conformity. In the early history of the University of Dublin this liberal spirit was freely displayed. Its first elected fellows were two Scotch Presbyterians, one of them tutor to the celebrated Usher. Its first two regular and official provosts, Travers and Alvey, were also nonconformists. The latter, persecuted in England by Whitgift for his nonconformity, found refuge and freedom and honor in Ireland. The presence of both men was welcomed, and their services were in demand and were valuable to the country in the honored positions they occupied. There was truly great need in that country of educated men, and particularly of a pious clergy who would care for the spiritual welfare of the people. Even so late as 1596 the poet Spenser, describing the people of Ireland, says: "Not one amongst an hundred knoweth any ground of religion or any article of his faith, but can, perhaps, say his Paternoster or his Ave Maria without any knowledge of what one word thereof meaneth." The common clergymen he represents as leading disorderly lives and guilty of the grossest vices, while the bishops in the remoter dioceses retain the benefices in their own possession "and set their own servants to take up their tythes and fruits."

This was the deplorable condition of the Irish Church in the closing years of Elizabeth's reign and after seventy years had passed since Protestantism was introduced into the kingdom. For the very limited progress which the Reformation had made two causes are apparent—the first, the formidable rebellions which almost constantly agitated the kingdom, and which produced a state of things most unfavorable to the spread of the truth; the second, the inadequate means employed for its propagation, the defence of the kingdom occupying the almost exclusive attention of the government. But peace was at length restored through the military triumphs of the English forces, the authority of the laws was extended over the entire island, and Elizabeth left to her successor the more pleasing duty of promoting peace and social order among the inhabitants and diffusing throughout the community the blessings of education and of true religion.

A better era dawned upon the Protestant Church of Ireland when James I. ascended the throne, April 5, 1603. His claims were recognized by all parties, and the country enjoyed great tranquillity. The victories in the former reign had prepared the way for the adoption of a more peaceful, humane and civilizing policy, which the king's love of peace and his attachment to religion disposed him to take advantage of and improve to the utmost. He accordingly adopted the wisest and most conciliatory measures toward the natives. He proclaimed a general pardon to all who had been concerned in the late rebellions, and admitted the natives for the first time to the privileges of subjects. The estates of the nobility, held on precarious titles, were now secured to them by the formalities of law. Courts were renewed in the southern provinces and established for the first time in the north, and the administration of justice secured to all classes.

These prudent measures to promote civil order met the general approval of the people. The only exceptions were some of the northern nobles, who, instigated by the Romish clergy, entered into conspiracies against the king; and being subdued, their lands were forfeited to the Crown. The most of this territory James resolved to plant with English and Scottish colonies. In this way the lands would be rendered more valuable by skillful cultivation, peace and prosperity would be promoted and the Reformed faith more speedily disseminated. The province of Ulster, where this scheme of colonization was first tried, had been reduced to a truly wretched condition. It had been the chief seat of the rebellions, and the inhabitants were rendered destitute and the country desolate by the ravages of war. Except a few fortified cities, its towns and villages had been leveled to the ground; scarcely a building remained in the country except the native huts, which were too poor to be plundered;

and the remnant of the inhabitants suffered the horrors of both pestilence and famine. The grain and the cattle, in which the wealth of the people consisted, had been destroyed by the rebels, so that the few remaining proprietors were without even the means to cultivate their lands. And the moral and religious state of the province was still worse. In some parts religious worship had entirely disappeared, and in most others, in consequence of the indolence or the vices of the clergy, or the ruinous condition of the church-edifices, " divine service had not for years together been used in any parish church, except in some city or principal towns."

In 1610 the colonization scheme began to be generally carried into effect, especially in Ulster. Sir Arthur Chichester, lord-deputy of the kingdom, on whom the king had conferred a large estate, was the chief agent. His first act was to have a careful survey made of the forfeited lands, and then to draw up a plan for their settlement. They were allotted to three classes, under certain and fixed regulations of occupancy. First were voluntary emigrants from England and Scotland, then servants of the Crown, consisting of civil and military officers, and finally natives, whom it was hoped this liberality would make orderly and loyal subjects. The colonists were bound to erect substantial dwellings, to clear the lands and cultivate them; and to do this they were obliged to procure and induce to settle on their estates a number of families proportional to the extent of their possessions. Especial care was taken by the king for the support of the Church. He restored to the sees all their ecclesiastical possessions, parochial churches were repaired, glebes allotted to ministers, and a free school was endowed in the principal town of each diocese.

Owing to the nearness of Scotland to Ulster, as well as to the enterprise of the Scotch, the larger part of the colonists came from that kingdom. At first they occupied the northern part of the province, but subsequently spread themselves over the remoter districts. The southern and western parts were settled chiefly by emigrants from England. Londoners gave its name to Londonderry. Other cities bore titles indicating the preponderance of the Scotch element. By means of this scheme the almost deserted cities were again peopled with inhabitants; towns were built and manufactures and trade revived; the lands were cleared of woods and brought under cultivation; farmhouses and homesteads took the place of robbers' castles, wattled huts and ruined cabins; and everywhere the industry and the peaceable character of the new occupants were apparent. Religion in a good degree also flourished. The sees were filled with Protestant prelates, and a convocation of the clergy was summoned in 1615. Its principal work was to draw up a *Confession of Faith* for the Irish Church. It was at first proposed to adopt the Thirty-nine Articles of the sister-Church of England, but the majority decided to have a new confession of their own. Dr. James Usher, already distinguished for his theological learning, and as professor of divinity in the College of Dublin, was entrusted with this duty. This he discharged to the entire satisfaction of all the parties concerned, and the Confession was ratified by the king in council, and also by his deputy in Dublin.

The difference in the religious sentiments of England and Ireland appears very clearly in this important document. In the former a rigid conformity was enforced, the hierarchy refusing to consult the scruples of the Puritans. Instead of seeking by some comprehensive plan to retain within the Church the learning and piety of the nonconforming clergy, new tests were devised to detect them and to punish them or compel their removal from the kingdom. But in Ireland a different and a wiser policy was pursued. Many of the exiled clergymen of Scotland, who had accompanied their countrymen to Ulster, had been promoted to high offices in the Church and were universally esteemed, and the confession of faith now adopted indicated the presence and influence of the Scotch and nonconformist element in the Irish Church. It was an honest and praiseworthy effort to compromise the differences between the High Church clergy and the nonconformists. Calvinistic in doctrine, it retained, almost word for word, the Nine Articles of Lambeth, which the English Puritans vainly sought to have adopted at the Hampton Court Conference in 1604. It asserts strongly the morality of the Sabbath and clearly implies the validity of ordination by presbyters, while many other tenets cherished by the Puritan party in the Church are set forth in the Confession. It is remarkable also in that it claims no authority for framing or enforcing ecclesiastical canons or decreeing rites and ceremonies, and makes no allusion to the mode of consecrating the higher orders of the clergy. Nor was this an unintentional omission. It was designed to sink out of sight that distinction between bishops and presbyters which was so much opposed by nonconformists. To prevent future trouble, the convocation decreed that there should be no public teaching of any doctrine contrary to the articles thus solemnly agreed upon.

Such was the comprehensive foundation upon which the Irish Church was settled. Its terms of communion were limited only in respect of doctrine. It embraced all faithful ministers of the gospel, neither compelling them to submit to objectionable ceremonies nor unchurching them for conscientious scruples respecting the government or methods of worship in the Church. This spirit of mutual forbearance showed an honest desire to have devoted ministers settle and exercise their office among the people, however they might differ on minor questions of ecclesiastical discipline.

Nor was it long before this liberal plan bore abundant and precious fruit. Many ministers speedily removed to Ireland, and especially to Ulster, induced by the security they were promised and by the great need of their services.

Among the most efficient and useful of these clergymen were the Presbyterian ministers from Scotland. Persecuted at home, they found a refuge and a welcome across the Channel. Of these pioneer laborers were—Edward Brice, who for opposing Archbishop Spotiswood's attempt to introduce prelacy into Scotland was obliged to leave the kingdom; Robert Cunningham, of whom Livingstone said that "he was the one man who most resembled the meekness of Jesus Christ in all his carriage that I ever saw;" James Glendenning, under whose preaching the great revival of 1625 began; the celebrated Robert Blair, formerly professor in the College of Glasgow; and the devoted James Hamilton, nephew of Lord Claneboy. Hubbard and Ridge, natives of England, were men of kindred spirit. These seven brethren possessed the true missionary spirit, and began at once the work of evangelizing the land, and with extraordinary success. The spirit in which they were received, even by the highest clergy in the Church, is to be seen by the conduct of Bishop Echlin, who was himself a native of Scotland. It was known to both Mr. Blair's patron, Lord Claneboy, and to the bishop, that Mr. Blair had conscientious scruples respecting episcopal ordination. But when the latter applied for ordination, the bishop said to him, " I hear good of you, and will impose no conditions on you. I am old and can teach you ceremonies, and you can teach me substances, only I must ordain you, to comply with the law. Whatever you account of episcopacy, yet I know you account a presbytery to have divine warrant. Will you not receive ordination from Mr. Cunningham and the adjacent brethren, and let me come in among them in no other relation than that of a presbyter?" "This," said Blair, "I could not refuse, and so the matter was performed."

The labors of these faithful and pious ministers were remarkably blessed. A revival of religion soon occurred, which, in some of its features, resembled the great work of grace that subsequently attended the ministry of Whitefield and Wesley in England, and a similar awakening in this country at a later period. It began in connection with the preaching of Mr. Glendenning, the weakest and the least discreet of the seven pioneer ministers, and extended over nearly the entire northern part of Ireland. Almost his only theme in preaching, says Blair, was " law, wrath and the terrors of God for sin." "And, indeed, for this only was he fitted, for hardly could he preach any other thing. He was a man who would never have been chosen by a wise assembly of ministers, nor sent to begin a reformation in this land. Yet this was the

Lord's choice to begin with him the admirable work of God." The truths which he proclaimed were what was needed "to awaken the consciences of a lewd and secure people." Wonderful spiritual results followed. Multitudes were brought to see their sinful and lost condition, and to cry out in their anguish of soul for deliverance. "I have seen them myself," says Blair, "stricken into a swoon by the word—yea, a dozen in one day carried out of doors as dead—so marvelous was the power of God, smiting their hearts for sin, condemning and killing." Some of the boldest and most incorrigible, who had attended the meetings to scoff and oppose, were subdued and cried out for mercy. The same authority states that "multitudes who sinned and still gloried in it, because they feared no man, became patterns in society, fearing to sin because they feared God."

The revival spread rapidly in all directions. Some of high rank and standing were numbered among the converts. The ministers made the most of these favorable opportunities to sow the seed, and reaped an abundant harvest. The awakened and inquiring people thronged to hear them preach, and by the judicious counsels and labors of the clergy the converts were instructed and established in the faith. Monthly meetings were appointed at convenient points, at which large numbers assembled. The hearers sometimes came even from a distance of thirty or forty miles.

Intelligence of the remarkable awakening having reached Scotland, a number of prudent and faithful ministers came over to the help of the exhausted laborers. Among these was Josias Welsh, a grandson of John Knox, formerly professor in the University of Glasgow, which situation he resigned on account of his nonconformist principles. His spirit resembled in no slight degree that of the illustrious Scotch Reformer, Knox, as the testimony of Blair shows: "The last time I was in Scotland I met him; and finding of how zealous a spirit he was, I exhorted him to hasten over to Ireland, where he would find work enough, and I hoped success too. A great measure of that spirit which wrought in and by the father" and the grandfather "rested on the son." Acting on Mr. Blair's advice, he came to Ireland in 1626, and took charge of Mr. Glendenning's parish, which had become vacant by the latter's departure to visit the seven churches of Asia. Here and at Templepatrick "he convinced the secure and sweetly comforted those that were dejected, and had many seals to his ministry."

Other clergymen of like spirit followed Welsh. Of these were Andrew Stewart, George Dunbar, Henry Colwort, John M'Clelland, John Semple, and the celebrated John Livingstone, whose name has become historic from his connection with the kirk of Schotts. These additional ministers were of great service to the settled pastors, and through them the revival was greatly extended. Most of them were from Scotland, where they had suffered from prelatical bigotry; and finding freedom in their land of exile, they labored with great zeal and success. Livingstone was ordained by Bishop Knox, and with an indulgence most honorable to that distinguished prelate. With letters from Lord Claneboy, the earl of Wigton and others, he repaired to the bishop, who at once divined the object of his visit. "He told me," writes Livingstone, "that he knew my errand, that I came to him because I had scruples against episcopacy and ceremonies, as Welsh and some others had done before, and that he thought his old age was prolonged for little other purpose but to do such offices; that if I scrupled to call him 'my lord' he cared not much for it; all he would desire of me, because they got there but few sermons, was that I would preach at Ramallen the first Sabbath, and that he would send for Mr. Cunningham and two or three other neighboring ministers to be present, who after sermon should give me imposition of hands; but although they performed the work, he behoved to be present." The latter was necessary to fulfill the requirement of the government. To accommodate still further the scruples of Mr. Livingstone, the bishop gave him the book of ordination and desired him to draw a line over whatever he objected to, and assured him it should not be read. "But," says Livingstone, "I found it so marked by some others before that I needed not mark anything."

Such liberality on the part of the ecclesiastics left the preachers with the necessary freedom to prosecute their work successfully. Their labors for the instruction of the people were indefatigable. With singleness of purpose, with intensity of desire and with untiring diligence, they gave themselves to their sacred duties. Through their instrumentality the Church of Christ increased rapidly, and far and wide a marked change was visible in the character of the whole population.

While carrying forward this work of reform, Blair and his brethren were careful to maintain Presbyterian discipline. "In my congregation," writes Blair, "we had both deacons for the poor and elders for discipline, and so long as we were permitted to exercise it the Lord blessed that ordinance." Livingstone adopted the same method, and speaks of his session meeting weekly, adjudicating cases of discipline and debarring unworthy persons from the communion-table. The communion was observed twice a year in each church, and it was customary for the people of the neighboring parishes to attend with their pastors. The same custom was afterward transferred to America, and memorable scenes were witnessed here also in connection with these communion-seasons. Nearly all the clergy of the north of Ireland were nonconformists, and generally strict Presbyterians.

While comprehended within the pale of the established Episcopal Church, its liberality toward them was then such that they were enabled to exercise their office without violence to their scruples, and to introduce and maintain, as we have seen, the peculiarities both of discipline and worship of the Scotch Church. For their firmness and zeal, our grateful regard is due to them as the founders of the Presbyterian Church in Ireland.

Though these Presbyterian ministers were for a considerable period unmolested by Episcopal prelates, yet was the progress of the gospel impeded by other obstructions. The first opposers were Romanists. Two friars from Salamanca, Spain, challenged the clergy to a public dispute; but when Blair and Welsh accepted the challenge and appeared at the appointed time and place, the friars shrunk from the contest. Again they were assailed by Separatists from London, allured to Ireland by the promise of religious freedom, and subsequently by English conformists zealous for Arminian tenets. All these in turn were discomfited and were obliged to withdraw, and these several trials were overruled for good, and finally served to exhibit more clearly the eminent piety, learning and prudence of these remarkable men.

But other and more formidable difficulties were soon to be encountered by these honored ministers. From being their friend and patron, Bishop Echlin became their determined opponent. This change was caused by jealousy and dislike, arising from the great success attending their labors. His animosity was first manifested by a refusal to ordain any more ministers unless they would promise strict conformity to the English Church. He next set a trap to catch Mr. Blair, hoping either to silence him or impair his influence. But one of the lords-justices interposed, and he escaped. Disappointed in this scheme, the bishop suspended both Blair and Livingstone for their alleged irregular preaching at the kirk of Schotts. These brethren were visiting their friends in Scotland, and being present on the Sabbath assisted at the celebration of the Lord's Supper, and, on Monday, Livingstone preached with great power to a vast concourse of people. The envy of the prelatical clergy was excited; and charging these Irish ministers with uncanonical and schismatic conduct, they prevailed upon Bishop Echlin to suspend them from the exercise of their offices. This was the first open blow directed against the Presbyterian clergy of Ulster.

The suspended ministers at once applied for relief to Archbishop Usher, and not in vain. He immediately interested himself in their behalf, and, convinced of their piety and prudence, wrote to Echlin "to relax his erroneous censure." And in a conference with Blair, after expressing the fear that there were those who would endeavor to mar their ministry, he added "that it would break his heart it our successful ministry in the north were interrupted."

Though foiled in their endeavor, the enemies of these devoted pastors did not cease their opposition. The next resort was to the English court, for they feared that an appeal to the civil powers of Ireland might result no more favorably to their wishes than had their representations to Primate Usher. Their charges were laid before the king himself, and they depended upon his co-operation, knowing as they did that he was guided in religious matters by Laud. The infatuated sovereign gave ready ear to their charges, and sent letters to the lords-justices of Ireland, directing them to enjoin the bishops of Down and Conner to try, and if found guilty censure, the alleged "fanatical disturbers of the peace of his diocese." Accordingly, Blair, Livingstone, Dunbar and Welsh were cited to appear before the bishop; and upon their refusing to conform, on the ground that there was no law or canon requiring it, they were deposed from the office of the ministry. Again application was made to Archbishop Usher. "But he told us," says Blair, "that he could not interpose, because the two lords-justices had an order from the king respecting us." And when the justices were applied to, they referred them to the king, who alone could remedy their grievance. But from this source they had little to expect by a direct appeal. Yet so anxious were they for a reversal of their unjust sentence in order that they might engage in their loved work that they resolved to make one more effort. Livingstone visited Scotland and obtained recommendatory letters to their friends at court from several of the Scotch nobility. Taking these, with others, which he himself had procured from his Irish friends, Blair visited London, and was granted the privilege of laying his case before the king. A favorable letter was written in his behalf by King Charles, which, though it did not take off the sentence of deposition, enabled these ministers to labor unmolested among their people under certain restrictions. These Livingstone could not endure; and seeing no hope of relief, he left the country and retired to Scotland.

The other clergymen continued to teach their flocks as before, only refraining from entering their pulpits when they preached. This they did with the expectation that on the arrival of Lord-Deputy Wentworth, the famous earl of Strafford, to govern Ireland, he would put an end to their privations. In this, however, they were grievously disappointed, for a more unfortunate choice of a deputy, as respects Presbyterian interests, could not possibly have been made. Haughty in manner, vindictive in temper and intolerant in his religious opinions, he was incapable of the least sympathy for those who suffered for any scruple of conscience. Soon after his arrival in Dublin, Blair laid before him the king's favorable letter, but in place of the relief expected the overbearing deputy replied "that he had His Majesty's mind in his own breast," and began at once to "revile the Church of Scotland" and upbraid Blair, "bidding him come to his right wits, and then he should be regarded." This was all the answer he deigned to give to the petition. Blair went with this intelligence to Usher, who, as he listened to the reply of the bold, vindictive man, shed tears.

# CHAPTER VII.

## From the Accession of Charles I. to the Irish Rebellion.

Gloomy in the extreme were the prospects of Presbyterian ministers in Ireland on the accession of Charles I., and little or no hope remained that those deposed would ever be restored. The policy of the king, both in England and Scotland, favored a rigid imposition of Episcopal forms. Nor could it reasonably be expected, therefore, that the mean and truckling Wentworth would show any leniency to nonconformists. So far as it was thought politic to do so, Romanists were recipients of kingly favors. They were encouraged to exercise their former ecclesiastical jurisdiction, new religious houses were opened, and even in the metropolis a college was founded for the training of priests. On the other hand, Protestants were so impeded in their work, and their freedom of worship so restricted, that large numbers of the people, together with their pastors, began to turn their attention toward a home in the New World. The visit of a son of Governor Winthrop of New England, at this time, afforded them an opportunity to learn of the prospects which America offered to emigrants who wished to enjoy religious freedom. So impressed were they by his statements that they resolved to send a minister and a layman thither to report upon the country, and, if desirable, to select a place of settlement. Livingstone and Wallace set out upon this mission, but were prevented from leaving England. On their return to Ulster their brethren determined to endure these privations with what patience they could, and await the further developments of the policy of the government.

Charles, by reason of his expensive wars with Spain and Austria, found it difficult to secure the funds necessary to maintain an adequate army in Ireland, and had recourse to the landed proprietors for assistance. As many of these were Roman Catholics, who were aware of the king's pecuniary embarrassment, they conceived that it would be a favorable opportunity to secure the abolition of the penal statutes which were in force against them. The king was disposed to yield to their demands, and on their proffering a large voluntary subsidy he promised to grant them the solicited privileges. Under the impression that the toleration of the Romish faith was about to be purchased by a contribution to the State, Archbishop Usher and the most influential of the Irish prelates protested strongly against the measure. This retarded for a time the proposed project.

But as the sovereign's needs were pressing, and the Romanists firm in their demands for concessions favorable to their religion, the execution of the penal laws was still further relaxed. This indulgence both offended and alarmed the Protestants, and led to a tumult in Dublin, where an attempt was made to disperse a meeting of Carmelite friars, and afterward instructions were sent to the English consul to suppress all such assemblies and to dissolve their religious houses.

At the instigation of the sycophantic and despotic Laud, the deputy turned his attention from civil to ecclesiastical affairs. The former had encouraged the introduction of superstitious rites into divine worship in the English Church, such as changing the communion-table into an altar and adorning it with candlesticks and crucifixes, and placing pictures and images in the churches. He now solicited the willing aid of Wentworth to carry forward like changes in the Irish Church, so as to have its service approximate as nearly as possible to that of the Romish ritual. The first and most important measure was to fill the sees with men who would be in sympathy with the scheme, and who would be ready to obey the orders of Wentworth as he received them from Archbishop Laud. The place of the mild and tolerant Knox was filled by the violent churchman John Leslie. The pious Downham, bishop of Derry, was succeeded by Bramhall, a servile creature of Laud's, whom he so resembled in spirit and in his intolerance of Puritans that he was styled "the Canterbury of Ireland." Usher was compelled to do the bidding of these bad men, who ordered him to call in and suppress a work on the covenant of grace which had been issued by the bishop of Derry, condemning Arminianism. Rather than comply, and thus stain his own fair fame by evincing so timid and irresolute a spirit, he should have maintained and defended the standards of the Church of which he was a custodian. Bedell, the saintly bishop, who resigned his office the better to promote reform in his diocese, and whose earnest Christian efforts to spread the gospel will ever be memorable in Ireland, was constantly thwarted in his self-denying labors. In preparing young men to preach in Irish to the natives, in establishing schools in every parish, in compiling and printing scriptural books, and in translating the Bible into the language of the country, he displayed an untiring zeal. These benevolent and valuable services for his adopted countrymen, in connection with his well-known liberal sentiments toward nonconformists, made him a shining mark for the poisoned arrows of Laud and Wentworth. They resolved that the work of reformation, which he was carrying forward so successfully, should be brought to an end, and to accomplish their purpose suits at law were instituted against him. Though of too frivolous a character to justify his suspension, they served to place obstacles in the way of his work of evangelization. When thus oppressed by the civil authorities, he turned for sympathy to Usher; but Usher declined to extend to him the friendly assistance which he had a right to expect, assigning as a reason that "the tide went so high against him." Bedell replied nobly "that he was resolved, by the help of God, to try if he could stand by himself." Still, his solitary efforts could accomplish but little for the Church.

Attention was next directed to the University of Dublin. There was too large a Puritan element in its management to suit the Romanizing party in England. Laud had already introduced innovations at Oxford in favor of popery, and was resolved that a similar change should be made at Dublin. Its provost, Dr. Robert Usher, a relative of the archbishop, and holding the same liberal sentiments, was removed, and a violent Arminian from England was put in his place. The statutes of the university were subjected to the revision of Laud and altered to suit his wishes, and under his direction the new provost urged conformity with unsparing intolerance.

One thing more was needed in order to accomplish the work on which the archbishop and the deputy had set their hearts. This was to bring the Church of Ireland into a more perfect conformity to the English Establishment. The latter undertook 'he task, and accomplished it in a summary manner. By his order a convocation of the clergy was summoned to meet in November, 1634, and in furtherance of his designs he did not hesitate to employ intrigue, deception and menace. The Calvinistic confession, prepared by Usher, adopted by the Irish Church, and ratified by Parliament twenty years before, was the chief obstacle in the way of the deputy. In order merely to manifest the agreement between the Churches of England and Ireland, he proposed to Usher that the Thirty-nine Articles of the former should be received and recognized, and promised that this should not displace or in any way interfere with the Confession of the Irish Church. Obtaining the assent of Usher, the Thirty-nine Articles were received. But no sooner were they adopted than it was claimed that they were the sole accredited standard of the Church's faith, and that the Irish articles, by construction, had been wholly abrogated. The deception was discovered too late to correct the error, though an effort to do so was immediately made by attempting to amend the English canons. The convocation was overruled by Wentworth in the most arbitrary and insulting manner. He sent immediately for the chairman, and commanded him to bring the book of canons, together with the draft of the proposed changes, and as soon as he had read these he began to pour out on him the vials of his fierce wrath. He told him that "certainly not a dean of Limerick, but an Ananias, had sat in the chair." He was "sure an Ananias had been there in spirit, if not in body, with all the fraternities and conventicles of Amsterdam." Hamilton was the boldest champion of the independence of the Church. But his influence, with that of kindred men in the convocation, was crushed by the despotic will of the deputy, ably seconded as he was by Bramhall and Leslie. In this violent and summary manner was the constitution of the Irish Episcopal Church finally settled. The Thirty-nine Articles of the English Church became the standard of the former, and the clergy were forced to accept them with their Arminian interpretation.

Having carried out his plan with such wonderful success, it might be supposed that Wentworth would be content. But not so. He desired increased power. Accordingly, he applied to Laud and Charles for authority to erect a High Commission court in Dublin. In his letter he says: "I hold it most fit that there were a High Commission settled here in Dublin to support ecclesiastical courts and officers, to bring the people here to a conformity in religion, and in the way of all these to raise perhaps a good revenue to the Crown." In this proposal the wily statesman bids for the sanction of the *prelate* by his expressed intention of persecuting nonconformists, and for that of the *king* by the hope of augmented revenues. The authority sought was granted, and with this unconstitutional tribunal he subjected the freedom and property of every individual to his arbitrary will and pleasure, and by its summary processes, from whose judgment there was no appeal, he was enabled to crush out the slightest opposition to his tyrannical measures.*

The Presbyterians of Ulster were soon made to feel the power that had been thus entrusted to the deputy, and their condition grew worse day by day. The four ministers suspended by Echlin were denied a fair trial, which they had requested, and were reproached for their unwillingness to conform. For a brief period, and as a matter of public policy, and not because of any favor entertained for these pastors, their sentence of suspension was relaxed. They were restored for six months to the office of the ministry, with the hope that this might allay the irritated feelings of the Scotch planters, whose lands had been threatened with confiscation. But at the expiration of this period their license was revoked, and at the instigation of Bramhall they were formally deposed.

Bishop Echlin, dying in July, 1635, was succeeded by that violent bigot, Henry Leslie, who immediately began the work of persecuting non-

---

* "A High Commission court sat in Dublin, canons were passed for ecclesiastical government, and dissent, under any Protestant form, was utterly prohibited. All who refused to obey the bishops and introduce and use the English liturgy, were deprived of their cures."—*Froude*, vol. i., p. 77.

conformists. On his requiring from the clergy of his diocese their subscription to the canons, five of the most zealous and influential of them refused to comply. For this reason alone these faithful ministers were summarily deposed from their office, deprived of their support, and finally obliged to leave the kingdom. These unjust and arbitrary proceedings still more fully convinced Presbyterians that there was no liberty to be expected by either pastors or people so long as they were subjected to prelacy, and that it was their duty to abandon a country in which their religious privileges were so flagrantly violated. Accordingly, they determined to carry out their previous design to remove to New England, and commenced work at once on a ship called the Eaglewing, in which they proposed to embark in the spring. After many disappointments and much delay the preparations for the voyage were completed, and one hundred and forty emigrants, accompanied by Blair, Livingstone and Hamilton, set sail from Loch Fergus in September, 1636. But contrary winds and a fierce tempest, that caused the loss of the rudder and the ship to spring aleak, compelled them to return to Ireland, and convinced them "that it was not God's will that they should go to New England."

But there was no rest for them in Ireland while the Episcopal authorities, through the power of the High Commission, could arrest and imprison all persons at their pleasure. Numbers were committed to prison or forced to fly the country. Armed with extraordinary powers by the English court, Wentworth pursued his rapacious schemes with new energy. He subjected the titles of the Ulster colonists to a rigorous examination; and where they had failed to fulfill in any particular the numerous and expensive conditions of their grants, he obliged them to renew their patents, for which he extorted large sums of money. Not only were the rights of property violated, but the personal liberty of the people was invaded and the lives of the highest in the realm endangered if they dared to oppose the deputy's authority. Severe and unwarranted punishment was inflicted at his mere caprice. He authorized the bishop of Down to arrest and imprison in a summary manner all who refused to subscribe to the canons. Suffering under these great grievances, both civil and religious, many of the Presbyterians of Ulster fled to the west of Scotland, where a number of their former pastors, who had preceded them, were settled over parishes. This served to keep up frequent communication between the two countries, and enabled the people to be of mutual service to each other in the common struggle for civil and religious liberty. Not a few of these Ulster Presbyterians, when visiting their native country, had subscribed the Covenant. Witnessing the beneficial results of the victory which had been obtained over prelacy by their Scotch brethren, they were the more dissatisfied with the tyranny under which they were living, and the more determined in their resistance.

Such was the spirit manifested that Wentworth became alarmed lest the people of Ulster should openly resist his authority. He, therefore, took measures to cut off all correspondence with Scotland, and to collect an army either to invade Scotland in co-operation with Charles, or to hold in subjection the Scotch residents in Ulster. He also called to his aid the prelates, and directed them to enforce conformity, to preach against the Covenant, and to obstruct the settlement of any more Scotch ministers within their dioceses. His final expedient was the imposition upon all the Scots of North Ireland of an oath called THE BLACK OATH, from the terrible evils it occasioned. It was a suggestion of Charles I. to his obedient deputy, and it is scarcely possible to conceive of anything more objectionable than this oath, or more in conflict with the principles of the civil and religious rights of subjects. It compelled the party to swear never to oppose any of the king's commands and to abjure all covenants and oaths to the contrary. All the Scotch residents in Ulster over sixteen years of age were required to take it on their knees and swearing "upon the holy evangelists," without even the privilege of perusing it in most instances. Women as well as men were sworn; the only exception was in favor of those Scots who professed to be Roman Catholics. In administering the oath the commissioners were required to proceed in the most expeditious manner possible, and permit no one to evade them from any want of vigilance on their part. The ministers and churchwardens were obliged to make a return of all the Scots who resided in their parishes. If any refused to take the oath, their names were forwarded to Dublin, when officers were dispatched by Wentworth to execute his pleasure on the recusants.

The deputy supposed that the people would generally, through fear, take the obnoxious oath. They had no objection to pledge their allegiance to their king, but very many refused to yield unconditional obedience to all that he might command, whether just or unjust. On these the highest penalties of the law, short of death, were frequently inflicted. Many were fined, others were cast into dungeons, while multitudes deserted their homes and fled to the woods, leaving their valuable properties to speedy ruin. So many of the laboring population fled to Scotland that it was found very difficult to gather the ripened grain in the fields. The severity of the sufferings endured by these Christian patriots may be inferred from the punishment meted out to a Mr. Stewart, who refused to swear to the unconditional terms of the oath. He and his family were dragged up to Dublin, placed in close confinement, speedily brought to trial in the Star-Chamber—a court in which even the forms of law and justice were despised—and fined in the sum of *sixteen thousand pounds*, and were ordered to be imprisoned at their own charges until the exorbitant fine was paid. This sentence they were told to consider as *an act of leniency* on the part of their judges, for had they been punished as they deserved they would have been declared worthy of death for treason. Among their judges was Primate Usher, who, while evincing more moderation than the other prelates in the trial, was swept along by the power and fear of royal prerogative, and led to concur in the judgment required by the cruel Wentworth, who then and there expressed his determination to prosecute "to the blood" all who declined the oath and drive them "root and branch" out of the kingdom; and he was as good as his word, for he imposed it with the greatest cruelty upon all ages, ranks and sexes of the nonconformists in Ireland.

For the time being the power of the deputy was irresistible. No one dared to oppose his oppressive measures. If any person evinced the least sympathy for those persecuted for their religious scruples in taking the oath, it was sufficient to incur his severest censures. Archibald Adair, bishop of Killala, having expressed his contempt of the conduct of a renegade Scotchman who had reviled his brethren for their attachment to the Covenant, was committed to prison and tried before the High

Commission court. At the instigation of Bramhall, and with the consent of the other bigoted and sycophantic prelates, he was deprived of his see, fined two thousand pounds and ordered to be imprisoned during the pleasure of the court. Bishop Bedell was alone in his opposition to this despotic measure, and by an able argument founded on the scriptural qualifications of a bishop sought to befriend his calumniated and injured brother.

Charles did not fail to reward the services of his unscrupulous and faithful servant, Wentworth. He was appointed lord-lieutenant of Ireland, elevated to the rank of an earl, and received other marks of royal approval and confidence. In return he entered with ardor into the king's plans, contributed largely to them out of his own private fortune, and immediately issued orders to raise an army to occupy Ulster and to aid his master, who had resolved to renew the war in Scotland whenever the opportune time should arrive. This army, consisting of eight thousand foot and one thousand horse, was almost entirely composed of Roman Catholics. It was stationed at several points along the coast where it could be employed to crush out any popular rising of the nonconformists, or, if needed, could be readily transported to Scotland for the purpose of an invasion of that country.

These unresisted efforts to keep the north of Ireland in peace and submission, Strafford hoped would prove effectual. In this belief he retired to

England to consult with his sovereign and mature further plans for maintaining the royal cause, leaving the government in the charge of a deputy. But scarcely had he taken his departure when a spirit of resolute opposition manifested itself. Those who had long suffered in silence under the most severe oppressions began to complain of their grievances and burdens. The evils of his administration were freely exposed, and the people earnestly and forcibly demanded relief from its intolerable abuses. Equal discontent prevailed in England, and for very similar causes. This led to frequent communications between English patriots and their oppressed brethren in Ireland, where were found many congenial spirits who not only valued civil and religious liberty, but stood ready to resist the usurpations of the Crown. Well was it for Great Britain that there arose at this time a party who both held correct views of constitutional freedom and had the courage to maintain them. Though the epithet "Puritans" had been derisively applied to them, yet even Hume himself was obliged to make the remarkable admission, "So absolute was the authority of the Crown that the precious spark of liberty had been kindled and was preserved by the Puritans alone, and it was to this sect that the English owe the whole freedom of their constitution."\*

Their brethren in Ireland had finally resolved

\* *History of England,* vol. v., p. 134.

upon bold measures. They drew up a *Remonstrance*, setting forth the evils they had suffered during the government of Strafford, and appointed a committee of six to present it to the king in person, and to demand that their worst grievances should be speedily redressed. At this opportune moment the LONG PARLIAMENT met, having been called together by the king to supply his urgent need of money. But instead of voting the required sums of money, one of the first motions made was to take into consideration the affairs of Ireland. The result was the bold measure of impeaching Strafford for high treason. A committee was appointed to prepare charges against him, and the same day he was formally impeached, sequestered from his seat and committed to the Tower, and in the following May, in less than six months from the time he was in the zenith of his power, he was beheaded on Tower Hill—a memorable example to all unprincipled statesmen.

Freed from the restraints of the earl of Strafford's presence and authority, and encouraged by their friends in England, the nonconformists of Ulster now earnestly sought deliverance from the evils under which they had so long suffered. They drew up a petition detailing their many grievances, both civil and religious, and praying for the enjoyment of liberty of conscience. This was presented to the Long Parliament, and helped to swell the tide of national indignation that was rising against royal and prelatical usurpation. In this petition the northern Presbyterians evinced their strong attachment to their own faith and order, for, next to the privilege of worshiping God as their consciences approved, they asked for the restoration of their banished pastors. Without an educated and pious ministry, they felt there could not be permanent peace and prosperity in the kingdom; and while they had been deprived of the services of their honored ministers, who were obliged to escape to Scotland, the more learned of the laity were accustomed to call their neighbors together and expound the Scripture to them. By this means the knowledge and love of the truth were preserved among the people, and they were eager to embrace the first opportunity which offered to engage again in the methods of worship to which they had been accustomed.

The representations contained in this petition, reciting as they did the persecutions to which they had been subjected, were not unavailing. They had great influence in securing the conviction of Wentworth for violating the fundamental laws of the kingdom during his tyrannical administration, and in obtaining in 1641 a complete change in the government of Ireland. Two lords-justices were appointed, both belonging to the Puritan party, who labored earnestly to repair the evils wrought by the former rulers, in which work they received the hearty co-operation of the English Parliament.

The High Commission court was summarily abolished, many of the illegal penalties imposed by ecclesiastical courts were declared null and void, Bishop Adair and five Presbyterian ministers of the diocese of Down were restored to their offices, the sentence of confiscation of the lands in the county of Londonderry was rescinded, and the army which Strafford had collected in Ulster to overawe the nonconformists was disbanded. The removal of these and kindred evils ensured a peace and tranquillity in Ireland such as had not been known for a long period.

## CHAPTER VIII.

### From the Irish Rebellion to the Death of Charles I.

The immunities and privileges secured through the overthrow of Wentworth and the High Commission court were shared equally by Roman Catholics and Protestants, as was both just and right. While the Romanists were suffering the common grievances resulting from the wicked government of the earl of Strafford, they were ready to make common cause with the Protestants. But when they were freed from the oppression they had so long endured, and their religion and their clergy were no longer molested in their religious rites, they began to cherish the hope that they might attain to that political ascendency which their preponderance of numbers seemed to warrant. Incited alike by their own ambitious leaders, their hatred of Protestantism and the promises and intrigues of the king, they ere long aimed at nothing less than the entire overthrow of the British power in Ireland. The native Irish, many of whom were descendants of the ancient chieftains, and who were the hereditary enemies of the English, joined in the insurrection, with the expectation of recovering their forfeited landed property, and from a desire to re-establish Romanism. They were encouraged by promised assistance from their friends on the Continent, by whose aid they hoped to drive out all English usurpers and to restore the nation to its former independence. They were incited to rebellion also by the priests, who had taught them to hate and abhor both the persons and religion of the Protestants, and their prejudices, as also the great ignorance in which they were kept by their spiritual advisers, rendered them the easy dupes of designing leaders. The priests, in their turn, were instigated by the emissaries of the pope, ambitious to recover his supremacy over a country which had been regarded as "the especial patrimony of the Romish see." A prominent object, therefore, of the rebellion was the destruction of Protestantism, and from the first the watchword was the extirpation of all heretics.

The plan contemplated, on a certain fixed day, the simultaneous seizure of Dublin and the principal forts and castles throughout the kingdom, and the disarming and securing those who would not join in the insurrection. Though the conspirators carried on their proceedings with the utmost caution and secrecy, the lords-justices and some of the Protestant nobility received information of the plot in time to secure the safety of the metropolis and some of the most important castles and towns. Through intelligence furnished by a converted Romanist who had been urged to join the conspirators, measures were hastily adopted whereby Belfast, Enniskillen, **Derry,** Coleraine, Carrickfergus and the town and castle of Antrim were secured against capture and pillage by the rebels. These towns served as places of refuge for the persecuted and famishing Protestants who were driven from their desolated homes, and where the Scots of Ulster rallied and held in check the insurgents in their otherwise unimpeded progress until English arms could be sent to aid in their subjection.

Notwithstanding these precautionary measures, such was the success of the uprising that in little more than a fortnight from its commencement the rebels were masters of the greater part of Ulster, together with the two neighboring counties, and had collected a force of thirty thousand men actuated by hatred of the English as conquerors and heretics, and thirsting for their blood. The undisciplined and revengeful soldiers were encouraged to give free scope to their worst passions by the native Irish leaders, who aimed at nothing less than the extirpation of all Protestants. Their orders were, "Spare neither man, woman nor child. The English are meat for dogs; there shall not be one drop of English blood left within the kingdom." Well did they obey the commands of their superiors. The havoc was terrible. "An universal massacre ensued; nor age, nor sex, nor infancy was spared; all conditions were involved in the general ruin. In vain did the unhappy victim appeal to the sacred ties of humanity, hospitality, family connection, and all the tender obligations of social commerce; companions, friends, relatives, not only denied protection, but dealt with their own hands the fatal blow." The houses of the victims were either consumed with fire or leveled with the ground. Their cattle, because they had belonged to abhorred heretics, were either killed or covered with wounds and turned loose to abide a lingering, painful end. Their valuable stores of grain were wantonly squandered and destroyed, so that famine ensued, owing to the scarcity of food. The refusal of the rebels to bury the corpses of their murdered victims in many places induced a pestilential fever, which carried off great numbers of the inhabitants who had escaped the fury of their enemies. So destructive was the pestilence that it was computed that in Coleraine *six thousand* died in four months, in Carrickfergus *two thousand five hundred*, in Belfast and Malone above *two thousand*, and in Antrim and other places a like proportion.

But we will not dwell upon this terrible scene of blood, which rivaled in its carnage that of St. Bartholomew. History records no more dreadful massacres than were perpetrated by the bloodthirsty savages who were let loose upon Ulster. Not satisfied with slaying defenceless women and children, they took a fiendish delight in first tormenting them, and their appeals for mercy and cries of pain were answered with revilings and insults.*

---

* Lest any one may think we have exaggerated the horrors of this insurrection, we append what the historian Froude says respecting it: "The order was to drive the English settlers and their families from their houses and strip men, women and children even of the clothes upon their backs. . . . On the morning of the fatal Saturday there appeared before the houses of the settlers gangs of armed Irish, who demanded instant possession, and on being admitted ejected the entire families, and stripped most of them to the skin. Many resisted and were killed, many sought shelter in the houses of their Irish neighbors, with whom they had lived in intimacy. The doors of their neighbors were opened in seeming hospitality, but within they were not human beings—not even human savages —but ferocious beasts. The priests had so charmed the Irish, and laid such bloody impressions on them, that it was held a mortal sin to give relief or protection to the English. . . . Savage creatures of both sexes, yelping in chorus and brandishing their skenes, boys practicing their young hands in stabbing and torturing the English children,—these were the scenes which were witnessed daily throughout all parts of Ulster. The distinction between Scots and English soon vanished. Religion was made the new dividing-line, and the one crime was to be a Protestant. . . . The priests told the people 'that the Protestants were worse than dogs—they were devils and served the devil—and the killing of them was a meritorious act.'"—*Froude,* vol. i., pp. 97, 107, 108.

Roman Catholic historians in vain deny these charges. Depositions filling forty volumes are still preserved in the library of Trinity College which tell the tale with perfect distinctness and consistency.

On no class did these sufferings fall more heavily than on the Protestant ministers. Being marked out specially for persecution by the priests who instigated the rebellion, they were shown no quarter. In a small part of Ulster alone thirty were murdered, while a much larger number died in circumstances of extreme wretchedness and poverty. Bishop Bedell was the only Englishman in the whole county of Cavan who was permitted to live undisturbed in his own house. Even he, though he had labored so earnestly for the good of the Irish people, and with a humility and disinterestedness that had commanded the respect of the most bigoted Romanists in his diocese, was at last arrested and imprisoned, and only released a few weeks before his death. As an evidence of the respect entertained for him, the privilege of burial by the side of his wife in the churchyard of Kilmore was granted, and a large force of rebels attended his funeral, who, when they fired a volley over his grave, expressed the wish that the last of the English might rest in peace. Having esteemed him as the best of the English bishops who had labored among them, they were resolved he should be the last left in Ireland.

No trustworthy record remains of the number of Protestants who perished in the rebellion by the sword, or from famine and pestilence. Suffice it to say that the lowest possible estimate to be made presents an awful sacrifice of human life.

In Ulster the devastation produced by the exterminating warfare, which was carried on for months, was so terrible that the Presbyterian interest was wellnigh destroyed. Yet the Presbyterians, as a body, did not suffer so severely as the Episcopalians. The reason for this was that the previous persecutions of Wentworth, by his agents Leslie and Bramhall and the court of High Commission, had compelled many of the most influential Presbyterian clergy and nobility to retire to Scotland, where the pastors had been joined by many of their parishioners, who were induced to go mainly by a desire to attend upon their ministry. Thus multitudes were providentially preserved, and what was designed to ruin the Presbyterian Church proved in the end its preservation. But those who did remain and were saved from the terrible carnage were rendered poor in property, and were destitute of the public ordinances of religion. They, however, continued steadfast in their love of their Church; and when the rebellion was finally subdued and peace restored, they heartily united with their brethren who returned from Scotland in re-establishing the Presbyterian Church in Ireland.

After the devastation had continued several months, Charles, by reason of the intelligence conveyed to him at Edinburgh, was induced to issue commissions for the raising of regiments to defend the kingdom, and the lords-justices adopted measures to furnish arms to the levies that were ordered. These regiments were commanded by men who had the respect and confidence of their soldiers. This was especially true of Sir William and Sir Robert Stewart, who had command of the forces raised in the counties of Derry and Donegal, which were afterward known as the LAGAN FORCES. With these the insurgents were held in check. Learning more fully the dangerous situation of the Protestants in the north of Ireland, the Scottish Parliament offered a supply of three thousand stand of arms and ten thousand men for their relief. Before these, however, could become available, it was necessary to obtain the sanction of the English authorities, and their aid in supporting the army. This was promptly given, and the English Commons not only voted a liberal supply of money, but an additional levy of men. Still, owing to many vexatious delays, it was some months before these latter regiments arrived in Ireland and joined the forces operating against the insurgents. After their junction an active warfare was prosecuted, but it was not until several fierce conflicts had taken place that the rebellion was subdued. Finding that they could not oppose successfully the combined forces of the Scotch and English, the principal leaders resolved to disband their followers and seek safety in flight.

The cessation of hostilities, though partial and temporary, prepared the way for the re-establishment of religion. The Episcopal Church, which had been so arrogant and intolerant in the day of prosperity, was now overthrown. Not a single bishop and but very few of her clergy continued to live within the province. Most of the Protestant laity who remained and had survived the rebellion were not in heart friends of the Irish Episcopal Church, having been constrained by penal laws to conform to its service. Consequently, when previous restraints were withdrawn, the great majority of them naturally returned to the Church of their choice—the Scottish Church, with whose forms they were familiar. Others, who were from preference Episcopalians, forsook the Establishment, because they had seen that their prelates and clergy were hostile to the cause of civil liberty. Thus out of the ruins, and largely from the incongruous fragments temporarily incorporated into the Episcopal Church of Ireland, arose speedily the simpler fabric of Presbyterianism. The Presbyterian element increased rapidly by the return to the country of the original Scottish settlers who had fled from Ireland; and being largely in the majority, they at once began the re-establishing of Presbyterian churches in Ulster. In this they were assisted by the chaplains of the Scottish regiments, who were strongly attached to the doctrines, worship and government of their national Church, the characteristic features of which were preserved in the

Irish. These chaplains were ordained ministers and having received calls from congregations to settle, they remained in the country after the return home of their regiments. By their prudence and zeal they rendered valuable aid in the organization of the Irish Presbyterian Church upon the scriptural foundation which it has ever since maintained.

It was by these clergymen that the first regularly constituted presbytery was held in Ireland, which met at Carrickfergus, June 10, 1642. Five ministers and four ruling elders were in attendance, the elders representing the sessions previously constituted in four of the regiments. Correspondence was opened with Lords Claneboy and Montgomery, the commanding officers of two other regiments, requesting permission for their chaplains to attend the meetings of presbytery. This privilege was freely granted, and was accompanied with the assurance that they would support the measures of the presbytery in establishing anew the Protestant Church in Ulster.

Intelligence having gone abroad that a presbytery had been formed, applications immediately began to be received from destitute parishes, for the organization of churches and for the supply of ministers. These requests were granted so far as the presbytery had the ability to comply. It was soon found, however, that it was impossible to provide ministers for all the places destitute of preaching, and where the people were desirous of enjoying the regular services of a pastor. A petition for aid was sent to the Scottish Assembly; and in response to the request of their Irish brethren, it commissioned six of its best-qualified ministers, giving them instructions to proceed to Ireland and labor for a period of four months each, "there to visit, comfort, instruct and encourage the scattered flocks of Christ, to employ themselves to the uttermost, with all faithfulness and singleness of heart, in planting and watering according to the direction of Jesus Christ, and according to the doctrine and discipline of this Church in all things."

In compliance with the appointment of the General Assembly, Rev. Messrs. Blair and Hamilton returned to Ireland in September, 1642, and were very warmly received by the brethren of the presbytery. The commission which they bore from the Assembly was ordered to be preserved among their records and inserted in their minutes. For three months they itinerated, performing missionary labor, organizing churches and preaching almost daily. Through the efforts of these experienced ministers, who were intimately acquainted with the circumstances and needs of the country, Presbyterianism rapidly revived. The seed previously sown now began to spring up with a vigor and a fruitage that gladdened the hearts of the laborers. Everywhere the people received these ministers with the utmost respect and gratitude.

Multitudes who formerly belonged to the Episcopal Church declared themselves in favor of the Presbyterian, and asked to be permitted to join her standards and partake of the privileges of her communion. In a brief period numerous Presbyterian congregations were gathered, and many of the Episcopal clergy came forward and united with the newly-formed presbytery. These were received into fellowship, but not until they had openly professed repentance for their former evil ways, and particularly for taking the Black Oath, and for their persecutions of the nonconformists.

In all these proceedings we are to notice and admire the overruling providence of God. These ministers, restrained by Scottish prelates from the exercise of their ministry in their native country, removed to Ireland, and there introduced Presbyterianism. Banished from their adopted country, they returned to Scotland, where they were the chief instruments in overthrowing prelacy and re-establishing the Presbyterian Church; and now, the sword of the rebels having either slain or driven away the most noted and violent of their persecutors, they are recalled to Ireland to accept the acknowledgments and repentance of the few remaining conformists, and to aid for the third time in reconstructing the Presbyterian Church on the ruins of prelacy. This duty they discharged with eminent prudence and faithfulness, and with such success that a peaceful and prosperous career now seemed open to the Presbyterian Church of Ireland.

Freed from the restraints hitherto imposed, and encouraged by the policy now predominant in England, the Presbyterian ministers, increased in numbers by the kind sympathy and aid afforded by the General Assembly of Scotland, were abundant in labors and successful in gathering congregations. Few disturbing influences were felt, apart from the turbulence of the Roman Catholic Irish, and the local conflicts growing out of the rebellion, which had been only half suppressed. Two Baptist preachers at Antrim, where a few Separatists still lived, attempted to spread their peculiar principles, but found such small encouragement that they soon abandoned their fruitless mission. Meanwhile, the subject of ecclesiastical reform had assumed such importance in England, and opposition to prelacy had become so general and decided, that Parliament passed an ordinance convening an assembly of divines at Westminster, with the hope of establishing uniformity of doctrine, worship and government throughout the entire empire. Though they did not accomplish all that was hoped, they did succeed in framing a confession of faith which served as a bond of union to Presbyterians throughout the three kingdoms.

This was followed by sending commissioners to Scotland to the convention of Estates and the General Assembly, for the purpose of securing a *civil* league between the two kingdoms. The Scots would not assent unless it was made also a *religious* covenant. The result of the negotiations was "THE SOLEMN LEAGUE AND COVENANT," which was ordered to be taken in England and Scotland by all persons over the age of eighteen years, under pain of being punished as the enemies to religion and the peace of the kingdom.

As Ireland was included in its provisions, measures were promptly taken to transmit it thither, and to furnish the inhabitants an opportunity to subscribe it. This they did with becoming solemnity and deliberation, when presented for their approval by the ministers who were sent over for this purpose from Scotland. Its effects were the same in Ulster as in England and Scotland. It served to make known and to unite the friends of civil and religious liberty, and inspired them with fresh courage to resist their enemies. It increased the attachment felt for the cause of Presbyterianism, and aided in re-establishing the Church where it had been overthrown either by prelacy or the rebellion. But, what was of much greater moment, the Covenant was the means of so reviving true religion, and of promoting the zeal and efficiency of both ministers and people, that from this period the Reformation made rapid progress, and a marked improvement of society was everywhere discernible.

During succeeding years, and up to the time when the *Rump Parliament* proceeded to the trial and execution of Charles I. in 1649, the interests of religion continued on the whole to advance, notwithstanding the ever-recurring hindrances arising out of the unsettled state of Ireland. The ministers of the presbytery were very zealous in their efforts to repress immorality and vice, and to establish throughout the province the regular administration of religious ordinances so far as their influence extended. Their successive petitions, addressed to the General Assembly of Scotland for more pastors, attest the increasing number of the congregations and the prosperous condition of the Presbyterian Church. As these ministers arrived, after a period of trial, they were ordained and installed over congregations, and sessions in each church were regularly constituted. Such was the growth of Presbyterianism, even in these troublous times, that at the beginning of the year 1647 there were, besides several chaplains of Scottish regiments and the occasional supplies sent over from Scotland, nearly *thirty* ordained ministers permanently settled in Ulster.

The presbytery of Ulster, though surrounded by the anti-monarchical party, did not hesitate to express their detestation of the murder of Charles and the overthrow of lawful authority in England. Irish Presbyterians sympathized with their brethren in Scotland in their preference for a hereditary and limited monarchy, if the proper securities of civil and religious freedom could be obtained. But they were not disposed to resort to any violent measures in behalf of Charles II. The rapid and decisive victories of Cromwell soon led them to assent, under protest, to the government *de facto;* and as they saw more of the man, and understood better his motives and his measures, they were less inclined to place obstructions in the way of his government.

Cromwell's course with respect to Ireland while lord-lieutenant, though open to censure in some particulars, was on the whole quite judicious.* The ignorant and vicious Romanists were made to tremble at the terror of his name. He was ever ready to listen to any proposal which promised to promote the spread of Protestant truth, and he was careful to secure to the clergy and the people full liberty of worship. And when once assured of their good and peaceable disposition, he was not rigorous in imposing any oath of allegiance. He seemed at least to respect the scruples of those who preferred the recognition of Charles II. as king, but were content to live quietly under his own government. He had prosecuted the war

* "He meant to rule Ireland for Ireland's good, and all testimony agrees that Ireland never prospered as she prospered in the three years of the Protectorate. Ireland's interests were not sacrificed to England's commercial jealousies. He recognized no difference between the two countries."—*Froude*, vol. i., p. 137.

with such vigor and with such resources, from the very day of his landing in Ireland, that the royalists were speedily dispossessed of all their garrisons in Ulster, and the republicans became masters of the province, which they continued to hold till the Restoration.

In connection with Cromwell's army there came over large numbers from England who were strong adherents of Independency. John Owen, their most noted divine, accompanied him as chaplain, and preached regularly in Dublin. Many of these Independents were more zealous than discreet, and relied mainly for the advancement of their interests upon the patronage of the government. Considering the condition of parties in England at this period, it was very natural that differences should arise between some of these new comers and the older clergy. The most of their number, however, were more devoted to the spread of gospel truth than to the triumph of party principles, and with all these the Irish Presbyterian ministers strongly sympathized and were ready to co-operate. To promote education and religion in Ireland a bill was passed by Parliament to increase the endowments of colleges and schools, to abolish the hierarchy and the use of the Common Prayer-book, and to "send over forthwith six able ministers to dispense the gospel in the city of Dublin." To each of these ministers it voted a liberal salary of two hundred pounds per annum, to be paid out of the public revenue of Ireland. So anxious was Cromwell to secure an adequate supply of ministers that he wrote to New England, offering most liberal inducements to such as would come over to Ulster. How many, if any, were persuaded to come there is no method of ascertaining, but it is known that a number of Independent and Baptist preachers were admitted to officiate, to the exclusion of the Presbyterian clergy, in the few garrison-towns.

One of the first measures adopted by Parliament after the death of Charles was the Engagement Oath, requiring all persons to swear to be "faithful to the Commonwealth of England as now established, without a king or House of Lords." To taking this oath many of the Presbyterian clergy were opposed, and so great was their popularity among the people, and so fully did they justify their refusal, that the attempt to enforce it proved a failure at the time. But the opportunity was seized by the sectaries, who in their councils urged the government to summon the recusant ministers and compel them either to take the oath or withdraw from the country. The crowning of Charles II. at Scone by the Scottish nobles, January 1, 1651, only increased the jealousy felt toward the Presbyterians and subjected their ministers to still severer treatment. The engagement was pressed with much greater rigor. As a result, many Presbyterian clergy were violently excluded from their pulpits, and their means of subsistence withdrawn; and, by a council of war held in March, 1651, some of them were formally banished from the kingdom. Those who ventured to remain, being deprived of their stipends and the houses of worship in which they were accustomed regularly to officiate, were forced to preach in the fields or in barns and glens.

An event took place at this time which deserves mention, for it shows the religious state of the country. While these faithful men were enduring great privations, the Independent ministers invited them to a conference at Antrim with the professed purpose to arrange some plan of agreement or accommodation between them. This invitation was accepted; but when the Presbyterians arrived at the place of conference, they found, to their surprise, that the Independent clergy designed to use the occasion to hold a public discussion before a large assembly respecting the merits of the two systems of church government. With very great reluctance the Presbyterian ministers engaged in the debate; and though wholly unprepared for the discussion, the result proved favorable to them. They were adjudged by the public to have had the best of the argument, and on returning to their people were left for a period unmolested.

An unfavorable change for Presbyterians had recently taken place in the Board of Commissioners for Ireland, the majority of whom were now strong adherents of the Baptists. Already a number of Baptist preachers had come over from England, and, propagating their peculiar tenets with great zeal, had gathered several churches. Among the most active of these propagandists were Thomas Patient, a former chaplain in Cromwell's army, now residing at Waterford; Christopher Blackwood, who accompanied Fleetwood when he came to Ireland in 1652, and who settled in Dublin; and Claudius Gilbert, another of Fleetwood's favorites, who was pastor of the church at Limerick. At their instigation, and influenced by political interest, the new deputy and commissioners resolved to silence or banish all the Presbyterian ministers in Ulster who refused to take the engagement oath. But in this attempt they failed. The ministers declined to subscribe, while they professed a disposition to do all they could to promote peace and order in the kingdom. The matter was brought before Fleetwood at Dublin, who referred it to a council of officers. From the known character of the army, it might have been supposed that all measures of persecution would have been abjured; but when the accused placed their refusal to take the oath on the ground of conscience, Allen, an Anabaptist, replied, "A papist would and might say as much for himself, and pretend conscience as well as they." To this charge Adair, one of their number, responded that "*their* consciences could digest to kill Protestant kings, but so would not ours, to which our principles are contrary." This was a home-thrust, and silenced the council. Some who were in heart opposed to the execution of the king drew their hats down over their faces, and others were angry because of the reflection on their conduct. The ministers were not called to appear again before the council, and were permitted to leave Dublin, though no pledge was given them that they would in future be secure from persecution.

The respite enjoyed was very brief, for in six weeks from their dismissal by the council the commissioners sent a party of soldiers to each minister's house, to seize all papers and letters they could find. They had determined to press the engagement upon all classes, beginning with their pastors. The danger was imminent, and they only escaped by the opportune arrival of the news of the dissolution of Parliament by Cromwell. This intelligence stayed the hands of the commissioners. Their authority was now at an end, and they dared not proceed. Accordingly, the ministers were permitted to return to their homes with fair words, and blessing God for the unexpected deliverance from their troubles.

Cromwell's accession to supreme power brought great relief to Nonconformists. Differences existed among themselves which produced no little friction in their final adjustment. But they were freed from persecution by Romanists and by the High Church party. Henry Cromwell was sent over to Ireland by the Protector to ascertain the condition of affairs, especially the disposition of the army toward the new government. His visit did much to allay the violence of parties and restore peace to the country. The suspicions which Cromwell at first entertained respecting the loyalty of the Presbyterian ministers were allayed, and they were permitted to pursue their proper calling without any serious restraints. Under their culture the churches began to revive and new ones were established, and during the Protectorate of Cromwell Presbyterianism in Ireland enjoyed almost uninterrupted prosperity. Many of those ministers who had fled to Scotland again returned. The differences which so divided their brethren in the Church of Scotland were not permitted to enter the Irish Church and work a division in it. It required, however, the utmost prudence and vigilance to guard the Church against the ruinous schism, since there was constant danger that the causes of dissension would be introduced by the return of the exiled ministers and the accession of new men from Scotland. Great caution was observed in receiving candidates for the ministry. If from abroad, they were required to produce testimonials as to their piety, their literary attainments and their theological views, and none were received until they could furnish ample proofs of their qualifications for the sacred office. Accepted candidates were put for a time on special trial, and appointed to preach not only in the congregations which wished to call them, but in neighboring ones also, so that ministers and people might have an opportunity to judge of their gifts. If they passed this scrutiny, approving themselves good and faithful preachers of the word, the presbytery gave its assent to their settlement, and proceeded to ordain and install them over the parish.

These wise and faithful measures were successful not only in preserving harmony in the presbytery, but in promoting the growth and spirituality of its churches. The gospel was preached in places which it had never reached before, and churches were multiplied and very generally had the services of a regular pastor. While in 1653 the number of ministers was only twenty-four, in a few years it reached eighty. The presbytery, having become too large to meet conveniently in one place, and extending over too large a district of country to provide properly for destitute places and maintain strict discipline in its churches, was divided so as to compose "five meetings." The order of the Church of Scotland, as heretofore, was carefully observed. Though these "meetings" were not strictly presbyteries acting on their own authority, but by commission, yet they performed most of the duties of such bodies, visiting congregations, giving advice to sessions and seeing that ministers, elders and congregations performed their respective duties. Thus they greatly facilitated the work of the presbytery, and helped to maintain a proper oversight of the wide and rapidly extending field. It was during this period of comparative tranquillity, extending to the death of the Protector, September 3, 1658, that the Presbyterian Church of Ireland was established on a permanent foundation.

Richard Cromwell, who succeeded his father in the Protectorate, soon proved himself wholly incapable of holding the reins of government, and Charles II. was invited to resume the crown as his hereditary right. But a fatal mistake was made when the king was invested with power without assigning proper limits to the royal prerogative, and thus protecting the freedom of his subjects. Unfettered by any conditions, Charles II. soon exhibited the same disposition to exercise arbitrary authority which his father had attempted, and with like results.

Notwithstanding his fair promises to Presbyterians, who, having so steadily refused to take the engagement oath, were surely entitled to his favor, it was soon apparent that they were to expect nothing but severity at his hands. Everything indicated the approach of a season of suffering and persecution. In the face of all his solemn declarations, he determined to replace the Episcopal Church on its former basis, and only desired to quiet all opposition until he could carry out his resolution. The effects of his policy were soon felt in Ulster, when Bramhall and Leslie, who still survived, were returned to their vacant sees and began to evince all the bitterness of their old intolerance. Other bishops were appointed, and measures adopted for crushing out the very existence of the Presbyterian Church. At the instigation of the bishops, the lords-justices issued a proclamation forbidding all unlawful assemblies and directing the sheriffs to prevent or disperse them. The object was to prevent the meeting not only of presbyteries, but also of congregations. Among the very foremost to incite the persecution of the Presbyterians, were those members of the court who had formerly renounced their allegiance to Charles I. and held office under Cromwell and his son Richard. These mercenary men were now the most active in denouncing, as disloyal and unworthy of toleration, those same ministers whom they had before persecuted for their loyalty and attachment to monarchy, when they themselves were the supporters of the usurper Cromwell.

While the bishops were preparing to put in force the proclamation of the lords-justices, the Presbyterian ministers held a meeting, and sent four of their number from their several presbyteries to Dublin, to remind the justices of the king's promises to them, and to remonstrate against the cruel measures contemplated to be employed. They reminded them also of their loyalty and sufferings under the Pretender, their present loyalty to Charles II., which was shown by the readiness with which they had welcomed him back to his throne, and their past peaceable spirit and their future resolution to remain loyal and dutiful subjects. But it was all to no purpose. The reply returned to the petition from the members of the presbyteries requesting liberty to exercise their ministry in their respective parishes, as they had formerly done, clearly indicated that nothing less than entire conformity to prelacy was intended by the council, instigated, as they were, by such bishops as Bramhall and Leslie. In their answer they said, "We neither could nor would allow any discipline to be exercised in church affairs but what was warranted and commanded by the laws of the land," and they told the ministers that "they were punishable for having exercised any other."

Even the celebrated Jeremy Taylor, bishop of Down and Connor, exhibited the same exclusive and intolerant spirit. The author of the eloquent work entitled *Liberty of Prophesying* tarnished his fair reputation by repudiating his avowed principles. In his conference with the nonconformist clergy he treated them sharply, and even rudely; and in reply to the conscientious scruples which they had assigned for not appearing at his visitation services, he declared that "a

Jew or a Quaker would say so much for his opinions." The Presbyterian ministers, though grievously disappointed with their reception, returned to their congregations resolved to breast as best they could the coming storm. Nor had they long to wait; for this bishop shortly afterward, in a single day, declared *thirty-six* of their churches vacant, and sent curates to take possession of part of them, while in others the regular pastors were violently arrested as they were entering their pulpits.

The situation of these ministers was peculiarly distressing. They were not only excluded from their pulpits and deprived of their means of living, but were forbidden, under heavy penalties, to preach, baptize or publicly exhort among their people. These privations, however, they willingly endured rather than violate their consciences and submit to a form of government and worship which they considered unscriptural.

Other prelates of the Established Church speedily followed the example set by Jeremy Taylor—"the impersonation and special jewel of Anglicanism," as Froude calls him—so that in Ulster alone *sixty-one* Presbyterian ministers were deposed from the ministry and ejected from their charges. Of these, sixteen were of the presbytery of Down, fourteen of Antrim, ten of Route, eight of Tyrone and thirteen of Lagan.

Of the Act of Uniformity, which was thus enforced, Mr. Froude says: "To insist that none should officiate who had not been ordained by a bishop was to deprive two-thirds of the Protestant inhabitants of the only religious ministrations which they would accept, and to force on them the alternative of exile or submission to a ritual which they abhorred as much as popery, while, to enhance the absurdity, there were not probably a hundred episcopally ordained clergy in the whole island. Yet this was what the bishops deliberately thought it wise to do. . . . Every clergyman had to subscribe a declaration that a subject, under no pretence, might bear arms against the king, and that the oath to the League and Covenant was illegal and impious. . . . Nonconformists became at once the objects of an unrelenting and unscrupulous persecution."

Only seven out of nearly seventy clergymen conformed to prelacy. The trials and hardships of the ejected ministers, though terrible, were heroically endured. "They set an example," says the historian, "of fortitude and integrity which prepared and encouraged their brethren in the sister-kingdoms to act with similar magnanimity, for they enjoyed the painful though honorable pre-eminence of being the first to suffer in the three kingdoms, and are therefore eminently entitled to the admiration and gratitude of posterity." Had they proved faithless in their day of trial, Presbyterianism in Ireland would have scarcely survived the subsequent persecutions of the prelates and the disastrous wars of the Revolution.

After an interval of nearly twenty years the Irish Parliament assembled in 1661. In the mean time, the prelatical party had acquired such ascendency that there was but a single member in the House of Lords, Lord Massareene, who sympathized with the persecuted Presbyterians. In the Commons also they had but few favorable to their interests, so strongly did the tide run in favor of prelacy. Many were anxious to remove all suspicion of their new-born loyalty by denouncing and punishing those who declined to conform, and therefore were ready to support the measures of the bishops and to enable them to enact just such laws as they desired. Parliament passed an act for burning the Solemn League and Covenant, ordering it to be burned in all cities and towns by the common hangman, and requiring the chief magistrate of the place to be present and see the order executed. It was further declared " that whosoever shall by word or deed, by sign or writing, defend or justify the said *treasonable Covenant*, shall be esteemed as an enemy to His Sacred Majesty, and to the peace and tranquillity of his Church and kingdom." In all cities and towns throughout the kingdom the Covenant was burned, the magistrates directing and witnessing the proceedings.

All hope of relief seemed to have fled. No

matter how loyal and well disposed their past history showed them to have been, nor what were their conscientious scruples to prelacy, there was not the least leniency extended to any of their number. The wickedness and obduracy of heart of their fellow-men made prayer their only resource, and "the ministers in this juncture gave themselves especially to prayer and did cry to God for help." Though forbidden the public exercise of their ministry, they deemed it to be their duty to remain with their people, and to embrace such opportunities as they had to converse with them in their homes, and to instruct them in the Word as they might assemble in small private companies.

During the brief administration of the duke of Ormond the persecution of Presbyterians was somewhat relaxed. Through the influence of their noble friend, Lord Massareene, the duke was led to sympathize with them for their previous sufferings in behalf of the king, and was disposed to be lenient toward them so long as they lived peaceably and did nothing to excite the jealousy of the bishops. Though denied the right of preaching in public, they were not molested in the discharge of their more private duties in their respective parishes. But this condition of peace and freedom was ere long disturbed by a secret conspiracy which was formed by a few restless spirits, chiefly those who had been attached to the Pretender's party, and with whom one or two ministers in

Ulster chanced to be very remotely connected. This is known in history as *Blood's Plot*. Notwithstanding the conspirators met with no encouragement from the Presbyterians of the north, with the single exception noted above, yet some of the ministers were arrested on mere suspicion, and many more exposed to great inconvenience and suffering. The apprehension of danger was so great that orders were issued to disarm all the Scotch in the country, which was done in the most summary manner. Before the disorder caused by the conspiracy had subsided, the jealousy and animosity excited against the ministry were so great that the larger part of them were obliged to return to Scotland, or retire into some obscure part of the country. But when the most rigid scrutiny had failed to identify them with the plot, and had shown that they had been quiet and peaceable citizens, the duke was induced to grant them certain indulgences, and to relax somewhat the severity of the penal statutes respecting conformity to Episcopacy. Bramhall dying at this time, his successor, a man of mild spirit, wishing to ingratiate himself with the people, continued to be lenient in his treatment, and the lords-justices, when not instigated by the prelates, were not inclined to trouble the people for nonconformity.

The little liberty granted them they received with thankfulness and used with prudence. By degrees those who had remained began to exercise their ministry in their own congregations. Seeing that their brethren were not molested, some of those banished to Scotland again returned to their former parishes and resumed their labors. Growing bolder by reason of the indifference of the civil rulers, they began to preach more publicly in barns and other places, administering the sacrament to the people at night, until finally, in 1668, they ventured to build "preaching-houses." Their monthly meetings also were revived. The magistrates, convinced of their loyalty and peaceableness, grew less jealous of them. Their old congregations, observing and admiring their constancy and fidelity during their severe trials, eagerly gathered around them and gladly listened to the gospel. As early as the beginning of the year 1669 the church in Ulster, by almost imperceptible advances, had attained a considerable degree of freedom. Presbyteries were again organized, though, as a precautionary measure, they were held in private houses and without the attendance of ruling elders. Parishes were supplied, as far as possible, with regular preaching, and the ordinances of the gospel were administered publicly to large congregations. New buildings were erected to accommodate the crowds of people who flocked to hear their old pastors, and sessions and presbyteries once more began to exercise discipline on offenders, and finally, with much caution, the presbyteries again ventured to license and ordain candidates for the ministry.

The administration of Lord Robarts, the successor of the duke of Ormond as lord-lieutenant of Ireland, was, on the whole, favorable to the Nonconformists. While a strict Episcopalian himself, he was indisposed to press the statutes passed in the interests of the bishops, and used his influence, moreover, to restrain them in their intolerant measures. The chancellor urged him to suppress the meetings of Nonconformists in Dublin, but he told him that "if they were not papists, and were peaceble and civil, he had no commission to meddle with them." This leniency toward Presbyterians, encouraging them to use the little liberty they had enjoyed under the former administration, joined with his enforcing strict discipline upon the officers of the army and his discountenancing all forms of vice, rendered Lord Robarts' government unpopular with the dominant party, and led to his early return to England.

Even during this period, while the ministers were left to exercise their ministry for the most part without disturbance, they had no permanent security, for their freedom depended on the caprice of the bishops and the use they made of the almost unlimited power committed to them. One of their number, Bishop Leslie, envying the limited liberty and ease which these faithful pastors now enjoyed, imprisoned four of them for a period of six years. Another bishop would have excommunicated twelve of them if he had not been restrained by a letter from the archbishop, who was prevailed upon by Sir Arthur Forbes, an enlightened statesman and a friend of Presbyterians, to interpose and prevent the persecution. This seasonable interposition, at a time when conventicles both in England and Scotland were violently suppressed, was of great service to the Irish Church. It put a check upon the persecuting policy of the bishops and inspired the ministers with confidence and hope. Shortly after this, measures were taken by the lords-justices whereby the four ministers who had been confined for refusing to conform were released, and Ireland for a brief period became a refuge for the more severely oppressed brethren of the sister-kingdoms.

The minor grievances which the Presbyterians still suffered did not seriously impede the revival of religious worship and discipline, so that the Irish Church for several years had a steady growth. Occasional differences which sprung up in its ecclesiastical affairs were speedily settled, and the discreet and loyal conduct of the ministry won the favor of the king. Such representations were made at court of their orderly lives, and of their sufferings on account of poverty, that Charles resolved to give them an expression of his approbation. Sending for Sir Arthur Forbes, their friend and protector, he informed him that it was his wish that *twelve hundred pounds* should be taken from the revenue of Ireland and given to those worthy ministers whose congregations were unable to pro-

vide them a comfortable subsistence. Such was
the destitution of most of them, and so great were
the necessities of the widows and orphans of those
who had been removed by death, that they were
frequently in great straits both for food and clothing. They therefore accepted with grateful feelings the king's contribution to their support. Although the *pension* only amounted to six hundred
pounds\*—and this was not paid regularly—it
proved a timely aid to these ministers, not only relieving their temporal wants, but stimulating them
to greater labors for the spiritual improvement of
their congregations, and to supply destitute places
with the ordinances of religion. They also encouraged the organization of schools and established a seminary of theology at Antrim, and had
the good fortune to secure as the president of the
same the celebrated John Howe, Lord Massareene's
chaplain. For several years he labored in this extended sphere of usefulness, for which he was so
eminently fitted, impressing his large views and
earnest, devoted spirit upon the future ministry
of the Church.

The unfortunate enterprise of the persecuted
Presbyterians of Scotland, which terminated in
the disastrous battle of Bothwell Bridge, June 22,
1679, had an unfavorable effect upon their brethren in Ireland. Ormond, who had again succeed-

---

\* After examination the secretary of the revenue reported
that only six hundred pounds were available for this object.

ed to the office of lord-lieutenant, was alarmed at the news of the insurrection, and took measures to stop all communication between the two kingdoms. Exaggerated reports were spread by their enemies to their prejudice; and though the Presbyterians of Ulster endeavored to remove these unfounded suspicions by presenting an address to Ormond, vindicating themselves from all the aspersions of want of loyalty, yet they only in part allayed his apprehensions. He pressed the oath of supremacy anew, and with great rigor. The soldiers of Lagan, who were mostly Presbyterians, refused to take it, except with certain explanations. These were not admitted. The magistrates believing that they were influenced in their conduct by their ministers, some of the latter were summoned before them and examined, and subsequently brought before the court at Dublin and indicted for holding a fast which was declared illegal. A packed jury of High Churchmen found them guilty, sentenced them to pay a fine of twenty pounds each, and required them to subscribe an engagement not to offend in this way again. Refusing to comply with this, they were imprisoned.

This action of the government encouraged the prelates to renew their persecution of the Nonconformists. The Presbyterian meeting-houses were closed and the public exercise of their worship was interdicted. Penalties for recusancy were inflicted with great severity both upon ministers and people. For the two following years harassing restrictions were continued. A servile compliance with the will of the court was demanded, and to be a friend of civil or religious freedom was sufficient to incur the suspicion and hatred of those in power. So deplorable was the condition of the Presbyterians in the counties of Derry and Donegal in the year 1684 that the greater number of ministers belonging to the presbytery of Lagan intimated to the other presbyteries their intention of removing to America, whither some of them had been already invited. They were brought to this determination "because of persecution and general poverty abounding in those parts, and on account of their straits and little or no access to their ministry." From this purpose they were dissuaded by the death of Charles II. in the following year and the appointment of Lord Granard as one of the lords justices. These events led to a mitigation of the pressing evils under which they then suffered.

At first no very manifest change took place in Irish affairs on the accession of James II. (1685) to the throne. But it was not long before it was clear that a change of policy in favor of Romanists had been resolved upon by the king, and the successive steps taken to effect his designs rendered clear his ultimate purpose to overthrow Protestantism in Ireland. Any doubt on this point has long since been removed by the production of a letter written by the king himself to the Pope, in which he avowed his intention. In the prosecution of this scheme Lord Clarendon was recalled and the notorious Tyrconnel was sworn into office as lord-deputy. His appointment was the most objectionable to the Protestants that possibly could have been made. He was the most obnoxious Romanist in the empire, violent, bigoted, and ready to disregard law and justice when they interfered with the royal projects to establish the papal Church. "Chancellor Porter was dismissed and his office given to Sir Alexander Fitton, who had been convicted and imprisoned for forgery."* Tyrconnel's first step was to remodel the army. Protestant officers were weeded out and their places filled exclusively with Roman Catholics, while priests were advanced to military chaplaincies. Having succeeded in placing the army of the State under the control of Romanists, his next effort was to transfer to the same party the civil authority of the kingdom. Three vacant bishoprics were virtually suppressed and their revenues ordered to be paid into the treasury to create a fund for the ultimate endowment of the Catholic hierarchy. All controversial discourses against the tenets of popery were forbidden. Three irreproachable judges were superseded in the most summary manner, and their places filled with Roman Catholic lawyers. In defiance of the law, Romanists were admitted mem-

* Harris' *Life of William II.*

bers of the privy-council and of corporations, and allowed to act as magistrates and sheriffs without taking the oath prescribed by Parliament. Of the high sheriffs but one was a Protestant, and he owed his appointment to a mistake. The corporate rights of towns and cities were disregarded with impunity. Where intimidation or flattery could not induce them to surrender their charters, these were wrested from them by process of law, the servile judges promptly obeying the wishes of their superiors in authority. Charters were recalled and new corporations formed, and their control vested in the hands of the Romanist party. Strahane. Derry, Newry, Armagh and Belfast were in this way subjected to their power.

The papal clergy were exultant over these changes. Liberal pensions were granted their prelates out of the revenues of the vacant episcopal sees, and in some instances priests appropriated the tithes of the legal incumbents of parishes to their own use. To all Protestants it was a period of gloom and depression, for all these acts of the court were especially detrimental to them. While done under the guise of toleration, their evident design was to give the Roman Catholic party complete ascendency, knowing that as soon as it acquired the necessary power it would use it to the prejudice of Protestantism. The popular feeling, moreover, was continually aggravated by new acts of usurpation in the interest of Rome, so that the very word *toleration* became offensive to those who had labored and prayed for liberty of conscience and worship.

But notwithstanding the insidious designs of James and the illegal nature of his declaration in April, 1687, suspending "the execution of all the penal laws for religious offences and prohibiting the imposition of religious tests as qualifications for office," the Presbyterians were for a time relieved from persecution. Nor did they fail to take advantage of the leniency which they now shared in common with Romanists. Places of worship which had been shut for years were once more opened. Stated meetings of presbytery were publicly held, and ruling elders again took their seats as members. The fears of the Episcopalians for their own Church induced them rather to court the assistance of Nonconformists than to inflict severities upon them.

Thus for a brief period religious freedom was enjoyed. But it rested on a very precarious and unconstitutional basis. It depended upon the illegal declaration of a king obnoxious to and distrusted equally by both Presbyterians and Episcopalians, while it encouraged those whom they had every reason to regard as their common enemy. It was not long before the measures of the court began to work disaster in Ireland. Through the solicitations of Tyrconnel and his agents, some of the nonconformist bodies were prevailed upon to forward addresses to the king, thanking him for the indulgence. The greater part of the Presbyterians, however, felt that the declaration was an unwarrantable exercise of the royal prerogative, and either declined signing such addresses or were careful to qualify their language so as not even by inference to approve of the illegal measure. Though peace was restored, yet there were many things that indicated that it could not be lasting, and that the present calm would soon be followed by a storm. A despotic and bigoted monarch was employing all the means at his command to destroy the constitutional rights of the people, and all of the latter, with the exception of the favored Romanists, were now of one mind in their resistance to arbitrary power. Yet they could do but little more than patiently observe the progress of events.

An incident occurred, December 3, 1688, which roused the Protestants to a sense of their imminent danger and constrained them to resort to active measures for their own protection. An anonymous letter addressed to the earl of Mount-Alexander was found in the streets of Comber, warning him that a general massacre of the Protestants by the Irish was to take place on the following Sunday. Letters of similar purport were addressed to others, and scattered through the neighboring towns. Fearful apprehensions were everywhere excited lest the horrid scenes which took place in 1641 were about to be again witnessed. The intelligence of the expected massacre was quickly conveyed to all parts of the kingdom, and Protestants armed themselves and stood prepared for any emergency. Protestant associations were formed in the several counties, which elected councils of war and a commander-in-chief for each county. A general council of union was appointed, composed of members from all the associations of Ulster. These county councils collected voluntary contributions for their defence and nominated officers to command the organized regiments, and the Presbyterian ministers exerted their influence to induce their people to enrol themselves in the ranks. Fortunately, no massacre was attempted, but the alarm had the good effect to put the Protestants on their guard, and it led them to adopt measures which were of the greatest importance in their bearing upon the interests of the three kingdoms.

While the Nonconformists were adopting these precautions for their own security, Tyrconnel was rapidly strengthening his army by forced levies of Romanists, who subsisted mainly by plundering the defenceless inhabitants. Detachments were sent to seize the principal fortified towns and castles before the Protestants were prepared to offer a successful resistance. Some of them, however, having received timely warning of what was contemplated, closed their gates and refused admission to the king's soldiers. The most important of these were Enniskillen and Derry. The inhabitants of the former, though deserted by their magistrates, resolved to shut their gates against the Romish troops that had been sent by Tyrconnel to occupy their garrison. They were encouraged to take this decisive step by a Presbyterian minister by the name of Kelso, who, like the rest of his brethren, " labored both publicly and privately in animating his hearers to take up arms and stand upon their own defence, showing example himself by wearing arms and marching at the head of them when together."

Derry was a still more important place to hold for the king, and the garrisoning of it was entrusted by Tyrconnel to a regiment composed exclusively of Romanists, under command of a Catholic nobleman, Lord Antrim. On the approach of these troops, the Rev. James Gordon, a Presbyterian minister, advised that they should not be allowed to enter the city. Its bishop, Hopkins, though Puritan in doctrine, was a non-resistant, and strongly opposed the closing of the gates. But Presbyterian zeal could not be restrained. Several young men took forcible possession of the keys and closed the gates against the earl of Antrim's "Redshanks," who were about to enter. In vain did the bishop and the more grave and prudent portion of the citizens urge them to desist from their bold and hazardous enterprise. They were resolute in their purpose, and by this decisive step they saved Derry to the Protestants; and in preserving this important post, an effectual barrier was raised between the victorious armies of the king and the purposed invasion of Scotland. Had a popish garrison occupied the city of Derry, James' soldiers would have had an easy conquest of all Ulster, from whence they would have passed without obstruction into Scotland, to the possible overthrow of the religion and liberties of the three kingdoms.

While these events were taking place in Ireland, the prince of Orange had landed in England. The Presbyterian ministers of Ulster were the first in the kingdom to hail his arrival, and to transmit an address to him congratulating him on his success and beseeching him to take speedy care for *their preservation and relief.* To their petition an answer was returned, addressed to the Protestants in the north of Ireland, approving of their past conduct and promising them effectual support. On the reception of this communication, they proclaimed William king in all the towns subject to their authority, and Ireland now became the grand scene of conflict for the sovereignty of the three kingdoms. Here the power of James was predominant, and here he hoped to regain his throne. But to attempt to give an account of the various battles between the troops of the two contestants for the possession of the country would lead us away from the purpose of this sketch. The superiority in numbers and discipline of Tyrconnel's army enabled him to overrun most of the kingdom, only a few fortified places, which had been seized at the first alarm of the massacre, being held by the Protestants.

Of these, as previously stated, **Derry** was by far the most important, and every preparation was made by their enemies to wrest it from them. King James and his formidable army laid siege to it on the 18th of April, 1689, and continued the investituer for a period of *one hundred and five days*. The siege was closely pressed and the city subjected to frequent bombardments, but it was valorously defended by its brave garrison. By far the larger number of the officers were Episcopalians, while among the soldiers and citizens there were *fifteen* Presbyterians for one Episcopalian. So resolute and successful was their defence that the enemy resorted to an inhuman expedient to secure the surrender of the city. All the Protestants who could be collected within ten miles, men, women and children, were driven under the walls, and ordered to be kept there without shelter, protection or food until the terms of capitulation should be accepted. This barbarous act was of no avail, for the governor of the city erected a gallows on the walls and threatened to hang the Irish prisoners in his possession unless these wretched people were permitted to return to their homes. But the garrison, as well as the inhabitants, were now suffering from scarcity of provisions.* Nearly all their resources of food had been exhausted, such had been the closeness of the blockade maintained by the enemy, and the relief sent to the people from England had failed to reach them by reason of the incompetency or treachery of the commander of the squadron. Although disappointed in their expectations of relief from the fleet from day to day, and with their numbers fearfully reduced by famine and sickness and death, the brave garrison resolved to perish rather than surrender the city. History shows few parallels to the valor and endurance exhibited on this occasion, and rarely have more memorable services been performed in behalf of civil liberty than by the brave and heroic defenders of Derry.† At length, through the urgent representations and remonstrances of the Rev. James Gordon, Major-General

---

* Speaking of the endurance of these brave men, Froude says: "Fever, cholera and famine came to the aid of the besiegers. Rats came to be dainties, and hides and shoe-leather were the ordinary fare. They saw their children pine away and die. They were wasted themselves till they could scarcely handle their firelocks on their ramparts."

† "Now was again witnessed what Calvinism, though its fire was waning, could still do in making common men into heroes. Deserted by the English regiments, betrayed by their own commanders, without stores and half armed, the shopkeepers and apprentices of a commercial town prepared to defend an unfortified city against a disciplined army of twenty-five thousand men, led by trained officers and amply provided with artillery."—*Froude*, vol. i., pp. 81, 82.

Kirk was induced to permit an attempt to be made to relieve the city, and two vessels of the English fleet, the Mountjoy and Phœnix, reached the quay in safety, to the great joy of the famishing garrison. Two days afterward the Irish army abandoned their trenches and raised the siege of the city.

Enniskillen was defended with similar bravery and success. Its stubborn defence compelled James to divide his forces in order to cut off all communication between Derry and the former place, and this division contributed to the security of both. In one of their many severe conflicts with the enemy, and only three days after Derry had been relieved, the Protestants gained a decisive victory over the Irish, routing their army, whose strength was three times that of their own, and killing nearly two thousand men, besides capturing the general and most of the officers. After this signal defeat the several sections of James' army that had been engaged in the sieges of Enniskillen and Derry beat a hasty retreat, plundering and burning everything in their way. Inspirited by this success, the adherents of William employed more vigorous means to drive the enemy out of the country. In this they were aided by the arrival of a formidable armament from England, consisting of ten thousand horse and foot commanded by the duke of Schomberg. Most of the strongholds of the enemy were quickly wrested from him, and James and his Irish forces retired to Dublin.

Although defeated and driven to take shelter in Dublin, the forces of James were still formidable, and he had the promise of large reinforcements from France to assist him to subdue his rebellious subjects. At this juncture King William announced his purpose to repair to Ireland and conduct the war in person. He was received on landing with every possible demonstration of joy and welcome, and one week after his arrival he took the field and conducted his military operations with his characteristic vigor. Within a fortnight the two armies were brought face to face in battle array on the banks of the Boyne. Here, on the first day of July, 1690, was fought that memorable battle the results of which were the total defeat of the Irish army, the flight of James to Dublin, his subsequent retirement to France, and the occupation of the metropolis of Ireland by the troops of King William. Thus was the power of James II. finally overthrown, and in the very quarter where he expected an easy triumph, and the prince of Orange secured in possession of the crown, and the liberties of the empire once more established on a *constitutional basis.* During all these troubles and conflicts the Irish Presbyterians vindicated their claims to the sympathy and gratitude of the English king, as well as the English people.

Episcopal bishops and curates hastened to congratulate King William just as soon as they saw that victory perched upon his banners. Within a day or two after reaching Dublin he was waited upon in his tent by an Episcopalian committee, who, in their address, assured him that during King James' reign in Ireland they had been "guilty of no compliances but such as were the effects of *prudence and self-preservation*," and that they now acknowledged William to be their king and prayed for his prosperity. Such an assurance was certainly needed, for only a few months before, nearly the same persons had presented an address to James in which they declared their "resolution *to continue firm to that loyalty* which the principles of their Church obliged them to, and which, in pursuance of those principles, they had hitherto practiced." Whatever may be thought of the sincerity of their professions to William, they were undoubtedly sincere in the avowal of their principles before King James. They were believers in the doctrine of non-resistance, and were keen to discover whose kingly fortunes were in the ascendant, and their "prudence and self-preservation" led them speedily to range themselves on the side of the victorious monarch. When James' authority dominated in Ireland, they prayed for him and his reputed son, the prince of Wales, and that all his enemies, William included, might be brought into confusion. In the course of a single week, so rapid a change had the sword wrought on the banks of the Boyne that these same clergy were praying, with the same apparent fervor, for William as their lawful king, whom they had so recently denounced as a usurper and his supporters as rebels. As each contestant for the crown obtained the ascendency the prayers of the Established Church had to be changed to suit the new condition of affairs, and thus its clergy in Ulster had been, as stated by one of their own number, "four times in one year praying forward and backward, point-blank contradictory to one another." But all were not so inconsistent or inconstant in principle and conduct. Many were the warm friends and most determined and valiant defenders of constitutional liberty when imperiled by the illegal measures of James. Of these the Rev. Dr. Walker, the celebrated governor of Derry during its siege, was a worthy and noted example.

When King William arrived in Ireland, he received from the commander of his army very favorable accounts of the loyalty of Presbyterians and the support they had given his cause. Their continued fidelity, and their subsequent distinguished services in his behalf, but served to deepen His Majesty's impressions and incline him to return a gracious response to a petition of their clergy for protection and relief. Recognizing their influence both as to numbers and worth, the king proceeded to redress their grievances and vindicate their rights by establishing civil and religious freedom, which was all that was needed from the government to restore prosperity to the Presbyterian Church of Ireland.

During the commotions caused by the war between the rival claimants for the throne, the Presbyterians of Ulster suffered terrible privations and losses. Their clergy were especially obnoxious to the troops of James and his adherents, and were forced to leave the country. **Public** religious worship as a consequence **was very** generally suspended. **Many of their churches** were either pulled down or burned, and their people scattered and impoverished by the interruption of all methods of industry. But the few who remained under the protection of King William labored with great zeal to repair the evils which former persecutions and the war had inflicted upon the Church. **Not**withstanding the many difficulties they encountered from the scarcity of ministers and the poverty of the people, Presbyterians not only held their own in Ulster, but increased in numbers. Though **their** clergy had been prohibited during previous reigns from the public exercise of their ministry, except at brief intervals when the severity of the penal statutes was relaxed, the ordinances **were** secretly administered by them, and their people were gathered in private houses and instructed in the word of God, so that the great body of them adhered steadfastly to their principles. In 1692, as we learn from the best authority, the Presbyterians constituted by far the largest portion of the Protestants in the north of Ireland. "Some parishes," says a dignitary of the Episcopal Church, **"have** not ten, some not six, that come to church, while the Presbyterian meetings are crowded with thousands, covering all the fields." In some regions, he admits, the Episcopal population did not bear a greater proportion to the Presbyterian than *one to fifty*. The sixty congregations of 1661 had increased to one hundred, of which three-fourths had settled pastors.

With the close of the war presbyteries and synods were again held, ministers ordained, houses of worship erected and congregations gathered. Ministers and their people returned from their enforced exile, and the Presbyterian Church once more entered upon a period of peace and prosperity. Nor were the loyalty and friendship which the Presbyterians had exhibited in behalf of King William forgotten by that monarch. Moved by their necessities, and by a wish to express his appreciation of the services rendered by their clergy in the maintenance of constitutional freedom, he authorized the payment to them yearly of *twelve hundred pounds*. This royal grant, known as the REGIUM DONUM, was designed as a testimony, so says His Majesty, to "the peaceable and dutiful temper of our said subjects, and their constant labor to unite the hearts of others in zeal and loyalty toward us," and because we are "sensible of the losses they have sustained."

The extent of these losses, and of the ravages occasioned by the war, may be inferred from the fact that nearly or quite fifty of the Presbyterian ministers of Ireland fled to Scotland, whither they were followed by a large number of their people. So great was the number of Ulster Presbyterians in Glasgow that the meeting-houses sanctioned by law for the use of indulged ministers were inadequate for their accommodation. As a number of the Episcopal churches were unoccupied, and had been closed for months, an application was made to the convention-parliament at Edinburgh to permit these Irish exiles with their ministers to occupy some of these deserted churches. This request was at once granted, and two churches were appropriated to their use, and Rev. Messrs. Craighead and Kennedy were appointed to officiate statedly therein. This they continued to do until their return to Ireland to their own parishes, and with such acceptance that they were earnestly entreated by their brethren in Glasgow to protract their stay in Scotland as long as possible. In a letter to the Irish ministers they say, "We cordially bless the Lord for the help and comfort that we have gotten by their ministry hitherto, and continue to supplicate that if you find it necessary to send any of your number to Ireland, you may spare these two reverend brethren for the present to carry on the great work which is now begun by them." A still more important circumstance was that this large influx of Irish Presbyterians gave occasion to the Scottish estates to take the first practical step toward abolishing the prelatical establishment and setting up the Presbyterian Church in its place. This action probably had a direct and decided influence in inducing many of the Irish ministers to remain in Scotland; for, from the many applications made by congregations to the synod at Belfast for a return of their former ministers, it appears that twenty-five of them settled in Scottish parishes and remained permanently connected with the Church of Scotland.

Presbyterian ministers were left for a period comparatively free to reorganize and build up their Church in Ireland. The laws against dissenters, it is true, were still in force; but owing to the known wishes of the king in favor of toleration, and the impressive lessons of the war enforcing the importance of Protestant unity, the penal statutes were not enforced. The conduct of King James had convinced the Episcopalians of the necessity of forgetting all ecclesiastical differences, and uniting with their Presbyterian brethren for the protection of themselves and their common faith. But scarcely had the impending danger passed by when symptoms of a renewal of the former unfriendly feelings were displayed by the High Church party. Instances of prelatical intolerance again occurred, and the dormant penalties of the law were revived in a few places against Presbyterian clergymen. Such bigotry, however, met with little sympathy. Besides, the Irish government, in accordance with the promises of William to the Presbyterians, protected them in the free exercise of their worship and discipline.

Still, while the laws against dissenters remained unrepealed, there was danger of their revival at any time when it became the interest and policy of the prelates to use the power left in their hands. To relieve Nonconformists from this danger, King William obtained from the English Parliament the abolition of the Irish oath of supremacy, which had been in force since the commencement of the reign of Elizabeth, and had substituted in its place the English oaths of fidelity and allegiance. These the Nonconformists did not object to; and as no sacramental test was in force in Ireland, this English act would have opened all public employments, civil and military, to the Presbyterians. But the liberal policy of the king was opposed by the Irish Parliament, which, after an interval of twenty-six years, met in Dublin. To it was submitted a bill for toleration similar to the one in favor of dissenters in England, but through the paramount influence of the bishops it was defeated, they refusing to give their consent to the legalizing of the public worship of Presbyterians unless the sacramental test was at the same time imposed. To this the king would not assent, and, consequently, Presbyterian worship was continued merely upon sufferance. These *magnanimous prelates*, moreover, wished to impose additional burdens upon those who had freely shed their blood for their common faith, and without whose assistance the Protestant religion would have been overthrown in Ireland. Among other things, these bigots demanded that all Presbyterians holding office should be required to partake of the communion three times each year in an Episcopal church, and that none of their clergymen should preach against the Established Church, under very severe penalties.

The absence of an act of toleration was at this period no great grievance to Presbyterians. Their loyalty was well known, and their recent valuable services in behalf of civil and religious freedom were still so fresh in the remembrance of the government and of the people that public opinion and the favor of the civil magistrates supplied the place of a legislative enactment. To nearly the close of King William's reign the isolated cases of attempted persecution, or of hardship suffered by them, could be readily brought before the agents of the government and prompt justice obtained. The failure of the attempts that were made to molest them in the enjoyment of their religious rights discouraged those who, moved by jealousy in seeing their prosperity and rapid increase in numbers, would have been pleased to obstruct their public ministry. Causes of irritation, however, were not wanting, occasioned by attacks made upon the worship and discipline in use among Presbyterians. One of the most noted of these was by Bishop King, of Derry. This High Church bishop, in 1693, published an anonymous pamphlet entitled *A Discourse Concerning the Inventions of Men in the Worship of God*, which contained very many unworthy insinuations and unfounded charges against Presbyterians. The tractate was written in a spirit of affected friendship for those whom it attacked, and with the design to show that their modes of worship were not only very defective, but were without any warrant from Scripture. The writer claimed to have been moved to his work by his concern " for a well-meaning people so strangely misled as to content themselves to meet together for years with a design to worship God, and yet hardly ever see or hear anything of God's immediate appointment in their meetings." He charged that Presbyterians, as a rule, were very inadequately instructed by their ministers in the principles of religion; that the Bible was rarely read in their religious assemblies; that few of them attended public worship; and that the Lord's Supper was undervalued and neglected, being celebrated only at very distant intervals.

The Rev. Robert Boyse of Dublin, and afterward the Rev. Robert Craighead of Derry, replied to the bishop's accusations, exposing the inaccuracy of his statements and refuting the reasoning based on the false charges. Not content with producing unimpeachable testimony expressly contradicting the bishop's alleged facts relative to the religious ignorance of Presbyterians, their disuse of the Scriptures in divine service and their neglect of the Lord's Supper, they proceeded to discuss the subject of church government, and called in question, in their turn, the divine authority of many of the rites and ceremonies in the Established Church. This opened wide the field of controversy, which continued for many years and called forth many publications.

By the able discussion which these subjects received, Presbyterians were more fully convinced than ever that their simple forms of worship were more in accordance with the word of God than those of the Episcopal Church. This in itself was a good, but the controversy was not without attendant evils. It excited animosities among Protestants when they should have stood shoulder to shoulder in resisting their common enemy. It led the ministers of the Establishment to preach frequently against the sin of schism, and those of the Presbyterian Church to defend their position as nonconformists and make prominent their objections to Episcopacy. Without doubt it embittered the clergy of the Established Church against all dissenters and had a great influence with other bishops, besides King, of Derry, to cause them to resist every measure of toleration which the liberal monarch and his ministry were anxious to grant. They began at this period to exhibit their unfriendly feelings toward the laity as well as the ministry of the Presbyterian Church. In some parts of Ulster the people were not permitted to bury their dead, as formerly, unless an Episcopalian officiated at the funeral and read the burial-service of his Church; in other places they were compelled to hold the office of churchwarden and take certain official oaths which were opposed to their consciences; in some instances they were prohibited from having their families instructed by tutors of their own religious faith, all teachers being required to conform to the Established Church; and strenuous efforts were made to prohibit Presbyterian ministers from celebrating marriages even among their own people.* These efforts to annoy and harass Nonconformists continued through succeeding years, until, on the accession of a Tory ministry in England and the ascendency of the High Church party, a bill was passed requiring "all persons in office, civil, military or ecclesiastical, to take the oath of abjura-

---

* After speaking of the persecutions of nonconformists subsequent to the Restoration, Mr. Froude states "that the full and free equality of privilege which they (nonconformists) had honorably earned, it was William's desire to secure to them by law. But in this he was prevented by the 'Irish Established clergy, the Irish peers and the great landowners, who were ardent High Churchmen,' and who were but a third of the nominal Protestants. In the opposition the bishops took the most prominent part, and were most vindictive and unrelenting."—*Froude*, vol. i., p. 237.

tion." And in 1704 the Irish bishops succeeded in having the sacramental test imposed, by which Presbyterians were deprived of all public offices and places of trust which they then held, and were rendered incapable of ever afterward being appointed to similar offices. Thus was a most flagrant act of injustice finally consummated through the influence of the bishops and the High Church party. To carry their end in Parliament, and to obtain votes for its passage, they promised to pass an act of toleration giving the same *legal security* to the Presbyterian Church in Ireland that was by law allowed Protestant dissenters in England. But all such promises were forgotten when their main object had been obtained, and the Irish Presbyterians were left in a much worse position than their English brethren.

The history of the many endeavors of the Irish Presbyterians to secure a legal toleration, and to have the numerous grievances under which they suffered removed, differs but slightly from what has been already narrated. Their efforts were largely directed to correcting the misrepresentations of their High Church adversaries, and to assuring the court of their loyalty and their desire to lead quiet and peaceable lives as good citizens. Strange as it may appear, they were not unfrequently charged with persecuting members of the Established Church, and with deliberate attempts to infringe upon the rights of its clergy. Easy of refutation as were these baseless accusations, they yet show to what lengths their adversaries were willing to go in order to prejudice them in the estimation of the persons who were in authority in the government. For more than half a century longer the Presbyterians were subjected to many civil disabilities and to unfounded suspicions of a want of loyalty, and in every attempt to secure their rights they were successfully resisted by the adherents of Episcopacy. It was not until 1780 that the Test Act was repealed, and this was followed two years later by an act declaring that marriages solemnized by Presbyterians *were valid in law*. Temporary relief for short periods was enjoyed, as at the accession of George I. to the throne, but the liberal projects of sovereigns and their ministers were in the end thwarted by the bigotry and narrow-minded jealousy of the Irish Established Church, and the indulgence extended at times to dissenters was so curtailed as to be of little use to them. Against all these illiberal influences and these evils of intolerance the Presbyterian Church of Ireland was obliged constantly to contend.

Notwithstanding their many hindrances and hardships, and the various inducements held out to both pastors and people to unite with the Episcopal Church, Presbyterianism during all this period was steadily on the advance in Ireland. New congregations sprang up, houses of worship were erected, vacant congregations were gradually supplied with ministers, principally from the Church of Scotland, and increased facilities for education were afforded young men desirous of preaching the gospel in their native land. The congregations in 1709 had increased to more than *one hundred and thirty*, and it became so inconvenient for their ministers and elders to meet annually in one Assembly, to attend to the business of the Church, that proposals were made to make it a delegate body, and to limit the number of attendants. The five original presbyteries had been divided into two particular synods, and some of the presbyteries, having grown too large for the proper discharge of their duties, were also divided. In this way two new presbyteries were formed out of Tyrone, and one out of that of Lagan.

Much difficulty was now experienced in obtaining an adequate supply of ministers to keep pace with the rapid growth of congregations. This, however, did not lead the Church to lower the standard of qualifications demanded of its ministry. It required that all candidates for licensure should have studied divinity for four years after they had completed their course of philosophy; and to prevent candidates from entering the Church who were not sound in the faith, the synod of 1698 enacted that all persons licensed or ordained should subscribe the Westminster Confession of Faith as their Confession. By these means the ministry of the Presbyterian Church became yearly more respected for its literary and theological attainments, and by these wise and continued efforts most of the congregations enjoyed the services of pious and educated men.

At the same time, the missionary operations of the Church were carried on with vigor and success. To meet the necessities of the scattered and neglected members of its communion, the synod in 1706 established a GENERAL FUND, and appointed a number of persons in each presbytery to solicit subscriptions. With the means thus obtained labor was actively begun among the Irish-speaking population—a class which had been wellnigh neglected since the time of the revered Bishop Bedell. That commendable progress was made in this needed work is seen from the statement, by the synod of 1710, that seven of its ministers and three of its probationers were able to preach in the Irish language, and that a plan had been formed for employing these men in this work and supplying them with Bibles, Confessions of Faith and Catechisms, all in the Irish language. With this missionary fund, to which large additions were made by wealthy members of the Church, the principles of Presbyterianism were much extended and the ordinances of religion provided in many destitute parts of the country.

Though the government and worship of the Presbyterian Church were finally legalized in 1719, its members still endured many privations. Episcopalian landlords possessing large estates refused to permit Presbyterian churches to be built upon them. Others exacted higher rents from Presbyterian than from Episcopalian tenants. By the sacramental test Presbyterians were still excluded from all places of public trust under the Crown. Presbyterian teachers could with difficulty keep open their schools, and private members were subjected to prosecution in the ecclesiastical courts for their marriages by their own clergy.* Is it any wonder they should grow weary of being thus constantly harassed, and should be led to look elsewhere for the relief they sought in vain in their native land, or that there should have been a growing desire among Presbyterians to emigrate to America? When the lord-lieutenant, the duke of Shrewsbury, reached Dublin in 1713, several ministers laid before him a paper in which they stated the evils that both ministers and people yet suffered from the continued imposition of the sacramental test. They stated also how discouraged they were by the fre-

---

* Mr. Froude shows how the bill for the repression of popery in 1704 was used against dissenters by the prelates: "The bishops fell upon the grievance, which had so long afflicted them, of the Presbyterian marriages. Dissenting ministers were unsanctified upstarts, whose pretended ceremonial was but a license for sin. It was announced that the children of Protestants not married in a church should be treated as bastards, and, as the record of this childish insanity declares, 'many persons of undoubted reputation were prosecuted in the bishops' courts as fornicators.'"—*Froude*, vol. i., p. 392.

quent disappointment of their hopes of relief, and assured him that "the melancholy apprehensions of these things have put several of us upon thoughts of transplanting ourselves into America, that we may there in a wilderness enjoy, by the blessing of God, that ease and quiet to our consciences, persons and families which are denied us in our native country." But it was in vain that they petitioned for redress. If, through a change in the office of lord-lieutenant, or in those of lords-justices, the severity of the penal statutes in force against dissenters was not inflicted, the relief was but temporary, and rested mainly upon the pleasure of those in authority, and not on legal enactments. The dissatisfaction felt at this state of affairs naturally increased from year to year, and determined many persons either to return to Scotland or to seek refuge in America. In 1729 the disposition to emigrate received a new impulse. After the Revolution the landed proprietors, anxious for the cultivation of their waste lands, had granted favorable leases, under which the Presbyterian tenantry had been stimulated to improve their holdings and extend their cultivation. But as these leases, usually for thirty-one years, expired, the rents were so raised that the farmers became greatly discouraged, and many were obliged to relinquish their farms and find a home in some other country where they might improve their condition. To add to their discouragement, there was proportionate increase in the demand for tithes, while the three successive harvests after that of 1724 had proved so scanty that the price of food in 1728 far exceeded what it had been in the memory of that generation. Added to all was the disqualification for office created by the SACRAMENTAL TEST. In these circumstances the thoughts of many were turned to the New World, not only as promising a better and a surer reward for their labor and capital, but relief also from the civil and social evils which they had so long endured.

# EMIGRATION OF SCOTCH AND SCOTCH-IRISH TO AMERICA.

## CHAPTER IX.

### EMIGRATION TO AMERICA.

The emigrants to this country from Scotland and Ireland had so many things in common, and they mingled so naturally and constantly wherever they settled, that it is impossible to trace, with any accuracy, the separate streams of emigration. An approximation is all that will be attempted.

During the bloody persecutions which prevailed in Scotland many of her best citizens were banished to America. Some of them were transported as felons because they would not violate their consciences; this was the only crime alleged against them by their accusers. Others fled because they saw no prospect in the future that in their native land they would be permitted to enjoy those modes of worship which they believed most in accordance with God's word; while still others were attracted to the New World by the prospect of improving their temporal affairs, which had been impaired or wholly ruined by the fines and imprisonments to which they had been subjected.

After the disastrous battle of Dunbar (1650), a large number of prisoners were sent to the Plantations, as they were called, to be sold for slaves. A like disposition was made of many who took part in the Pentland rising and the battle of Bothwell Bridge. The oppressed congregations also furnished many colonists, who, denied all religious freedom at home, fled to this country. A large number of these Presbyterians settled, from the years 1670 to 1680, on the Elizabeth River, Virginia, and in the lower counties of Maryland, and established several churches at least twenty years before the close of the century.

Several Scottish noblemen and gentlemen, who had been active in their opposition to the prelatic measures of their sovereign, and so incurred his displeasure, conceived the design of providing a home for their persecuted brethren in America, and in 1682 they contracted with the lords-proprietors of Carolina for a large landed property. In the same State, and previous to the year 1670, "several hundred able-bodied men formed a settlement on the west bank of the Ashley River and named it Charles' Town." * As early as 1662 a company of persons driven from Virginia by religious persecution settled on Albemarle Sound. They supposed they would be protected in their civil and religious rights, but no sooner did the Episcopal Church acquire the necessary prestige and power

* Howe's *History of the Presbyterian Church in South Carolina.*

than dissenters were taxed for its support, and were disfranchised if they failed to conform. Thus were they socially and politically degraded by intolerant laws designed to prop up Episcopacy, and to escape from this injustice they removed to another colony. This settlement and a previous one on Chowan River were visited by Governor Berkley of Virginia in 1663, who appointed William Drummond, a Scotch Presbyterian, the first governor of the colonies settled in North Carolina. At his death (1667) the colonists numbered about five thousand.

The congregations of Marlborough and Bladensburg, Maryland, were composed of Presbyterians who left Scotland during the persecution in the reign of James II. East Jersey subsequently received a considerable emigration, chiefly induced to remove there by George Scot of Pitloche, who had suffered everything short of death for his nonconformity. In his appeal to his countrymen to emigrate he dwelt especially upon the privilege they would have of enjoying their own modes of worship; and this appeal was seconded by letters from their friends who had previously settled in the province. Other companies of Scotchmen found homes in Delaware and along the York and Rappahannock Rivers in Virginia; while, as we have seen, a large number of colonists had entered the southern colonies, landing either at Wilmington or Charleston. Those who remained in Charleston united with Congregationalists from New England, who were already settled there, in forming an Independent church, but the pastors for many years belonged to the Church of Scotland. This church was gathered probably as early as 1682. In 1695 we know that a gift of one thousand pounds was made to it by Governor Joseph Blake. The French Huguenot church was established in 1686, and was the first purely Presbyterian church in South Carolina. Other churches were formed within a few years. A letter from South Carolina published in London (1710) states that there were at this time five Presbyterian churches in the colony, and the records show that a donation of three hundred acres of land was made in 1717 for the support of a Presbyterian minister on Edisto Island.

North Carolina was also largely indebted to these early Scotch colonists for many of her most useful and honored citizens. As early as 1729, and again in 1736 and 1739, there were large arrivals of emigrants, who occupied the fertile plains along the Cape Fear River. The rebellion of 1745 caused many Highlanders to leave their native land. Shiploads of them are said to have landed at Wilmington, and from thence they made their way into the interior of North and South Carolina. Some of these were voluntary exiles, but the most of them had fled from Scotland to avoid persecution, and even death itself. For many years the Gaelic language was retained among them, and was employed by their preachers in all public services.

As early as 1698 a colony of French Presbyterians (Huguenots), numbering more than one thousand persons, settled upon the Santee and Cooper Rivers, South Carolina. The emigration of Huguenots continued for many years, and various colonies were formed in the State. From these have descended some of the most worthy citizens in the South. Previous to the year 1700 seventy families of Swiss Presbyterians landed in the same State, and being largely mechanics and merchants made their permanent residence in Charleston.

Though the emigration from Scotland began at an earlier period than that from the north of Ireland, it never assumed the magnitude nor the organized form of the latter, especially from the years 1715 to 1750. During these years America received very large accessions to its Protestant population, most of whom were Scotch-Irish, and in hearty sympathy with the Presbyterian Church. So great were the numbers from Ireland who sought refuge in this country that the civil magistrates "deplored the hallucination" which seemed to have seized the inhabitants, and which led them in such multitudes to forsake their adopted land.

There were three causes impelling the inhabitants of Ulster to desert a country which they had reclaimed from barbarism. These were religious bigotry, commercial jealousy and the oppressive measures employed by landlords.

Of the first little requires to be said in this connection. In the course of the previous history we have seen what evils were inflicted upon nonconformists by an intolerant government, instigated by still more intolerant bishops. It may be well, however, to add here, and more in confirmation of previous statements than by way of elucidation, what Mr. Froude\* has said on this subject: "The Protestant settlers in Ireland at the beginning of the seventeenth century were of the same metal with those who afterward sailed in the Mayflower —Presbyterians, Puritans, Independents—in search of a wider breathing-space than was allowed them at home. By an unhappy perversity they had fallen under the same stigma, and were exposed to the same inconveniences. The bishops had chafed them with persecutions. . . . The heroism with which the Scots held the northern province against the Kilkenny Parliament and Owen Roe O'Neil, was an insufficient offset against the sin of nonconformity. . . . This was a stain for which no excellence could atone. The persecutions were renewed, but did not cool Presbyterian loyalty. When the native race made their last effort under James II. to recover their lands, the Calvinists of Derry won immortal honor for themselves, and

---

\* As Mr. Froude was educated for the ministry of the Established Church of England, though not now in orders, it is probable that as an Englishman and a churchman he would not speak with undue severity, not to say injustice, of any matter where Ireland and dissenters were concerned.

flung over the wretched annals of their adopted country a solitary gleam of true glory. Even this passed for nothing. They were still dissenters, still unconscious that they owed obedience to the hybrid successors of St. Patrick, the prelates of the Establishment; and no sooner was peace re-established than spleen and bigotry were again at their old work. Vexed with suits in the ecclesiastical courts, forbidden to educate their children in their own faith, treated as dangerous to a State which but for them would have had no existence, and deprived of their civil rights, the most earnest of them at length abandoned the unthankful service. . . . If they intended to live as freemen, speaking no lies and professing openly the creed of the Reformation, they must seek a country where *the long arm of prelacy was still too short to reach them*. During the first half of the eighteenth century, Down, Antrim, Tyrone, Armagh and Derry were emptied of Protestant inhabitants, who were of more value to Ireland than California gold-mines." *

Another cause for the large emigration from Ireland was the repressive measures adopted by the English government toward commerce and agriculture. At first these industries were fostered by the mother-country, and the encouragement given, particularly to the culture of flax, so increased the linen trade that there was danger of Ireland con-

* Froude, vol. i., pp. 129, 130.

trolling the market. When this became apparent, England repented of the magnanimity shown to Ireland's most flourishing branch of industry, and began at once "to invade the compact," and by indirect yet effectual means to steal away the trade from her colonists in favor of her own people.

A similar course was pursued with respect to agriculture. The prices at which the Irish farmers could afford to put their crops into market excited the fears of their English competitors, and so restrictions were put on the production, in order that English land should not be depreciated in value. "Her salt meat and butter were laid under an embargo when England went to war that the English fleets and armies might be victualed cheaply at the expense of Irish farmers." By such means a large portion of the people were remanded back to poverty and its attendant evils, and were rendered hostile to the oppressive government; and such of them as had property resolved to seek a home where they could escape from all these unnatural and unjust discriminations.

But the arbitrary treatment of tenants by their landlords had much to do in swelling the tide of emigration. At the time when the six counties of Ireland were escheated to the Crown, and a portion of the land placed in charge of Scotch colonists, agriculture was in a low state. Such was the character of the former inhabitants, and the unsettled condition of the country, that the proper culture of the soil was wellnigh impossible. A miserable peasantry dragged out a wretched existence. Great changes, however, rapidly took place with the introduction of a more frugal and industrious class of farmers. Lands were cleared and improved in productiveness through a better system of **farming.** Mud hovels and wattled huts gave place to commodious homesteads, and the entire country showed evidence of increasing **thrift and comfort.** By the time the tenants' leases had expired, the lands cultivated by them had **largely** increased in value.

This excited the cupidity of the landlords. Unwilling to share the benefits with the farmers, and only to raise their rents in a moderate degree, they extorted from them all they possibly could, irrespective of their improvements and what the tenants had done to make the property valuable. Instead of an effort to reach an arrangement which would have been just to both parties, the landlords, as soon as the leases expired, invited proposals in writing for the leasing of their lands. **This was an** invitation to every covetous and malicious person to bid for the possession of his neighbor's improvements. Catholics stood ready to bid more than their value, and to promise anything in the way of rent, in order to recover their hold upon the soil. Thus the stupid selfishness of the landlords expelled their Protestant tenantry by letting the land over

18

their heads to Romanists, and at once a whole countryside were driven from their habitations.

As the landlords were sustained in this oppression by the House of Commons, the Protestants had no hope of redress, and therefore hastened to leave a country in which they had been so cruelly dealt with. "In the two years," says Froude, "which followed the Antrim evictions, *thirty thousand Protestants left Ulster* for a land where there was no legal robbery, and where those who sowed the seed could reap the harvest.... The south and west were caught by the same movement, and ships could not be found to carry the crowds who were eager to go."

Similar testimony is borne by many other writers to the unprecedented exodus of the Protestants of Ireland, induced by the causes which have been described. Early in the year 1718 a minister in Ulster wrote to a friend in Scotland, "There is like to be a great desolation in the northern parts of this kingdom by the removal of several of our brethren to the American plantations. Not less than six ministers have demitted their congregations, and great numbers of their people go with them; so that we are daily alarmed with both ministers and people going off."

The tide of emigration was somewhat checked for a brief period by the passage of the Toleration Act, and by further promises of relief. It, however, began anew in 1728, ten years later, as appears from a statement which Archbishop Boulter sent to the English Secretary of State, and which he calls a "melancholy account" of the condition of the north, and of the extensive emigration which was taking place to America: "We have had for several years some agents from the colonies in America, and several masters of ships, that have gone about the country and deluded the people with stories of great plenty and estates to be had for going for in those parts of the world; and they have been the better able to seduce people by reason of the necessities of the poor of late." He proceeds to assign reasons why the people desire to leave the country, and then adds: "But whatever occasions their going, it is certain that above four thousand two hundred men, women and children have been shipped off from hence for the West Indies within three years, and of these about thirty-one hundred this last summer. . . . The whole north is in a ferment at present, and people every day engaging one another to go. The humor has spread like a contagious distemper, and the people will hardly hear anybody that tries to cure them of their madness. The worst is that it affects only Protestants and reigns chiefly in the north." In a private letter the following year the bishop states that "the humor of going to America still continues. There are now seven ships at Belfast that are carrying off about one thousand passengers thither."

James Logan, who at this period was president of the Proprietary Council of Pennsylvania and identified with the Quakers, and who was unfriendly to the emigrants arriving from Ireland, states that it is " the common fear that if they [the Scotch-Irish] continue to come, they will make themselves proprietors of the province." He further, in 1729, expresses " himself glad to find that the Parliament is about to take measures to prevent their too free emigration to this country. It looks as if Ireland is to send all her inhabitants thither; for last week not less than six ships arrived, and every day two or three arrive also." Another authority states that in 1729 " there arrived in Pennsylvania from Europe six thousand two hundred and eight persons, and of these more than five thousand were from Ireland." Dr. Baird, in his *History of Religion in America*, states that " from 1729 to 1750 about twelve thousand annually came from Ulster to America."

These emigrants entered the country mainly at the ports of Boston, Philadelphia and Charleston. Those landing at Boston settled chiefly in Maine, New Hampshire and Massachusetts. Previous to this period, and, in fact, from the first settlement of New England, a large number of Presbyterians had found homes in its several colonies. Cotton Mather tells us " that previous to the year 1640 four thousand Presbyterians had arrived." Writing a few years later, he says: " We are comforted with great numbers of the oppressed brethren coming from the north of Ireland. The glorious providence of God, in the removal of so many of a desirable character from the north of Ireland, hath doubtless very great intentions in it." Others estimate the number of Presbyterian colonists in **New** England as **high as** twenty-two thousand. These it is difficult **to** designate, **as** they united largely with Congregationalists in public worship, on the terms of union that had been agreed upon in London prior to 1640; which union Mather states " existed between these parties almost from the first settlement of the **country."** The evidence of this **union** and **the influence of** this Presbyterian element are seen in the fact that the early churches **of** Salem, Charleston, Boston and elsewhere in New England had ruling elders, while **in 1640 and in 1680** respectively all the ministers and elders from each church met in **synod** at Cambridge, and **by** distinct act recognized the Presbyterian form **of** church government.

Nor need there **be** any surprise expressed at the synod's action, for, independent of the leavening influence of Presbyterianism upon the churches, the form of order of the **church** of Leyden, the mother-church of the Plymouth colony, was the same as that of the French Presbyterian churches. Plymouth **was** modeled after Leyden, and the constitution of the Plymouth church was copied by all the other churches.

Presbyterians, in comparatively limited numbers, also settled in New England at the period when the largest emigration took place from Ireland. In 1719, Derry was settled, and subsequently congregations were organized at Pelham and Boston, Massachusetts, and a presbytery was formed in 1745, and a synod, consisting of three presbyteries, in 1775 at Seabrook. Presbyterianism, however, never acquired much strength, owing probably to the plan of union, and many of the Presbyterian settlers subsequently found their way into Pennsylvania, and helped to swell the tide which was pouring into that State through the port of Philadelphia.

These immigrants first occupied the eastern and middle counties of Pennsylvania and the adjoining regions of Delaware and Maryland. Such as landed at more southern ports located themselves on the fertile lands of North and South Carolina and Georgia, and were afterward joined by large numbers of their brethren who had originally settled in the more northern provinces. Owing to the rapid increase of emigration and the occupancy of the best farming-lands in central Pennsylvania, many of the Scotch-Irish in the latter State were led to turn their steps southward, and found homes for their families in the fertile valleys of Virginia. At a later period western Pennsylvania was occupied by the descendants of the settlers in the middle counties of the State, and those of the more southern colonies passed westward to the country then called " between the mountains," now known as Kentucky and Tennessee. From these points of radiation the Scotch-Irish have extended to all parts of the Union, and being an intelligent, resolute and energetic people have left their impress upon the institutions of all the States where they have settled.

Referring to this great exodus from the north of Ireland, the Rev. Dr. Foote, the historian of Virginia and North Carolina, says: " In the early part of the eighteenth century the emigration began, and, like the mighty rivers in the New World, went on in a widening and deepening current to pour into the vast forests of America multitudes of hardy, enterprising people. All the colonies from New York southward were enriched by shiploads of these people, that came with little money, but with strong hands and stout hearts and divine principles, to improve their own condition and bless the province that gave them a home." Many of these voluntary exiles landed at Philadelphia, and after a short stay with their friends and countrymen in Pennsylvania, removed to the inviting valley of Virginia, or the more distant banks of the Catawba in the Carolinas. It thus came to pass that "in the southern part of the valley of Virginia and in the Mesopotamia* of North Carolina and large districts of South Carolina, the Scotch-

* The country between the Catawba and Yadkin Rivers.

Irish had the pre-eminence both in time and numbers."

With very rare exceptions, these colonists were Protestants, and were either communicants in the Presbyterian Church or strongly attached to its doctrines and polity. Families generally united in forming settlements, fixing their residences sufficiently near each other to furnish mutual help and protection from the savage foes who lurked in the surrounding forests, to gratify their social feelings, and to enjoy the privileges of religious worship. Wherever they formed a settlement, among the first things they did, after providing a shelter for their families, was to organize congregations for Christian worship and erect a tabernacle to the Lord. This being their custom, we are not surprised to learn that in a decade from the time that these pioneer emigrants ventured into the valley of Virginia, there were at least twelve Presbyterian congregations organized. In answer to their earnest appeal, the synod of the Presbyterian Church appointed two of its members to visit them and to secure for them the favor of the governor, in order that they might enjoy their own methods of worship. And about the same period Samuel Blair, writing respecting a particular congregation, adds, "All our congregations in Pennsylvania, except two or three, chiefly are made up of people from that kingdom" (Ireland).

We have dwelt thus particularly upon the

extensive emigration from the north of Ireland because of the influence which it exerted on the Presbyterian Church of this country. It gave a sudden impulse to its growth. As we have seen, the emigration was so general that frequently, when pastors sought relief from the hindrances to which their ministry was subjected, they were accompanied to the New World by nearly their entire congregations, or were afterward joined by them in their voluntary exile. Thus they brought with them the framework of Christian institutions, ready to be set up on landing on these Western shores, and these emigrants gave bone and muscle to the religious body, the Presbyterian Church, of which they became at once members.

As was most natural, when these colonists, together with their ministers, came to organize the churches, they adopted the same system of church order and government with which they were familiar at home, and to which they were so strongly attached. All the essential elements of presbytery, parity of the clergy, the office of ruling elders, with their clearly defined duties, and the province and obligations of the "kirk session," from whose decisions an appeal could be taken to the higher court, were principles of church government well known to them. When Presbyterianism had extended over a wide extent of territory, and questions of common interest and importance had to be considered and decided, the formation of synods, and finally of a General Assembly, naturally and necessarily followed.

The mode of worship in use in Scotland and Ireland was also introduced wherever churches were formed, great care being taken in defining the limits of each congregation or parish. The Bible and the catechism held an honored place in the instruction of youth in their schools and in their families. On the Sabbath all the members of the household were regularly assembled, and parents, children and servants recited the catechism. This was followed by explanations of the precepts and doctrines contained therein, and finally the duty of obedience was enforced by showing that its doctrines were derived from the Scriptures and conformed strictly to their teachings.

A portion of the congregation was assigned to each elder, whose duty it was to look after the spiritual interests of the people in that particular field. The pastor, accompanied with one or more of his elders, was accustomed to meet his people frequently, either at a private house or in some other convenient place, in different parts of the congregation, to hear them recite the catechism, and to address to them words of Christian counsel and admonition. In this way, and largely through the fidelity of the eldership, impressions made by the preaching on the Sabbath were rendered permanent and fruitful. As a consequence, also, of this method of instruction, the members of the several churches were intelligent Christians, well grounded in the Scriptures, not tossed about by every wind of doctrine, and able to give a reason for the hope that was in them.

During the early history of Presbyterianism in this country, it was common for presbyteries to appoint committees to visit congregations, who were to question the pastor as to how fully and conscientiously he had discharged all his duties to his flock; how the elders had met the responsibilities of their office; and how his people had attended upon the preached word and the ordinances of the Church; and whether they had fulfilled to him the pecuniary obligations they had voluntarily assumed. Very similar questions were asked separately of each of these parties, and all complaints and causes of dissatisfaction were investigated, and, if possible, amicably arranged.

Twice a year the Lord's Supper was celebrated. Previous to it a day of fasting was observed, and appropriate sermons were preached on the three days preceding the Sabbath, by the pastor or neighboring ministers. Members of adjacent congregations generally attended in large numbers. On these occasions the preaching was often in the open air, as the congregations were too large to be accommodated in the church. These seasons were anticipated with much interest, and were frequently accompanied with wonderful manifestations of the presence and power of the Holy Spirit. The emblems were spread upon long tables, which extended oftentimes through all the aisles of the church from the pulpit to the doors. At these tables the communicants were seated, none being admitted to this privilege unless they had previously received tokens* from their pastor or the session. To them the "Lord's Supper was in its fullest sense a monument of the great facts of redemption, a memorial of the necessity of atonement, the glorious deity of the Son of God, the freeness of justification and the fullness of the promises. The mode in which it was administered rendered it necessary that the highest truths, the loftiest themes, should be preached, and with unction. Those were golden days, when the preacher spoke in the demonstration of the Spirit and with power, and when souls were enlightened by the knowledge of the grace of Christ."

So large an emigration, and of such a character, as flowed into the Middle and Southern States for nearly half a century, could not fail to exert a powerful and lasting influence upon the Presbyterianism of this country. For the most part, these colonists had been tillers of the soil in their native lands, and on their arrival on our shores went immediately to work to make homes for their families upon

---

* The tokens were small pieces of lead or spelter, and usually had the initial letter of the church stamped upon them. They were carried by communicants to neighboring churches when they desired to commune.

the fertile lands, which only needed the wise and persistent labors of these sons of toil to cause them to yield abundant harvests. They did not come as criminals fleeing from justice, or paupers to fasten themselves for support upon the industries of the country, but with money enough—the result of their previous energy and thrift—to purchase the choicest of the lands. As a consequence, prosperity attended their well-directed endeavors; plenty ere long smiled around their happy households; churches and schools at once took their proper places and flourished in all their settlements; and society received an impress which it retains to the present day.

# FOREIGN MINISTERS OF THE PRESBYTERIAN CHURCH IN AMERICA, 1681–1758.

## CHAPTER X.

### Foreign Ministers in America.

Much the largest proportion of the early Presbyterian ministers in this country were from the Irish Church. They, however, were originally either natives of Scotland or descendants of those who had removed to Ireland, and, with few exceptions, were educated in Scotland. Webster states that nearly two-thirds of the ministers of the Presbyterian Church in America, previous to 1738, were graduates of Glasgow University. It is now impossible, from accessible records, to determine the nationality of all these ministers, so intimate was the intercourse between Scotland and the north of Ireland, and so constant were the accessions from both these churches to the ministry in this country. We shall, therefore, not attempt this distinction, but content ourselves with giving, in the limited space at our command, the names of the clergymen, the time of their arrival in America, the places of their ministry, and, in some few instances, the character and results of their labors. Even this bare recital we believe will be sufficient to secure the conviction of the importance of the services they rendered not only to Presbyterianism, but likewise to civil and religious liberty, in the land of their adoption.

Francis Makemie, to whom the honor has been ascribed[*] of laying the foundations of the Presbyterian Church in this country, was born in the county of Donegal, Ireland, educated in a Scotch university, and licensed in 1681 by the Presbytery of Lagan. An application from Maryland for a minister to settle in that colony led the Presbytery to ordain him as an evangelist for America. Arriving in this country, by way of Barbadoes, either in 1682 or 1683, he organized a church at Snow Hill, Maryland, in 1684, which was, so far as now known, the first regularly organized Presbyterian church in America. The Eastern Shore of Maryland and the adjacent counties of Virginia continued to be his principal field of labor, though he extended his journeys at times as far south as the Carolinas. Over all this region he performed with great fidelity the duties of a primitive bishop, organizing a number of churches

---

[*] "Rev. Richard Denton, a graduate of the University of Cambridge, had charge of the Presbyterian church at Hempstead, Long Island, from 1644 to 1658, when he returned to England."—*Rev. P. D. Oakley, in the "New York Observer."*

If this statement can be fully established—and the evidence adduced is very strong—then must Rev. Mr. Denton be regarded as the first regular Presbyterian minister in this country.

and supplying them, so far as he could, with preaching. Feeling the need of help, he opened correspondence with Boston and London in order to obtain aid for destitute places, and made two journeys to England, returning in 1705 with two ministerial brethren. In 1705 or 1706 he assisted in forming the first presbytery, that of Philadelphia, consisting of seven ministers; and afterward continued until his death (1708) actively and usefully engaged in missionary-tours among the destitute settlers, in gathering congregations and furnishing them with competent ministers, thus exerting an extensive influence in behalf of Presbyterianism in the entire region. He is represented as "indefatigable in effort, clear-sighted and sagacious in his views, fearless in the discharge of duty, a man of eminent piety and of strong intellectual powers."

Samuel Davis was the next minister, in point of time, to Makemie. He preached at Lewes, Delaware, and afterward at Snow Hill, Maryland, and was moderator of Philadelphia presbytery in 1709. John Frazer and Archibald Riddel came to America 1685; the former preached at Woodbury, Connecticut, the latter at Woodbridge, New Jersey. David Simpson and John Wilson arrived 1686, and the latter was settled at New Castle, Delaware. George MacNish accompanied Makemie on his return from England in 1705, and labored at Monokin and Wicomico, Maryland, settling at Jamaica, Long Island, where he was instrumental in forming, 1717, the Presbytery of Long Island. John Hampton, the other associate of Makemie in labor and in imprisonment by Lord Cornbury for preaching without a license, was pastor at Snow Hill, Maryland.

Josias Mackie labored for nearly a quarter of a century in Virginia; John Boyd, 1706, pastor at Freehold and Middletown; James Anderson, 1709, pastor at New Castle, Delaware, and then in New York city; John Henry, 1709, was the successor of Makemie; George Gillespie, 1712, pastor first at Woodbridge, New Jersey, and then at White Clay Creek, Delaware; Robert Lawson, 1713; Robert Witherspoon, 1714, labored in Delaware; John Bradner, 1714, pastor at Cape May, New Jersey, and Goshen, New York; Hugh Conn, 1715, pastor at Patapsco and Bladensburg, Maryland; Samuel Gelston, 1715, labored at Kent, Delaware, in Virginia, and as pastor at South Hampton, Long Island; John Thomson, 1715, preached at Lewes, Delaware, Middle Octorara and Chestnut Level, Pennsylvania, and removed in 1744 to Virginia; he took a prominent part at the division of the synod, being the originator of the overture which resulted in the adopting act. His *Explication of the Shorter Catechism,*[*] his treatise on the *Government of the Church* and his sermons on *Conviction and Assurance* are pro-

---

[*] The only known copy is in the possession of Rev. B. M. Smith, professor in Hampden-Sidney College, Va.

nounced to be as "able, learned, judicious and evangelical as any of the writings of Dickinson and Blair."

William Tennent, 1716, was orginally a deacon in the Established Church of Ireland; he left it on account of conscientious scruples, and coming to America was received by the presbytery of Philadelphia. First settled at East Chester, New York, then at Bensalem and Smithfield, Pennsylvania, and in 1726 at Neshaminy. Here he established the celebrated "Log College," and made it his great lifework to educate young men for the Presbyterian ministry. In it some of the very best men of the Church were educated—men eminent alike for learning and piety. He was a warm personal friend and admirer of Whitefield, and a zealous promoter of revivals.

Robert Cross, 1717, pastor at New Castle, Delaware, and colleague pastor to Jedediah Andrews in Philadelphia, where he was the leader of the Old Side party and author of the protest that divided the synod. James Macgregor, 1719, came to Boston with one hundred families who had been connected with his church in Ireland. These settled near Haverhill, calling the place Londonderry, and electing Mr. Macgregor as their pastor. Many regard this as the first Presbyterian church in New England, and it grew rapidly under his able ministry. Though but a youth at the time, he was among the brave defenders of Londonderry, Ireland, and discharged from the tower of the cathedral the large gun which announced the approach of the relief vessels. Robert Laing, 1722, supplied Snow Hill, Maryland, and Brandywine and White Clay Creek, Delaware; Alexander Hutcheson, 1722, supply at Drawers, Delaware, and pastor of Bohemia Manor and Broad Creek churches, Maryland; Thomas Craighead, 1723, pastor of White Clay Creek, Delaware, then at Pequa and Big Spring, Pennsylvania; Joseph Houston, 1724, preached first at New London, Connecticut, then pastor of a church on Elk River, Maryland, and finally pastor at Walkill, New York; Adam Boyd, 1725, pastor of Octorara and Pequa churches, Pennsylvania, where he labored for forty-four years.

Gilbert Tennent came with his father to this country in 1716, and was installed pastor at New Brunswick, New Jersey, 1726, where he remained sixteen years. He accompanied Whitefield in 1740 on a preaching-tour to Boston, which they extended as far north as New Hampshire and Maine, and which was attended with great religious interest. He accepted a call to a new congregation in Philadelphia that had been formed of Mr. Whitefield's admirers in 1743, where he passed the residue of his life, twenty years, endeared to all by reason of his loving and compassionate nature. Few equaled him as a preacher. John Tennent, the third son of William Tennent, Sr., was licensed 1729, and ordained pastor of the church of Freehold, New Jersey, 1730, where he passed his brief ministry of three and one-half years, eminently successful in winning souls to Christ. John Moorhead, 1729, came to Boston, where he had charge for forty-four years of the "Church of Presbyterian Strangers," and where his labors were attended with great success; James Campbell, 1730, labored in Pennsylvania and North Carolina; John Cross, 1732, minister at Baskinridge, New Jersey, was a great promoter of revivals; and John Campbell, 1734, labored in Pennsylvania.

William Tennent was installed pastor of his brother's congregation at Freehold, New Jersey, where he remained until his death, 1777, occasionally making preaching-tours into Maryland, Virginia and New York. His ministry was attended with frequent revivals, and resulted in the establishment of a number of churches. He was an earnest and active patriot, and zealous in resisting the aggressions of the enemy.

Samuel Blair, 1733, accepted a call to Middleton, New Jersey, where he remained until 1739, and then removed to Fagg's Manor, Pennsylvania. Here he established a celebrated classical school. He was distinguished as a preacher for solemnity and impressiveness. President Davies refers to him "as the incomparable Blair," and stated that in his travels in England he had not heard his superior. His published writings were seven sermons, three of them on *Justification*, a *Vindication of the Excluded Brethren*, an answer to John Thomson on the *Government of the Church*, and to Alexander Craighead's *Reasons for Forsaking our Church*, also a *Treatise on Predestination*.

Alexander Craighead, 1734, pastor of Middle Octorara, from whence he removed to Virginia, 1749, and then to North Carolina, where he passed the remainder of his days in the active duties of the ministry; was an earnest, fervid preacher and a zealous promoter of revivals. His ardent love of personal liberty, and his advanced views on civil government and religious liberty, made him obnoxious to the civil governors of Pennsylvania and Virginia, and led to his removal to North Carolina, where he became an "apostle of liberty,"* to whom "the people of Mecklenburg county are indebted for that training which placed them in the forefront of American patriots and heroes."

Francis Alison, 1735, was pastor of New London, Pennsylvania, for fifteen years, where he established a classical school, which in 1744 was taken under the care of synod. He removed to Philadelphia in 1752, where he took charge of an academy, which in 1755 was erected into a college, of which he was vice-provost and professor of moral philosophy. He had the reputation of being the best scholar then in America; acted at the same time

* Rev Dr. Miller of Charlotte.

as assistant pastor of the First church, and had great influence in all the judicatories of the Presbyterian Church. John Elder, 1736, was installed pastor of Paxton and Derry churches, Pennsylvania, 1738, where he continued for more than half a century, sharing with his people the hardships and exposures of their frontier-life. He superintended the military discipline of his people, and acted as their captain in their warfare with surrounding savage foes. His ability and experience in this frontier warfare led to his receiving a commission as colonel in the colonial service, and to his being placed in command of the blockhouses and stockades from the Susquehanna to Easton; he was respected and beloved by his congregations, and very useful as a minister.

John Craig, 1737, labored first in Maryland, and then in Western Virginia. He was installed pastor of the congregations of Augusta and Tinkling Spring, and was the first Presbyterian minister settled in Virginia. His congregations extended over a territory thirty miles long by nearly twenty broad, and suffered greatly in the French-and-Indian war. By precept and example he encouraged his people to resist their enemies, which they did successfully, and from these congregations went forth many hardy soldiers to fight in the various Indian wars and in that of the Revolution. His memory is held in the highest veneration by the descendants of those to whom he preached for thirty-four years.

Charles Beatty came to this country in 1729, and was installed, 1743, pastor at Neshaminy, as successor of Mr. Tennent, where his entire ministry was spent. His services as a missionary to visit the frontier settlements and to ascertain the condition of the Indian tribes, and also in connection with the fund for the relief of destitute ministers, were of the most important character. He was an active patriot, and served as chaplain of the provincial forces raised to defend the frontier.

John Blair, brother of Samuel Blair, was settled, 1742–1748, as pastor in Pennsylvania, during which period he made two visits to Virginia, preaching with great power in various places and organizing several churches. His next pastorate was Fagg's Manor, Pennsylvania, from whence he was called to the professorship of divinity at Nassau Hall, in connection with the duties of vice-president of the college, and served as president until Dr. Witherspoon's arrival. His last pastoral charge was at Walkill, New York. He was a judicious and persuasive preacher, and eminently successful in the conversion of the impenitent. He published several works.

Samuel Finley, D. D., was pastor of the church at Nottingham, Maryland, for seventeen years, where he founded an academy to prepare young men for the ministry, which acquired a great reputation. He was an accomplished scholar and teacher. At the death of President Davies, of Nassau Hall, he was chosen his successor, and his administration proved of great advantage to the college. He was a distinguished pulpit orator. His learning was extensive, every branch of study taught in the college being familiar to him. The degree of doctor of divinity was conferred on him by the University of Glasgow. John Roan was licensed, 1744, and sent on a missionary-tour to Virginia, where great numbers were converted under his preaching. Returning to Pennsylvania in 1745, he was settled over the united congregations of Paxton, Derry and Mount Joy, where he remained until his death, 1775, proving an able, courageous and faithful minister of the gospel.

Robert Smith, D. D., was licensed, 1749, and settled over the churches in Pequa and Leacock, Pennsylvania. Here he opened a classical school, which was attended by a large number of young men, many of whom became distinguished in the ministry and in the professions; he was moderator of the Assembly, and highly esteemed as an able, faithful pastor. Three of his sons entered the ministry: Dr. Samuel Stanhope Smith, President of Nassau Hall; Dr. John Blair Smith, president of Hampden-Sidney, and afterward of Union, College; and Dr. William Ramsey Smith, pastor of the Second Presbyterian church, Wilmington, Delaware.

Other ministers who came from abroad and aided in establishing Presbyterianism in this country, to whose labors we cannot refer, were: Robert Orr, 1715; Henry Hook and Samuel Young, 1718; Archibald McCook and Hugh Stevenson, 1726; John Williamson, William Orr and David Sankey, 1730; William Bertram, 1732; Benjamin Campbell, 1733; Samuel Hemphill, James Martin and Robert Jamison, 1734; Hugh Carlisle and Samuel Black, 1735; John Paul, 1736; Charles Tennent, 1737; David Alexander, 1738; Samuel Caven, David Megregor and Francis McHenry, 1739; Alexander McDowell and James McCrea, 1741; John Steel, 1744; Andrew Bay, 1747; Samson Smith and Samuel Kennedy, 1750: Robert Smith, 1751; James Finley, 1752; John Kinkead and James Brown, 1753; Hugh Knox, 1755; and Henry Patillo, 1757, an author, and a patriarch in the churches of North Carolina.

In the above enumeration we have confined ourselves to those clergymen from Scotland and Ireland who entered the ministry of the Presbyterian Church in this country previous to the union of the synods in 1758. This was the period when the largest emigration took place, and the formative period of Presbyterianism in America. If we would give proper weight to this influence, we must bear in mind that at the union of the two synods of New York and Philadelphia, in 1758, there were but *ninety-four* ministers connected with the Presbyterian Church in this country, and of this number *forty* had come either from Ireland or Scotland. From the origin of the Church, at least *ninety ministers of foreign birth* had helped to plant Presbyterianism in the New World and aided in its subsequent growth. At the union of the synods more than half of these clergymen had ceased from their labors, their places, however, being largely supplied by their sons, who had been trained for the ministry in the humble yet efficient educational institutions of the Church. The indebtedness of the Presbyterian Church in America, therefore, to the churches of Ireland and Scotland can scarcely be overestimated; and this is as true of the membership of the Church as of the clergymen who ministered to them.

# PRESBYTERIANS
# THE FRIENDS OF EDUCATION.

## CHAPTER XI.

### PRESBYTERIANS AND EDUCATION.

PRESBYTERIANS have ever been the earnest advocates and patrons of general learning. The influence of their religious system, when in practical operation, inevitably tends to this result. The academy of John Calvin, established at Geneva, to which so many of the youth of Europe resorted, is well known to fame. One of the first things that the Church of Scotland did when its privileges were restored by the Prince of Orange, King William III., was, through its General Assembly, to make ample provision for the education of the people. Schools of different grades were established in every parish throughout the kingdom, which were so far supported by public funds as to render education possible to the poorest in the community.

As in Geneva and in Scotland, so wherever Presbyterianism has been planted, it has invariably shown a similar love for learning. The first emigrants to this country were no exception. Many schoolmasters accompanied them to America, and at an early period each Presbyterian settlement made suitable provision for its schools. Even among their servants it was a rare thing to find one that could not at least read God's word.

A higher education than could be acquired in the ordinary schools of the country, also, early engaged the attention of the colonists. The synod of the Carolinas *enjoined* upon all its presbyteries "to establish within their respective bounds one or more grammar-schools, except where such schools are already established." And thus, through the influence of an educated ministry, a large number of classical schools and academies were speedily organized, which acquired a wide and deserved reputation. In these many of the youth of the country received an education which fitted them for after-usefulness in the liberal professions of law and medicine, while their main purpose was to raise up and qualify ministers for the rapidly increasing congregations. As instructors of the rising generation the Presbyterian clergy exerted an immense influence for good upon society, then in a formation-state, and subsequently their example fostered a zeal for education in other denominations, and led them also to found schools and colleges.

In this connection some of the more important of these classical schools deserve special notice, as the efforts and sacrifices necessary to sustain them will show how devoted the ministers and members of the Presbyterian Church were to the cause of liberal education.

The first literary institution of the kind was established in 1728 by the Rev. William Tennent, and was known in after-years as the Log College—a name derisively given to the school by its enemies. The building was composed of logs, was about twenty feet square, and was situated in Bucks county, Pennsylvania, twenty miles north of Philadelphia, and "about a mile from that part of Neshaminy Creek where the Presbyterian church has long stood." Though the edifice was wanting in architectural grace and beauty, it vindicated its right to the title of a college, for it was a truly noble institution, and proved a fountain of rich blessing to the Presbyterian Church.

Its founder was a native of Ireland, a graduate of Trinity College and an accomplished scholar, "to whom Latin was as familiar as his mother-tongue, and who was an honor to the Church of his adoption." When received by the synod as a member, he delivered an elegant Latin oration before that body. He was also said to be a proficient in the other ancient languages, and to have the power to inspire his pupils with a love for learning.

His motive for founding the school was to provide a pious and educated ministry for the Church, which he saw must ultimately be furnished from within her own bounds. Hitherto the most of her ministers had received their education in the University of Glasgow, some in Ireland and others at New England colleges. As yet no college had been established in any of the Middle States, where young men looking forward to the ministry could obtain a proper education, and they had been obliged to resort either to Scotland or New England to study—an expense which at that time few were able to incur. This was a condition of things very unfavorable for the growth and prosperity of the Church, and one which Mr. Tennent determined to remedy so far as he could. To this work he devoted the remainder of his life; and in addition to the classics, he instructed his pupils in theology, and sent forth a large number of men into the gospel ministry who were eminent alike for piety and learning. "To him," says Webster, "above all others, is owing the prosperity and enlargement of the Presbyterian Church. He had the rare gift of attracting to him youth of worth and genius, imbuing them with his healthful spirit, and sending them forth sound in the faith, blameless in life, burning with zeal, and unsurpassed as instructive, impressive and successful preachers." Similar testimony is borne by Dr. Archibald Alexander to the influence of this honored teacher: "To him the Presbyterian Church is more indebted than to any other individual for the evangelical spirit that pervaded its early ministry." His three sons, the Revs. Samuel and John Blair, William

Robinson and Charles Beatty, and Dr. Samuel Finley, not to mention others of his pupils, are a sufficient justification of any eulogy that has been pronounced upon this school.

Soon after the division of the original synod of the Presbyterian Church, in 1741, measures were adopted to establish a classical and scientific institution which would be under the supervision of the synod of Philadelphia. For years the Old Side party had been dissatisfied with the Log College, and the rupture of ecclesiastical relations served to separate still more widely the former friends and supporters of the college, and to make it more necessary that another school should be started. After much discussion and consultation among those who favored the enterprise, a public meeting was held in 1743, when it was resolved to found an institution, under the direction of the synod, to which all persons who pleased might send their children, to be instructed, without charge, in the languages, philosophy and divinity.

An academy of the kind having been already established at New London, Pennsylvania, by the Rev. Francis Alison, the synod adopted it, and appointed a board of trustees to manage it. Mr. Alison was retained as principal, and had charge of it until his removal to Philadelphia, in 1752, to take the direction of an academy in that city, which in 1755 was merged into the University of Philadelphia.

With the reputation of being the foremost scholar at that time in the country, and a man of "unquestionable ability," as his pupil Bishop White testifies, he was admirably qualified to instruct the youth who in large numbers repaired to his institution. While it did not aspire to the name and dignity of a college, the school was justly celebrated and widely useful, and was "a powerful auxiliary to the cause of theological education." It not only furnished the early Presbyterian churches of this country with many distinguished pastors, but the State with many of its ablest civilians. Among the pupils of this school were the secretary of the Continental Congress and three of the signers of the Declaration of Independence.

The Rev. Alexander McDowell succeeded Mr. Alison as principal of the New London school, which, after a long and useful career, was subsequently removed to Newark, Delaware, and has been since known as Delaware College.

A classical school was instituted at Fagg's Manor, Pennsylvania, in 1739, by Rev. Samuel Blair, in which such distinguished ministers as Samuel Davies, John Rodgers, Alexander Cummings, James Finley and Robert Smith received their education. Mr. Blair is represented as one of the most learned as well as pious and excellent men of his day. Profound as a theologian, he was still more eminent as a preacher, and in every respect a burning and shining light in the Church.

Having been educated at the Log College, and sympathizing strongly with the Tennents in their views, and also in their efforts to promote revivals, the purpose and character of his school were similar to that at Neshaminy, and, like it, was celebrated both for the superior education imparted to its pupils and the high moral and religious purposes with which they were animated.

Soon after his settlement at Nottingham, Maryland, 1744, the Rev. Dr. Samuel Finley opened an academy in order to prepare young men for the ministry, which soon acquired such a reputation that students resorted to it from a great distance. Mr. Finley was eminent as a scholar and skillful as a teacher, and in his instructions religion was united to learning, according to the principles of Scripture. When president of Princeton College, to which office he was unanimously elected at the death of President Davies, in addition to his official duties, he taught Latin, Greek and Hebrew to the senior class, and superintended an English school held in one of the college-buildings.

With such superior qualifications as an instructor, we are not surprised that the Nottingham academy acquired a great reputation and sent forth from its walls some of the ablest and best men, both in Church and State, whose memories are cherished by their countrymen to the present day. Among these may be mentioned the names of Benjamin Rush, M. D., Governor Martin of North Carolina, Dr.

McWhorter, Ebenezer Hazzard, Dr. Williams, Mr. Tennent and Dr. James Waddell.

Dr. Robert Smith, when settled, in 1750, at Pequa, Lancaster county, Pennsylvania, opened a school in which Latin, Greek and Hebrew were taught. It soon became the resort of many young men, over whom the instructor exerted a strong religious influence. Large numbers of them were induced to devote themselves to the ministry, and afterward also studied divinity under him. After Princeton College was established, students continued to be prepared here to enter that institution. With scarcely an exception, those who were trained in this academy were the uniform friends of religion, and the Presbyterian Church was greatly indebted to Mr. Smith for the number of faithful pastors who received their education in his school.

The first classical and scientific school that was opened west of the mountains, and designed to train young men for the pastoral office, was that of the Rev. Joseph Smith, at Upper Buffalo, Pennsylvania, 1785. His kitchen, in the absence of any other building, was devoted to the school. Here, McGready, Patterson, Porter, Brice, Holmes and many other pious youth received their education, who were afterward the missionaries and ministers of the Redstone and Ohio presbyteries. In their course of study they were supported in part by the ladies of the neighboring churches, who provided them with their clothing.

The school was continued for several years, and then, by mutual arrangement, was transferred, and reorganized, near Canonsburg, under the care of the Rev. Dr. McMillan. It was the nucleus out of which grew eventually the Canonsburg academy, the log cabin being superseded by a building of stone in 1790, which served the double purpose of a church and a school. This led to the organization of Jefferson College, in 1802, so that the log cabin, the academy and the college may be considered one and the same institution, under progressive forms of enlargement and usefulness.

Similar institutions of learning, at an early period of the Church, were established by the Rev. Jonathan Dickinson at Elizabethtown, New Jersey, the germ of Princeton College; by the Rev. Thomas Evans at Pencader, Maryland; by Samuel Kennedy, a highly accomplished scholar, at Baskinridge, New Jersey; by Hugh Stevenson, who opened a grammar-school, 1740, in Philadelphia; and by Eliab Byram at Mendham, New Jersey. The Presbyterian colonists of Virginia also made as ample provision for the education of their youth as their circumstances permitted. In most of their congregations pastors established classical and scientific schools. West of the Blue Ridge such a school was carried on at New Providence, by the Rev. John Brown, while east of the Ridge a similar institution was conducted by the Rev. John Todd, under the patronage of Dr. Samuel Davies. The first of these, after removals to Mount Pleasant, where it was known as Augusta academy, and then to Timber Ridge, as Liberty Hall, finally became Washington College. The widespread desire for literary institutions of a high order led the presbytery of Hanover, as early as 1771, to take measures to establish an academy in Prince Edward county, which subsequently was chartered as Hampden-Sidney College. These institutions, so humble in their origin, awakened such a thirst for knowledge in the minds of large numbers of the youth of that State that not a few of them afterward became eminent for their literary attainments and were distinguished in the pulpit and at the bar.

Classical schools of great excellence were organized by Dr. David Caldwell at Buffalo, and afterward at Guilford, North Carolina, in which many of the most eminent men of the South—lawyers, statesmen and clergymen—were educated; by Dr. Samuel E. McCorkle, a thorough scholar and earnest student, whose school at Thyatira, North Carolina, bore the significant name of *Zion Parnassus*, and in which there was a department for the education of school-teachers, and provision was made to have poor and pious young men taught free of expense, of whom *forty-five* entered the pulpit; by the Rev. William Bingham at Wilmington, and subsequently at Chatham and Orange; by Dr. Joseph Alexander at Sugar Creek; by Dr. Alexander McWhorter, principal of "Queen's Museum," in whose hall the debates preceding the Mecklenburg Declaration were held, and which the legislature of North Carolina afterward chartered under the name of Liberty Hall academy. Other classical and scientific schools were taught by Rev. Dr. Robinson at Poplar Tent; by Dr. Wilson at Rocky River; by Dr. Hall at Bethany; by the Rev. Henry Patillo at Orange and Granville; and by Dr. Waddell at Wilmington, under whose instruction some of the ablest civilians of the State were educated.

A large number of Presbyterian families moved at an early day from Virginia and the Carolinas into Tennessee, who carried with them their love of education. Rev. Samuel Doak, a graduate of Princeton College, opened a classical school in Washington county, which was afterward incorporated under the name of Martin academy, and finally became known as Washington College. This was the first literary institution established in the Mississippi Valley. The books that formed the nucleus of the college library were transported from Philadelphia over the mountains in sacks on packhorses. After acting as president of the college for several years, Mr. Doak resigned and removed to Bethel, where he founded Tusculum academy, and continued to be the active advocate and patron of learning, as he had ever been the decided friend of civil and religious liberty.

Greenville College was indebted mainly for its origin to the Rev. Hezekiah Balch, and it was through his patronage that it subsequently rose to great usefulness, as was Blount College to its first president, the Rev. Samuel Carrick, the friend and co-presbyter of Balch. If Davidson academy was not originated by the Rev. Thomas B. Craighead, it was indebted to his untiring labors in its behalf for its subsequent prosperity. After serving for twenty years as president of its board of trustees, he was elected president of Davidson College when the academy was chartered as a college.

Without enumerating the other institutions of learning founded in these new and sparsely-settled regions of country, we perceive that the Presbyterian clergy of the South, like their brethren of the North, were the devoted friends of education. They felt the necessity of promoting the general intelligence of the people, but more particularly of training up an educated ministry for the rapidly extending missionary-field. Hence in nearly every congregation a classical school was taught by the pastor. And who can calculate the influence for good which such men as these exerted in training noble minds who have given impulse and direction to the intellect of the entire country? The names of many of these ministers and teachers may be forgotten, but their labors, by which they so largely contributed to the intellectual advancement of the people, are imperishable.

But these schools, though so excellent and useful in the communities where they were located, did not do away with the necessity of establishing still higher institutions of learning, in which the benefits of a regular collegiate education might be enjoyed. Without permanent funds, libraries, scientific apparatus and an enlarged corps of instructors, they could not meet all the intellectual needs of the young men of the country. And as it was extremely difficult, and in most cases impossible, for parents, on account of the great distances, to send their sons either to Scotland or to the colleges of New England, the synod of New York and Philadelphia turned its attention at an early period to making provision for a more liberal education nearer home. A charter to incorporate the College of New Jersey was procured from the governor of that province, mainly through the influence of Jonathan Dickinson, of Elizabethtown, where the infant institution was first established, with Dickinson as its first president. His death occurring the following year, the Rev. Aaron Burr was chosen his successor, and the college was removed to Newark, where it continued until 1755. Buildings for the accommodation of the students having been erected at Princeton, the college went into more complete operation at that place, where it has since been permanently located, and has continued more and more to realize the expectations of its founders.

It was with extreme difficulty that the means were provided during the first years for the current expenses of the institution and for placing it on a solid basis. Ministers freely contributed for its support from their meagre salaries, and the synod of 1752 ordered collections to be taken up in the churches on its behalf. A deputation of ministers was also sent to England and Scotland to advocate its claims. Their mission proved eminently successful. Between four and five thousand pounds was collected, which placed the college on a sure financial basis, and cheered the hearts of all the friends of liberal education in the Presbyterian Church.

The first commencement under the new charter was held at Newark in 1748. Governor Belcher, the friend of religion and the patron of learning, was on the platform, and around him was gathered a company of honored trustees—of ministers, Samuel Blair, Pierson, Pemberton, Gilbert and William Tennent, Treat, Arthur, Jones and Green; and of laymen, Redding, president of the council, Kinsey, Shippen, Smith and Hazzard. It was a great day in the annals of our Church and of the State.

Most of those who had been actively engaged in founding this college, whose fruits now began to appear, had been educated at the LOG COLLEGE or in schools taught by those who had been instructed there. Thus it came to pass that a humble institution established by a single godly minister was the means of training many talented youth for honor and usefulness in their generation, who in their turn founded other schools of learning, and eventually became the originators of not only the College of New Jersey, but of Jefferson and Dickinson College in Pennsylvania and Hampden-Sidney and Washington College in Virginia. These institutions, together with many others which have come into life of Presbyterian parentage, which have sent forth so many men of learning and piety to bless and adorn our country, evince the high character and intelligence of the early ministers of our Church, as also the wisdom of their labors and sacrifices in behalf of liberal education.

# PATRIOTISM OF PRESBYTERIANS.

## CHAPTER XII.

No people had a clearer perception of the essential principles of liberty, or had done and suffered more to assert and defend them, than the Presbyterians of Scotland. Their great and incomparable Reformer, Knox, when obliged to flee his native land, had repaired to Geneva, where he "studied with unwearied diligence" under Calvin, and became so charmed with that independent commonwealth, and with the simple scheme of church government there established and the spirituality of the worship connected with it, that on his return to Scotland he began to propagate his matured sentiments with great earnestness and success. The adoption of these wise and liberal views by his countrymen led eventually to the triumph of religious and political liberty. What these were, so far as rulers and subjects were concerned, was shown by Knox's memorable reply to Queen Mary when she asked him the question, "Think you that subjects having the power may resist their princes?" "*If princes exceed their bounds, madam, no doubt they may be resisted even by power.*" This the learned historian Froude calls "*the creed of republics* in its first hard form;" and so John Knox became the representative of civil equally with religious freedom in Scotland.

To this is to be added a sense of past wrongs and the remembrance of how their ancestors had been hunted like wild beasts by the soldiery, and had their houses pillaged and burned, while they were compelled to fly for safety to glens and mountain-fastnesses when the despotic attempt was making to impose prelacy upon Scotland. Thus it was that the history and the traditional memories of the Scottish people, who constituted so important a part of the Presbyterian Church of America, made them earnest and active patriots when called upon to choose between resistance or submission to arbitrary power.*

---

* The single exception was that of some Highlanders in North Carolina at the beginning of the Revolution. Banished from Scotland for taking up arms for the Pretender, their pardon was conditioned on a solemn oath of allegiance to their sovereign. Such obligations they regarded with peculiar sacredness, and they had required the king to swear to the Solemn League and Covenant. Not feeling to any great degree the evils complained of by the other colonists, they were slow to engage in the contest. Some of them at first sympathized with and aided the royalists; but when the monarchical government came to an end, they became the fast friends and supporters of republican institutions. We may respect their moral principles, while we deplore their error of judgment, that led them at first to battle with freemen who were only demanding their rights.

The causes were many and obvious why the patriotism of the Scotch-Irish should have been so universal and ardent in the war with England. Their antecedent history furnished abundant reasons why they should distrust the mother-country and dislike her methods of governing her colonies. Under the rule of those who had controlled the policy of that government, and through the oppressive measures which were imposed upon Ireland, they, and their fathers before them, had been made to feel all the evils that the arrogant bishops could inflict; they had seen their manufacturing industry paralyzed to please the mill-owners of Lancashire, their agriculture discouraged in order that English-grown corn might have a more lucrative market, and Ireland cut off from the sea by the navigation laws and compelled to sell her products to British merchants rather than in the open markets of the world. In a word, they had seen that England's policy was to use her colonies for her own interests, irrespective of their rights or their consent.

With their past experience, it would indeed have been strange if they had not been among the first to discern the threatened evils and the most earnest in resisting them. Ireland was but a colony of longer standing; and having seen to what a pitiable condition an English colony could be reduced whose rights and interests were disregarded, is it any wonder that these people were the earliest to take alarm? The question in both colonies was substantially the same. The same governmental measures were sought to be employed in America as had been in Ireland. The wrongs which the American people were called upon to resist had been inflicted upon the people of Ireland for generations. The trade of this country was already in English hands. Under the fostering care of the proprietary governors, active means were being employed to make the Episcopal the established Church of the country, and then farewell to all liberty of conscience. Oppressive laws which would destroy the manufactures and the agriculture of the new colony, as they had those of the older one, might be enacted at any time; and the only way to prevent the recurrence of the evils and the injustice from which they had fled was firmly to resist the first encroachments of irresponsible authority. So that if the Scotch-Irish were more suspicious than other settlers of the mother-country, and more positive and outspoken in their opposition, the reason was none had such cause for complaint on account of the grievances they had previously endured.

Their hostile feelings, moreover, were kept alive by the continued arrivals of their friends from Ulster, driven out, so to speak, from a country which they had reclaimed from desolation and made rich and prosperous. It required, too, more than the wide waste of waters which separated them from their former oppressors, to efface the resentment which these exiles carried with them to their new homes. It blazed up anew at every remembrance of the wrongs they had endured; and when the possibility of a recurrence of these evils confronted them, it is not surprising that "in the war of independence England had no fiercer enemies than the grandsons and great-grandsons of the Presbyterians who had held Ulster against Tyrconnel." They and succeeding colonists "were torn up by the roots and bid find a home elsewhere, and they found a home to which England, fifty years later, had to regret that she had allowed them to be driven."\*

The patriotism of the Scotch-Irish Presbyterians, as was true also of their brethren from Scotland, was influenced largely by deep religious convictions. Many of them were voluntary exiles for conscience' sake. These would be very naturally the faithful advocates and supporters of religious freedom. Here, in the land of their adoption, they wished to enjoy and to transmit to their children not only the blessings of a liberal civil government without the prescriptive rights of a nobility, but one in which they would be equally free from the impertinent interference of an ecclesiastical hierarchy.

They were ready to grant to others the rights and privileges they claimed for themselves. If any

\* Froude.

were enamored with the "trappings of Episcopacy," and preferred a Church with subordinate and superior orders of clergy, culminating finally in bishops with powers of supervision and control, they were not disposed to quarrel with them about their choice. But what they knew of the prerogatives of bishops beyond the sea induced them to deprecate their presence and power in the Church of Christ. "Our forefathers," said they, "and even some of ourselves, have seen and felt the tyranny of bishops' courts. Many of the first inhabitants of these colonies were obliged to seek an asylum among savages in this wilderness in order to escape the ecclesiastical tyranny of Archbishop Laud and others of his stamp. We dread the consequences as often as we think of this danger." And what was here said of Archbishop Laud by these Connecticut colonists, could have been uttered with equal truth of nearly every prelate of Scotland, including that arch-traitor and archbishop, Sharp.

Nor were they without good reasons for fearing that Episcopacy might be established in this country. The instructions given to the governors of the several provinces required them "to give all countenance and encouragement to the exercise of the ecclesiastical jurisdiction of the bishop of London," and particularly directed that "no schoolmaster be hereafter permitted to keep school within this our said province without the license of the bishop of London."* In 1730 an order of council was passed approving the instructions that had been sent to the governors of the provinces, directing them "to support the bishop of London and his commissioners in the exercise of such ecclesiastical jurisdiction as is granted to them."† In several of the provinces the Episcopal Church was either established by law or was peculiarly favored by the colonial governments. Already some of them had experienced the tender mercies of Episcopacy in Virginia, in the Carolinas and in New York, where it had secured a preponderating influence and was supported by the strong arm of the civil authority. In these colonies "dissenters" had been subjected to grievous and unjust hardships. In some instances they had been fined and imprisoned for being present at, and taking part in, religious services after the Presbyterian mode of worship; in others they were obliged to aid in the support of clergy upon whose ministry they did not attend, and were denied the rights of citizenship and the right of marriage by their own pastors.

Besides, the intention to introduce Episcopacy into this country, and make the Episcopal the established Church, was early and frequently avowed. "Americans in England were openly told that bishops should be settled in America in spite of all the Presbyterian opposition." The Episcopal clergy of New York and New Jersey pe-

* Maclean's *History of Princeton College*. † Ibid.

titioned for the episcopate, and at as early a period as 1748 it was proposed to introduce Episcopacy into New England by elevating some of the ministers to an ecclesiastical pre-eminence over their brethren. Thus the memories of the past, together with these avowed intentions and attempts, united all the other denominations in resisting the project to make the Episcopal the established Church in America. They wanted no Courts of High Commission, no lords-spiritual, no prelatical arrogance, in their new homes.

**It** was not only, then, because their civil rights were imperiled, but also because their religious freedom was in danger, that our Presbyterian fathers were such steadfast, earnest patriots. As in Scotland and Ireland, so here, they recognized the fact that civil and religious liberty stood or fell together. So that, while they protested against taxation without representation, they were equally opposed to any interference with **the rights of conscience.** Feeling it to be their duty to resist all arbitrary power in civil government, they naturally feared and distrusted the influence of Episcopacy, since in their former homes it had ever been found the strong ally of despotism, and in this country they saw that its clergy and their flocks "leaned, with very few exceptions, to the side of the Crown."

These principles and sentiments were common to the Scotch and Scotch-Irish colonists and their descendants, and sustained them through the sacrifices and perils of a seven years' conflict for independence. But while they were conspicuous in their zeal and devotion as patriots, they were not alone or singular in this respect in the Presbyterian Church. For its members, though coming from sources widely diverse, were yet wonderfully harmonious and united in support of the cause. So well known were the opinions and sympathies of Presbyterians that they were subjected to all the evils the enemy was capable of visiting upon their persons or their property, and wherever found they were regarded and treated as arch-rebels.

History accords to Presbyterians the honor of being the first to combine to resist the impositions of the mother-country upon the colonists. Mr. Adolphus, in his book on the *Reign of George III.*, uses the following language: "*The first effort* toward a *union of interest* was made by the Presbyterians, who were eager in carrying into execution their favorite project of forming a synod. Their churches had hitherto remained unconnected with each other, and their union in synod had been considered so dangerous to the community that in 1725 it was prevented by the express interference of the lords-justices. Availing themselves, with great address, of the rising discontents, the convention of ministers and elders at Philadelphia enclosed in a circular-letter to all the Presbyterian congregations in Pennsylvania the proposed articles of union. . . . In consequence of this letter, a union of all the congregations took place in Pennsylvania and the Lower Counties. A similar *confederacy* was established in all the Southern provinces, in pursuance of similar letters written by their respective conventions. These measures ended in the establishment of an annual synod at Philadelphia, where all general affairs, *political* as well as religious, were debated and decided. From this synod orders and decrees were issued throughout America, and to them a ready and implicit obedience was paid.

"The discontented in New England recommended a union of the Congregational and Presbyterian interests throughout the colonies. A negotiation took place, which ended in the appointment of a permanent committee of correspondence, and powers to communicate and consult on all occasions with a similar committee established by the Congregational churches in New England. . . .

"BY THIS UNION A PARTY WAS PREPARED TO DISPLAY THEIR POWER BY RESISTANCE, and the Stamp law presented itself as a favorable object of hostility."\*

Equally explicit testimony is borne in a published address of Mr. William B. Reed of Philadelphia, himself an Episcopalian: "The part taken by the Presbyterians in the contest with the mother-coun-

---

\* Undue political importance was attached to these measures, but it indicates the close connection between the religious and civil part of the contest now begun.

try was indeed, *at the time, often* made a ground of reproach, and the connection between their efforts for the security of their religious liberty and opposition to the oppressive measures of Parliament, was *then distinctly seen.*" Mr. Galloway, a prominent advocate of the government, in 1774, ascribed the revolt and revolution *mainly* to the action of the Presbyterian clergy and laity as early as 1764. Another writer of the same period says: "You will have discovered that I am no friend to the Presbyterians, and that I fix ALL THE BLAME of these extraordinary proceedings upon them." And Rev. Dr. Elliott, editor of the Western organ of the Methodist Church, in answer to an assailant of Presbyterians, says: "The Presbyterians, of every class, were prominent, and *even foremost*, in achieving the liberties of the United States, and they have been all along the leading supporters of the Constitution and law and good order."

The Synod of the Presbyterian Church, which met in Philadelphia a year before the Declaration of Independence, was *the very first body* to declare themselves in favor of open resistance, and to encourage and counsel their people, who were then ready to take up arms. But a few weeks before, the bloody conflict had taken place at Lexington, and created great excitement throughout the land. The General Congress was also in session in Philadelphia, consulting concerning the crisis which had been precipitated upon the colonies. At this important period the Synod gave expression to its deep sympathy for the cause of freedom, and its religious convictions respecting the rights of the people. "Rarely," says Dr. Gillett, "on any occasion, has there been a parallel utterance more significant or effective, and it came at the opportune moment when political zeal needed to be tempered and sustained by religious sanctions." Rev. Dr. Lang, in his volume entitled *Religion and Education in America*, thus speaks of the same document: "As a literary production, the letter is evidently of a superior order, highly creditable to the body from which it emanated; as a political document, it is unexceptionable; as a Christian testimony and admonition, it is all that could be possibly desired."

The spirit which actuated these men is shown by the following extract from the Synod's pastoral letter: "Perhaps no instance can be given, on so interesting a subject, in which political sentiments have been so long and so fully kept from the pulpit, and even malice itself has not charged us with laboring from the press, but things are now come to such a state that, as we do not wish to conceal our opinions as men and citizens, so the relation we stand in to you seemed to make the present improvement of it to your spiritual benefit an indispensable duty."

It proceeds to exhort those who belong to its communion "not to suffer oppression, or injury itself, easily to provoke you to speak disrespectfully of the king," but to " let it ever appear that you only desire the preservation and security of those rights which belong to you as freemen." With respect to union in defence of their rights, it says: " Be careful to maintain the union which at present subsists through all the colonies; nothing can be more manifest than that the success of every measure depends on its being inviolably preserved, and therefore we hope that you will leave nothing undone which can promote that end. In particular, as the Continental Congress now sitting in Philadelphia consists of delegates chosen in the most free and unbiased manner, by the body of the people, let them not only be treated with respect and encouraged in their difficult service, not only let your prayers be offered up to God for his direction in their proceedings, but adhere firmly to their resolutions, and let it be seen that they are able to bring out the whole strength of their vast country to carry them into execution."

The letter further urges "mutual charity and esteem among members of different religious denominations, vigilance in regard to social government and morals, reformation of manners, personal honesty and integrity, humanity and mercy, especially among such as should be called to the field."

In order that these sentiments might exert their appropriate influence over the people connected with their congregations, copies of the pastoral letter were transmitted to all the churches,\* and it aided largely in kindling and sustaining the patriotic zeal of the country. Particularly did it give prestige and influence to the counsel and acts of the Congress then in session, for whom, as we have seen, prayer was unceasingly to be offered, and to whose resolutions they were exhorted "firmly to adhere," in order that they may "be able to bring out the **whole** strength **of** this vast country to carry them into execution." From every Presbyterian pulpit in the land, and from every Presbyterian household altar, went **up** the voice **of** supplication **in** behalf of **a** suffering country. Thus it was that the Presbyterian Church, by the act of its highest judicatory, took its stand by the side of the American Congress, and helped to sustain the struggle for independence **by its wise,** brave and patriotic words.

Of the highest significance were the resolutions adopted by the Scotch-Irish Presbyterians of North Carolina in convention **at** Charlotte, May 20, 1775 which are known in history as the MECKLENBURG DECLARATION.† This high-spirited people had

\* This paper **had a wider** circulation than **the** bounds of the **Synod.** The official record of the provincial congress of North Carolina states "that two hundred copies of the letter **were presented** to the delegates by **Rev.** Mr. Boyd."

† All the members of this convention were connected with the seven Presbyterian churches and congregations that embraced the entire county of Mecklenburg. One was a Presbyterian minister, and nine were elders of Presbyterian churches.

carefully watched the progress of the controversy between the colonies and Great Britain; and when, in May, 1775, they received news of the address that had been presented to the king by Parliament, declaring the American colonists to be in actual rebellion, they concluded that the time for action had arrived, and accordingly proceeded to renounce their allegiance to the Crown. Two delegates from each militia company in the county were called together in Charlotte as a representative committee. The result of their deliberations was to form, in effect, *a declaration of independence*, as well as a complete system of government. All laws and commissions, civil and military, derived from the king or Parliament, were declared void, and the provincial congress of each province, under the direction of the great Continental Congress, was invested with all legislative and executive powers. This action was made binding on all; and to give effect to it, the freemen of the county formed themselves into military companies and entrusted judicial powers to men selected by vote of these companies, the tenure of all offices being conditioned solely on the pleasure of their several constituencies.

The importance of the resolutions adopted at Charlotte justifies the insertion here of two of them. In the second they resolve, "That we do hereby *dissolve the political bonds which have connected us with the mother-country,* and hereby *absolve* ourselves from all allegiance to the British Crown;" and in the third, "We hereby declare ourselves a *free* and *independent people;* are, and of right ought to be, a sovereign and self-governing association, under the control of no power other than that of our God and the general government of the Congress, to the maintenance of which we solemnly pledge to each other our mutual co-operation and our lives, our fortunes and our most sacred honor."

These extraordinary resolves were sent by a messenger to the Congress in Philadelphia, and were printed in the *Cape Fear Mercury* and widely distributed throughout the province. A copy of them was transmitted by Sir James Wright, then governor of Georgia, to England, in a letter of June 20, 1775, and the paper containing these resolutions may still be seen in the British State-Paper Office. Owing to the remarkable coincidence of language, as well as the many phrases common both to the Mecklenburg and the national declaration, the question has arisen which had precedence in point of time. However this may be decided, or whether they both were not indebted to some common source—such as the National Covenants of Scotland and England—it is certain that the Presbyterians of Mecklenburg were in advance of Congress and in advance of the rest of the country in proclaiming "the inherent and inalienable rights of man," and that the historian Bancroft was right in stating that "the first voice publicly raised in America to dissolve all connection with Great Britain came *from the* SCOTCH-IRISH PRESBYTERIANS."

The Presbyterians of Western Pennsylvania, assembled at Hanna's Town, May, 1776, after expressing sympathy for their Massachusetts brethren, and their abhorrence of the system of tyranny which England was attempting to enforce upon them, resolved, that it was "the indispensable duty of every man who has any public virtue or love for his country, by every means which God has put in his power, to resist and oppose this oppression; and as for us, we are ready to oppose it with our lives and fortunes."

A similar spirit was shown by the freemen of Cumberland county, Pennsylvania, who were among the first to conclude "that the safety and welfare of the colonies did render separation from the mother-country necessary." Their sentiments were embodied in a memorial presented to the assembly of the province, May 28, 1776, in which they say: "If those who rule in Britain will not permit the colonies to be free and happy in connection with that kingdom, it becomes their duty to secure and promote their freedom and happiness in the best manner they can without that connection." This, and other considerations, "induced us to petition this honorable house that the last instructions which it gave to the delegates in Congress, wherein they are enjoined not to consent to any step which may cause or lead to a separation from Great Britain, *may be withdrawn.*"

Besides expressing the present convictions of the people under their **new and** changed circumstances, the memorial shows that the citizens of the county, who were at the time almost exclusively Scotch and Scotch-Irish, were in advance of their representatives in the assembly and in Congress. These were brave words, but they were followed by equally brave deeds when the call **was made** upon them to meet the enemies of their country.

The presbytery of Hanover presented a memorial to the legislature of Virginia in 1776, in which, **as** will be seen, an earnest devotion to the cause of independence was expressed: "Your memorialists are governed by the same sentiments which have inspired the United States of America, and **are** determined that nothing in our power or influence shall be wanting to give success to their common cause. We would also **represent** that dissenters from the Church of England in this country have ever been desirous **to conduct** themselves as peaceable members of the civil government, for which reason they have hitherto submitted to several ecclesiastical burdens and restrictions that are inconsistent with equal liberty. But now, when the many and grievous oppressions of our mother-country have laid this continent *under the necessity of casting off the yoke of tyranny, and of forming independent governments upon equitable and liberal* *foundations,* we flatter ourselves we shall be freed from all the encumbrances which a spirit of domination, prejudice or bigotry hath interwoven with our political systems."

Further testimony of the same kind might be adduced were it necessary. But it is indisputable that Presbyterians were the *first* to combine in resistance of the arbitrary acts of England, and made the first practical declaration of independence in America.

Throughout the entire period of the war with Great Britain, the Presbyterian ministry bore a conspicuous and honored part. Their superior culture, the respect and the affection in which they were held by their people, their well-known principles and patriotism, and their resolute and unflinching courage,—all combined to make them leaders. They not only taught their people the duty of resisting oppression in every form, but many of them, by example as well as precept, encouraged the members of their churches to take up arms in defence of their country. And when disasters came upon the American army, and the future of the cause appeared dark and forbidding, they inspired their fellow-citizens with fresh courage, and with confidence in the God of nations. Many served as chaplains in the army, not a few as soldiers and officers, while others were of equal service in State and national councils; and others still placed their property and their lives upon the altar of their country with a devotion rarely paralleled.

The sympathy and services of the Presbyterian clergy were so universally on the side of the colonists that there is danger of appearing invidious in any endeavor to point out those who were prominent and influential advocates of the cause of liberty in the pulpit and in legislative halls, and who by their example as well as by their words greatly aided the patriots fighting the battles of their country.

**Dr.** Witherspoon, of Princeton, stands in the front rank of **those** who rendered eminent service in establishing a free government. He **was** a lineal descendant of John Knox, and, like the celebrated Scotch Reformer, was fitted to be a great leader among men. He **was** almost equally eminent as a scholar, a theologian, an orator, teacher, author and financier; and in all these relations he reflected honor upon his adopted country. Immediately on his arrival **in America he** identified himself with the colonial cause, and in the ensuing struggle with England his powerful advocacy of the rights of the colonists placed him by the side of Jefferson and Franklin, and the other noble defenders of freedom.

From the commencement of the Revolution he was a member of the various committees and conventions whose object was to obtain redress from the king of the evils the people endured.

In 1776 he was a member of the New Jersey convention that formed its republican constitution, and the same year took his seat in the Continental Congress, in which he helped frame the Declaration of our rights, and to which he affixed his name, "appealing to his God for the approval of his act, and to the world for the justice of the cause he espoused." And he urged the other delegates, some of whom were hesitating, to take the same patriotic stand. "That noble instrument upon your table," said he, "which ensures immortality to its author, should be subscribed this very morning by every pen in the house. He that will not respond to its accents, and strain every nerve to carry into effect its provisions, is unworthy the name of a freeman. For my own part, of property I have some, of reputation more. That reputation is staked, that property is *pledged*, on the issue of this contest. And although these gray hairs must soon descend into the sepulchre, I would infinitely rather they should descend thither by the hands of the public executioner than desert at this crisis the sacred cause of my country."* He remained a member of Congress until 1782, with the exception of one year, and contributed perhaps as largely as any other one man to the success of the patriot-cause. His labors were incessant, his industry untiring, his perseverance unyielding, and his patriotism fervid, and as pure as the crystal fountain.

* Rev. Dr. Krebs, as quoted in vol. i. *Southern Review*.

Most of the measures he proposed in Congress were either at the time or subsequently adopted.

His influence in the legislative hall was deservedly great, for he had a mind that was able to grasp and expound the principles of government. His perceptions were clear and his judgment acute; and when he **spoke he was listened to** with the utmost interest, and his clear and strong reasoning rarely failed **to** secure the **conviction** of his hearers. Several eloquent appeals, recommending the people to observe days of public fasting and **prayer, were** from his able pen. " Few men acted with more energy and promptitude; few appeared **to** be enriched with greater political wisdom; few enjoyed a greater share of public confidence; few accomplished more for the country than he **did in the** sphere in which he was called to act. In the most gloomy and formidable aspect of **public** affairs he was always firm, discovering the greatest reach and presence of mind **in the most** embarrassing situations."

Worthy allies of Dr. **Witherspoon, and** only less celebrated, were Dr. Patrick Allison of Baltimore, pronounced the ablest *statesman* in **the** Presbyterian Church, an earnest defender **of** his country's cause, and one of the committee of the Assembly of 1789 to draft an address to President Washington; William Tennent of Charleston, **a** member of the provincial congress of South Carolina, and appointed by the committee of safety to arouse the people in behalf of independence; George Duffield of Philadelphia, chaplain of the Colonial Congress, and often consulted on public questions by civil and military officers; and Dr. John Rogers of New York, one of the council of safety, and chaplain in the war, first of Heath's brigade, then of the convention of the State.

In Pennsylvania were John Carmichael, who before the military on several occasions preached by request a sermon on "the lawfulness of self-defence," which exerted a great influence; John Craighead, who raised a company from the members of his congregation, serving as captain and chaplain, and who is said to have "fought and preached alternately;" Dr. James Latta, who to encourage his people shouldered his knapsack and accompanied them on their campaign; Dr. Robert Davidson, who by his patriotic sermons before military companies inspired the soldiers with courage and fortitude; Dr. William Linn, chaplain, who was present at the taking of Fort Washington; Dr. Robert Cooper, who "bore arms, marched and countermarched through the Jerseys on foot so long as he was able;" John Elder, a colonel in the colonial service; John Steele, who served as captain, "and led the advance company of nine hundred men in their march to the seat of war, and often preached with his gun standing by his side;" John Rosbrugh, first a private soldier, then a chaplain, and who was killed in cold blood by the Hessians; Dr. John

King, eminent for his patriotic zeal, doing duty as a chaplain, and by his many addresses increasing the devotion of the people to their country's cause.

In New Jersey were **Dr. Alexander McWhorter**, who was appointed by Congress in 1775 to visit North Carolina to promote independence among the people; who was afterward at the battle of Trenton, and at General Knox's request acted as chaplain while our army lay at White Plains; Dr. Asa Hillyer of Orange, who assisted his father as surgeon in the army; James Caldwell, chaplain of the Jersey brigade and assistant commissary-general, in which position his services were very valuable, who had a price set upon his head, and who was subsequently killed by the enemy; James F. Armstrong of Elizabethtown, "chaplain of the Second brigade of the Maryland forces;" John Miller of Dover, bold in the expression of his freedom-loving views, preaching to his people prior to the Declaration of Independence from the text, "We have no part in David, nor any inheritance in the son of Jesse; to your tents, O Israel!" Dr. Ashbel Green, an orderly sergeant in the war, risking his life repeatedly in defence of his country; and Dr. Elihu Spencer of Trenton, who was conspicuously engaged on the side of the patriots, and employed by the provincial congress of North Carolina to convince some of her colonists of the justice of the American cause.

In Virginia were Dr. John Brown, who "fought

with intrepid spirit by the side of Sumter," and was afterward president of Georgia University; William Graham, who encouraged the members of his congregation to enlist, and served as a captain; John Brown and Archibald Scott, neighboring pastors, who entered warmly into the American cause, and exhorted their people to fight for their freedom; Dr. James Waddell, who was one of the first and most earnest vindicators of liberty from the pulpit; Dr. Moses Hoge, who served for a time, previous to entering the ministry, in the army of the Revolution; and Dr. John Blair Smith, who was an active patriot and captain of a company of students of Hampden-Sidney College, of which he was president.

In the Carolinas were Alexander Craighead, who, though not living to see the clash of arms, "sowed the seeds of the Mecklenburg Declaration;" Dr. David Caldwell, a distinguished patriot and educator, and member of the convention that formed the State constitution of North Carolina, and had his library burned by the enemy; Henry Patillo, a valuable member of the provincial congress of North Carolina, and active in carrying on the war against the enemy; Hugh McAden, who suffered the loss of all his property by the enemy; Dr. James Hall, a commander and chaplain; Dr. Francis Cummins, a Mecklenburg patriot, who fought in several engagements; John Simpson, who encouraged his people to deeds of heroism, and was himself in several battles; James White Stephenson, who served throughout the war, and had his gun shivered in his hand by the enemy's shot; Joseph Alexander, a fugitive from his home, which was used by the patriots as a hospital for their sick and wounded; Lewis F. Wilson, who served for many years as surgeon in the Continental army, having studied medicine previous to entering the pulpit; Dr. Thomas H. McCaule, a zealous patriot, who was by the side of General Davidson when he was shot by a **Tory**; and **Adam Boyd, one of the** earliest friends of **liberty, chaplain of the** State brigade, editor of the *Cape Fear Mercury*, and a member of the committee of safety of North Carolina.

These were some **of the** more prominent advocates and defenders of the independence of their country. Whether engaged in preaching to their own congregations, or **addressing** public assemblies, or deliberating in **legislative** halls, or serving in the army as **officers or soldiers or** chaplains, **they were known as earnest, active** patriots, **who fearlessly had committed themselves on** the side of **freedom.**\*

\* Though the Scotch and Scotch-Irish colonists were in point of numbers relatively small as compared with the **entire population** of the country, yet they furnished a great many of the general army officers. At this late day anything like a full or accurate designation is impossible, owing to the fact that in the biographical sketches of these men very frequently there is no mention made of their nationality. Enough, however, can be traced to justify the assertion that the Presbyterian colonists

With the exhibition of such patriotic zeal and devotion as was evinced by the clergy, we may be sure that the elders and members of their churches stood in the front rank of battle when their country needed defenders. From the investigations we have made, we are persuaded that, could the facts be properly presented, they would be as surprising to most persons as they would be honorable to the Presbyterian Church. In confirmation of this remark, our space will permit of but two illustrations.

In one county of Pennsylvania, settled almost exclusively by Scotch-Irish Presbyterians, it is on record in the State papers that fourteen days after the battle of Lexington over *three thousand men* had already united in military organizations, fif-

were conspicuous and able and brave in the battles of the Revolution.

Of MAJOR-GENERALS we may refer to Anthony Wayne, John Stark, Hugh Mercer, Thomas Sumter, Henry Knox, William Alexander (Lord Stirling), Alexander McDowell, Richard Montgomery, John Sullivan and William Moultrie. Of GENERALS, to Daniel Morgan, John Beatty, Francis Marion, Griffith Rutherford, George Graham, William Irvine, John Moore, Charles Stewart, John Armstrong, William Davidson, Joseph Graham, Isaac Hughes, Andrew Pickens, Arthur St. Clair and Joseph Reed. Of BRIGADIER-GENERALS, to John Armstrong, Jr., Jethro Sumner, Matthias Ogden, Otho H. Williams, Stephen Moylan, Francis Nash, Elias Dayton, Edward Hand, Andrew Lewis, Lachlan McIntosh, William Thomson, Andrew Porter, James Moore and William Macpherson. Of colonels and of other subordinate officers we attempt no enumeration, as in point of numbers they were almost legion.

teen hundred stand of arms had been returned, and that delegates from the different precincts of the county had met in convention and voted that five hundred effective men should be at once armed and equipped to march on the first emergency, and to be paid *by a tax on all estates, real and personal, in the county.* Reinforcements for the army continued to be sent forward as the public exigences of the **war required, so that** by its close " *almost every man able to carry* **arms** had **been in** the military service of his country." And while these volunteer forces, in such surprising numbers, were marching to battle, there were already in the Continental army a great many officers and soldiers from this county who had joined it the previous year. These patriots very generally selected their own officers, and as a rule were commanded by their loved pastors, or the elders of the churches to which they belonged, who cheerfully encountered with the common soldiers the privations incident to an active campaign.

To **give** proper weight **to the** patriotism here displayed, it should be known that this was a *frontier* county, with a comparatively sparse population, the people poor and obliged to defend themselves from the Indian savages, who were instigated by the enemy to commit deeds of violence and to murder the unprotected inhabitants.

The other illustration of the military services rendered by Presbyterians in the Revolutionary struggle we take from a widely separated part of the country. Referring to the war in South Carolina, Rev. Dr. Smith writes: "The battles of the Cowpens, of King's Mountain, and also the severe skirmish known as Huck's defeat, are celebrated as giving a turning point to the contests of the Revolution. General Morgan, who commanded at the Cowpens, and General Pickens, who made all the arrangements for the battle, were both Presbyterian elders, and nearly all under their command were Presbyterians. In the battle of King's Mountain, Colonels Campbell, Williams, Cleveland, Shelby and Sevier, as also Colonel Hamilton and Major James, were all Presbyterian elders, and the body of their troops were collected from Presbyterian settlements. At Huck's defeat, in York, Colonel Bratten and Major Dickson were both Presbyterian elders. Major Samuel Morrow, who was with Colonel Sumter in four engagements and in many other battles, was for fifty years a ruling elder in the Presbyterian Church."

Thousands of others identified with the Presbyterian Church, either as office-bearers or private members, freely risked their lives in defence of their country, and many of them sealed their devotion to it with their blood. As descendants of those heroic men who so successfully resisted oppression in all its forms in the Old World, they, in the hour that tries men's souls, proved themselves not unworthy of their lineage, and it was because the

American Presbyterian Church contained within it such elements as these that it was able to take the patriotic stand it did in establishing a free republican form of government.*

After the part taken by Presbyterians in achieving the independence † of the colonies, it would have been strange if many of them had not been called into the civil service of their country. This was the fact, but our limits will only permit the mention of a few of the more distinguished of the number.

General Moultrie of South Carolina was twice governor of that State subsequent to the war; General Joseph Reed served in Congress, and was thrice governor of Pennsylvania; General Sullivan was president of New Hampshire for three years; General Henry Knox was selected as secretary of war; General Sumter, member of Congress, minister to Brazil and senator from South Carolina; Governor Clinton, elected vice-president; Patrick

---

* As the Puritans of England were for a long time unquestionably Presbyterians, Robinson's church at Leyden having the same government as the Protestant churches of France, and as not less than from twenty to thirty thousand Presbyterians from the north of Ireland entered New England at an early period and united with the churches already established, and that were so similarly constituted to those they had left, Presbyterians should be credited with no "insignificant share of the splendid patriotism displayed by New England in the Revolution."

† Of the fifty-six signers of the Declaration of Independence, we recognize at least fifteen of them as having been of either Scotch, Irish or Huguenot ancestors.

Henry, appointed secretary of state and minister to France, which posts of honor he declined, and was elected governor of Virginia; Robert R. Livingston, minister to France; General Morgan, a member of Congress from 1797 to 1799; Richard Stockton, member of the Continental Congress, and one of the signers of the Declaration of Independence; General Stewart, a member of Congress in 1784–85; Samuel Spencer, judge of the Superior Court of North Carolina; General William Irvine, member of the committee on the war, and afterward in Congress—a judicious statesman and zealous patriot; James Wilson, representative in Congress, who gave the casting vote in the Pennsylvania delegation for independence, and a member of the war committee; John Meheling, member of the provincial congress of New Jersey, 1775, and quartermaster-general; Alexander Martin, governor of North Carolina and senator; General Anthony Wayne, a member of the committee of safety of Pennsylvania; General John Armstrong, member of Congress; Thomas McKean, member of Congress from 1774 to 1783, and judge of the Supreme Court of Pennsylvania; Richard Caswell, governor of North Carolina and president of the convention that framed the State constitution; Hon. William Killen, chancellor of the State of Delaware; George Read, signer of the Declaration of Independence, and honored with many civil appointments; George Bryan, judge of the Supreme

Court, and author of the plan to abolish slavery in Pennsylvania; John Montgomery, member of Congress and of the committee of safety of Pennsylvania; John Byers, member of the supreme executive council of Pennsylvania; Andrew Porter, surveyor-general of Pennsylvania, and declined the office of secretary of war; and John Armstrong, Jr., a member of General Gates' staff, and afterward ambassador to France and secretary of war.

We forbear further mention of those who sat in the legislative halls of the nation, or were elevated to positions of honor and great responsibility. Our object has been merely to show that these men, and those of like lineage and spirit, enjoyed the confidence of their fellow-citizens, and were chosen by them to frame, expound and administer the laws and government of a free people.

Thus called into the councils of the nation for the purpose of settling the forms of our government, it is not surprising that Presbyterians should seek to introduce into the Constitution the simple elements of representative republicanism contained in their own loved system. From the remarkable similarity between the constitution of the Presbyterian Church and the political Constitution of our country, it is evident that the former gave character to our free institutions. "The framers of *the Constitution of the United States*," says Chief-Justice Tilghman, " were greatly indebted to the standards of the Presbyterian Church of Scotland in modeling that admirable instrument." So, too, Hon. W. C. Preston of South Carolina states: "Certainly it was the most remarkable and singular coincidence that the constitution of the Presbyterian Church should bear such a close and striking resemblance to the political Constitution of our country. This may be regarded as an earnest of our beloved national Union. . . . The two may be supposed to be formed after the same model." Nor is this to be wondered at when we recall the agency which Dr. Witherspoon, the embodiment of Presbyterianism, had in framing and adopting that instrument, and the valuable services which so many other distinguished members of the Presbyterian Church rendered in establishing a constitutional, representative republic.

The elements of civil and religious liberty thus happily embodied in the Constitution did not spring, Minerva-like, from the brain of any one individual, but were the results of years of persecution, conflict and suffering endured by God's people in behalf of freedom in the Old World. And just so far as our Presbyterian fathers had shared in these struggles against religious and political tyranny, and so far as their descendants had imbibed the spirit and shared the opinions of their worthy ancestry, were they prepared to take a leading part as FOUNDERS OF NEW STATES.

Presbyterians, while lovers of liberty in the Old World, were not anarchists. While they resisted the establishment of a monarchy on the basis of non-resistance and passive obedience, they desired a constitutional government, with proper restraints on the royal authority and proper guarantees for the people in their religious worship. They clearly perceived the province and duties of the civil magistrate, and so long as he used his office to promote the welfare of his people he was to be respected and obeyed; but when he assumed the prerogatives of a spiritual ruler, and sought to bring the Church into bondage to the State, and deprive it of the rights and jurisdiction with which it was entrusted by Christ, his claims were to be denied. The temporal power of the civil ruler and the spiritual power of the Church they insisted should be separate, but harmonious; but when the former enjoins what the Head of the Church forbids, then God rather than the sovereign was to be obeyed. If they yielded their civil rights, their bitter experience in the past had taught them that spiritual despotism was sure to follow. For no sooner was the arbitrary will of the monarch supported by an obsequious Parliament, accepted as superior to the hereditary rights of the people, than Episcopal prelates, adopting the policy of Rome, immediately began to assume lordship over their consciences. The danger to which they were thus exposed they were quick to discern, and they met it with promptitude and calm decision. And it was their clear perception of these important principles that caused them to cling to them with such tenacity of purpose and led them to make the great sacrifices they did of ease, property, and life itself. In the hardships of persecution they learned to prize more than ever the privileges and truths of their simple and scriptural faith, and so, that they and their descendants in America might enjoy the same inestimable blessings, they were ready to lay all they had upon the altar of their adopted country, and resist, even unto death, every attempt to deprive them of their religious or civil liberty.

THE END.

www.ingramcontent.com/pod-product-compliance
Lightning Source LLC
Chambersburg PA
CBHW030314240426
43673CB00040B/1162